Louis Riel:
Rebel of the
Western Frontier
or Victim of Politics
and Prejudice?

ISSUES IN CANADIAN HISTORY

General Editor
J. L. GRANATSTEIN

ISSUES
IN
CANADIAN
HISTORY

# Louis Riel:
# Rebel of the
# Western Frontier
# or Victim of Politics
# and Prejudice?

Edited by
H. BOWSFIELD

THE COPP CLARK PUBLISHING COMPANY
TORONTO

To F.H.B.

971·0510924

[1620]

© 1969 The Copp Clark Publishing Company

# Contents

## Clash of Opinion

dered a musket to fight against the neglect of government and the shameless greed of speculators.

WILFRID LAURIER 1885

Whether we realize it or not, we of 1968 face a situation which is similar in some respects. If Riel could walk the soil of Canada again today, I am sure his sense of justice would be as outraged as it was in 1885.

ROSS THATCHER 1968

The God damned son of a bitch is gone at last.

BYSTANDER at hanging of RIEL 1885

He shall hang though every dog in Quebec bark in his favour.

JOHN A. MACDONALD 1885

Riel . . . was too cunning to allow anything to interrupt the current of events, which he felt would bring him into importance and satisfy his ambition and vanity. From my knowledge of Riel, at this time [1869], I venture to affirm that his motives were more those of personal ambition and aggrandizement than consideration for the good of his people, and his subsequent action confirms this opinion. He was clever enough to make tools of every one who came in his way, not even excepting the clergy, some of whom were his admiring supporters.

CHARLES A. BOULTON 1886

He was a young man of fair ability, but proud, vain, and assertive, and had the ambition to be a Caesar or Napoleon.

REV. GEORGE BRYCE 1900

Had I been born on the banks of the Saskatchewan I would myself have shoul-

To say they are a small number of dissidents is not sufficient. We know that the few become the many. . . . If they are men like Gandhi, or in my country, like Louis Riel, they live on.

PIERRE ELLIOTT TRUDEAU 1969

Riel and his followers were protesting against the Government's indifference to their problems and its refusal to consult them on matters of their vital interest. Questions of minority rights have deep roots in our history. . . . We must never forget that, in the long run, a democracy is judged by the way the majority treats the minority. Louis Riel's battle is not yet won.

PIERRE ELLIOTT TRUDEAU 1968

In essence the troubles associated with the name of Louis Riel were the manifestation, not of the traditional rivalries of French Catholic Quebec and English Prot-

1

estant Ontario, but of the traditional problems of cultural conflict, of the clash between primitive and civilized peoples.

GEORGE F. G. STANLEY 1954

By the Resistance Riel saved the French element in the North-West from neglect and oblivion. He saved them both from the heedless aggression of Ontario and the parochial indifference of Quebec. By the Resistance Riel challenged Quebec to play a positive part in Confederation, to maintain French institutions throughout Canada and not merely in Quebec.

W. L. MORTON 1956

But for the execution of Scott, Louis Riel today would probably be looked upon by English and French, white and métis, as the father of the province of Manitoba. The "rebellion" would have passed for a patriotic demonstration in arms of the unwillingness of the people of Red River to be sold like a piece of landed property.

GEORGE F. G. STANLEY 1954

I have come to the conclusion that he is not an accountable being, that he is unable to distinguish between wrong and right on political and religious subjects, which I consider well-marked typical forms of insanity under which he undoubtedly suffers, but on other points I believe him to be sensible and can distinguish right from wrong.

DR. F. X. VALADE 1885

So I see they have sentenced my poor friend Riel. By heaven they ought to string up a number of the Government officials if they hang him.

A. G. B. BANNATYNE 1885

How sad and silly it all seems—after sending those brave battalions to the front

—to start in with this childish twaddle about hanging a cur of a self-interested conspirator who has twice brought this country to rebellion and at last let loose savage Indians to murder White Men and even Priests. The idea that because a criminal is half-French it is to stop the sword of justice is outrageous. I would rather join in a war of extermination between French & English than to submit to live in a Country where such monstrously insolent pretensions were put forward by a part of the population.

GENERAL T. B. STRANGE 1885

. . . a mere domestic trouble, and ought not to be elevated to the rank of a rebellion.

JOHN A. MACDONALD 1885

If some one would arrest Dennis and Schultz and lock them up for a twelve-month there would be hope of a settlement.

SIR STAFFORD NORTHCOTE 1870

It was known by the Government and the country that the rebellion in the North West originated with the Roman Catholic priesthood. . . . The priesthood desired to secure certain advantages for themselves, their church or their people. And they advised their people to take the course they did.

WILLIAM MCDOUGALL 1870

We cannot believe that the "rebellion" amounts to anything worth feeling particularly anxious about. The "rebels" are nothing more than a mob of disaffected half-breeds, who are, without doubt, merely the agents of interested parties, who have not the courage to appear in the matter.

*The Daily Telegraph,* Toronto, 1869

Fundamentally the question is one of nationality and religion and the Métis are repeating the pages which mark in a melancholy colour certain events in the history of the Acadians and the Canadians, their ancestors.

*Le Nouveau Monde* 1869

Canada claims the North-West, and intends to have it. . . . [Canada] will not permit a handful of armed traitors to tyrannize over their unarmed brethren, or to sell to the foreigner lands which, by natural right and by money purchase, belong to herself. The question has arrived at the point of issue; and either Riel or Canada must go down.

*Toronto Globe* 1870

By 1869 Red River had had a government, courts, churches and schools for nearly fifty years. It had become a civilized society, largely of mixed white and Indian blood, it is true, but civilized by every test except that of self-government; and that test in no forced sense of the word it could also meet. Red River was not a frontier, but an island of civilization in the wilderness.

W. L. MORTON 1956

# Part I

# Interpretation

A hundred years have passed since Louis Riel resisted Canada's attempt to extend the new Dominion westward to the Pacific. In that century the flow of contentious words never ceased. Now, as a subject of both drama and opera, the *métis* leader has emerged as a genuine—and perhaps Canada's only—folk hero. In 1885 he went to the gallows in Regina amid a fierce political and racial controversy, and after death continued to arouse the same passionate and often irrational response that had made him in his own day a patriot and a traitor, a martyr and a rebel, a saint and a madman. He remained an object of idolatry and damnation.

The traditional interpretation of the Riel rebellions, particularly that of 1869-70, viewed the resistance at Red River as the extension of the racial and religious conflict between Ontario and Quebec to the western prairies. That interpretation, still accepted by many, is represented in this first section of readings by excerpts from the writings of Chester Martin and Mason Wade. In 1936 George Stanley added a new dimension to this interpretation by placing the rebellions within the context of the frontier thesis. He did not minimize the *métis* struggle as a racial or religious one but argued that the frontier problem—that of a clash between a civilized and a primitive society—underlay the traditional explanation. Joseph Kinsey Howard, an American writer, in *Strange Empire*, suggests a slight variation to the frontier thesis. To Howard, Riel was a symbol of the frontier, of the North American frontier, a figure doomed along with his race and the Indian by the North American war of extermination of the red man by the white.

While Stanley's thesis is still generally accepted by many historians it has been challenged in some aspects by W. L. Morton who questions Stanley's treatment of the 1869 and 1885 rebellions as identical movements. Morton's opinion is that the frontier thesis, though useful in understanding the 1885 uprising, has slight relevance to the disturbances of 1869-70. His argument in respect to the Red River Settlement is outlined in his introduction to *Alexander Begg's Red River Journal* published in 1956. The Settlement in 1869, he says, was not a primitive society within the meaning of the frontier thesis but had become a civilized society. The resistance of the *métis*, he claims, was the movement of a "unique ethnic and political reality" to secure guarantees for itself and protection in the face of a Protestant and English westward expansion.

The revival of a militant French Canadian nationalist movement in the 1960's has focused attention once again on the meaning of Canadian federalism and the interpretation of Confederation. The nature of the compact made in 1867 regarding the issue of biculturalism and bilingualism has been stated forcefully by Donald Creighton. In a paper presented to the Manitoba Historical Society in 1967 he criticizes the use to which "quiet revolutionaries" in Quebec, and "some English-Canadian associates," have put their version of Canadian history, and argues that Confederation was not a compact between two cultures or two nations. To their claim that the provisions of the Manitoba Act of 1870 represent the westward extension of the philosophy of cultural compact he counters with the argument that the bicultural and bilingual clauses of the Act resulted from Riel's "dictatorship," from the necessity of a quick settlement at Red River and security for Canada's continental destiny. They did not represent, he says, "the carrying out of a solemn commitment to biculturalism which had been made at Confederation." They were imposed by an "exceptional and transitory" set of circumstances and not by an ideal conception of what Canada should be.[1]

The opposite opinion has been expressed by most French Canadian historians, the writings of Lionel Groulx being representative of this viewpoint. W. L. Morton has noted that French Canadians looked upon Confederation as a treaty designed to preserve their culture and nationality. English Canadians, on the other hand, regarded the recognition of French rights only as a political concession and limited to Quebec. From this misunderstanding, he says, have come opposing interpretations of the Manitoba Act. The Red River Settlement in 1869, he points out, was already a "working duality" and the resistance an attempt to force recognition of the French rights in Red River and the entrance of Manitoba into Confederation on the basis of equality and duality.

1. Donald Creighton, "John A. Macdonald, Confederation and the Canadian West," *Papers Read Before the Historical and Scientific Society of Manitoba*, Series III, No. 23, 1966-67, pp. 5-13.

Mason Wade, *The French Canadians 1760-1945,* (Toronto, Macmillan, 1955), pp. 393-397. Reprinted by permission of The Macmillan Co. of Canada Ltd.

# French vs. English

The strife in Quebec in the years between 1867 and 1896 which was heightened by developments in the West, was remote at the outset of the period and dominated national life at its close. The same period saw the birth and death of hopes of building a new Quebec in the West, upon the foundations laid in the days of the fur trade, under both the French and English regimes.

The Red River colony had depended on Quebec for its religious organization since 1818, when Bishop Plessis answered Lord Selkirk's request for missionaries by sending out the Abbés Norbert Provencher and S.-J.-N. Dumoulin. With them went a few settlers from Quebec, also requested by the noble colonizer. These newcomers joined the French-Canadian and *Métis* (half-breed) employees of the fur trade settled about the missions of St. Boniface and Pembina, after the absorption of the North-West Company by the Hudson's Bay Company in 1821 left many without work. At the outset the Selkirk colony was two-thirds Scottish, with the remaining third made up of German Swiss veterans of the Régiments du Meuron and De Watteville which had served in the War of 1812, French Canadians from

Quebec, and veterans of the fur trade. As the years passed, the French, who tended to follow a semi-nomadic hunting life, came to equal in number the Scottish and English settlers, who inclined more to agriculture. Because of this ethnic mixture the colony was described as 'a little Quebec.' But the *Métis,* both French and English, increased far more rapidly than the pure-blooded whites, and developed a sense of nationality of their own, with Indian blood acting as a tie which offset ancient French and English differences.

The West was more of a British frontier than a Canadian one at this period, since after 1821 it was controlled and supplied from Britain through Hudson Bay, rather than over the barrier of the Laurentian Shield north of the Great Lakes, or by the roundabout and difficult route from Canada through the States. The English group in the colony, including the Hudson's Bay Company men who dominated both trade and government, the Anglican missionaries, and a few settlers, was the most influential; the group of Scottish settlers the most homogeneous; and the French-Canadian and *Métis* group the most numerous. Aside from the officials, the French Canadians had the closest economic relation to the Hudson's Bay Company, since they were largely nomadic trappers, *voyageurs,* and buffalo hunters who supplied the pemmican which was the basic ration of the fur trade. For this reason they were more restive under the company's monopoly than the agricultural Scots. Then from the North-Westers' bitter trade wars with the Hudson's Bay Company the French *Métis* had acquired a tradition of enmity to the latter; while from their Indian forbears they had inherited the belief that the West was their land, and that its natural resources were theirs, despite the company's strict regulations against unlicensed fur-trading. Gradually the *Métis,* both French and English, developed a sense of unity.

They called themselves the 'New Nation.' Accustomed to choosing their own leaders, Indian-style, and to acting together with disciplined unity for the purposes of the buffalo hunt, the *Métis* grew increasingly restive under the regulations of the Hudson's Bay Company officials of Assiniboia, and in 1849 this unrest exploded into virtual rebellion. . . . Jean-Louis Riel, grandson of the famous *coureur de bois* Lagimonière and himself the miller of St. Boniface, was the most influential figure among the French *Métis,* thanks to the prestige of his two years as an Oblate novice and his later industrial training in Montreal. . . .

The isolated little world of the Red River was gradually drawn into the life of the continent. There was an annexationist agitation in 1845-6, occasioned by the focusing of American expansionism on the Oregon boundary dispute, but its development was checked by a force of English troops who garrisoned the colony from 1846 to 1848. In the West as in the East the Church threw its weight behind loyalty to the British connection, and the Abbés Blanchet and Demers were sent from the Red River to the Oregon settlements at the request of the imperial authorities to offset the influence of American missionaries in the latter regions. Again from 1857 to 1861 a small force of the Canadian Rifles was stationed at Fort Garry to guard against Fenian raids and to offset the annexationist movement in Minnesota inspired by James Wickes Taylor, then a special agent of the United States Treasury, who reported to the Governor of Minnesota in 1860 that 'the frontier, hitherto resting upon the sources of the St. Lawrence and the Mississippi, is soon to be pushed far beyond the International frontier by the march of Anglo-Saxon civilization.' During the 1840's and 1850's the Red River region, which had previously been tied to eastern Canada only by the dependence of its missionaries on Quebec and Montreal, gradually became a bone of contention between Upper and Lower Canada. George Brown, the francophobe and anti-Catholic editor of the *Toronto Globe,* aroused English-Canadian interest in the West and preached annexation of the Red River colony to Canada. In this cause he was aided by the like-minded William McDougall, whose *North American* was soon absorbed by the *Globe*. Both men wanted to make the West an extension of English Upper Canada, with a view to dominating French Canada. Quebec, whose interest in the West had been stirred by the reports of the missionaries whom it supported and largely supplied, naturally opposed this program, which increased its chronic sense of insecurity.

With the project of Confederation already under discussion, Canadian pressure was brought to bear in London against the renewal of the Hudson's Bay Company charter in 1857; and in that same year a committee composed of George Brown and Joseph Cauchon was appointed by the Canadian legislature to consider Western affairs. Canada took the view that the Hudson's Bay Company title to the North-West was invalid, and, as its own expansionism developed, became somewhat concerned at the extension of American economic influence in the Red River region, which was linked to the United States by steamer in 1859 and by rail shortly afterward, when the railroad reached St. Paul. The Hudson's Bay Company itself began to import supplies by this route rather than by the traditional York Factory one. The authority of the company declined after the renewal of its charter was refused in London. The company's officials were left in the forlorn position of a lame-duck American president, obliged to round out his term of office after defeat at the polls.

In this situation Canadian and American annexationist parties grew up among the new settlers at Fort Garry, the English settlement about the Hudson's Bay post across the river from St. Boniface, the *Métis* and French Catholic center; while the older settlers agitated for Crown colony status. The American party received backing from Minnesota, and Taylor reported on December 17, 1861: 'The Americanization of this important section of British North America is rapidly progressing. Unless the British Parliament acts promptly . . . I shall confidently expect a popular movement looking to independence or annexation to the United States.' Two Canadians, William Coldwell and William Buckingham, founded in 1859 the first newspaper, the *Nor'Wester,* which was the organ of the Canadian party. In 1862 John Ross [*sic,*] a Scottish *Métis,* claimed that the 'New Nation' wanted responsible government, while J.-L. Riel denied it. Meanwhile the Canadian authorities, proceeding on their convenient view that Assiniboia had no legal government, provided for the admission of the North-West Territories into Confederation at the Quebec Conference of 1864, without consulting the wishes of the people of the region. When this news reached the Red River, it was proposed that one French and one English delegate should be sent to London to express the popular demand for Crown colony status.

Resentment of highhanded eastern determination of the fate of the West continued to grow along the Red River. . . . The population at this period numbered about 10,000, predominantly *Métis* and almost equally divided between English and French. Despite the urgent representations of Governor Mactavish, Colonel Dennis, and Bishop Taché—who warned Cartier at Ottawa in July 1869 and Cartier and Hector Langevin at Quebec in September on the eve of his departure for the Vatican Council—that trouble was brewing in the West, the land schemes of the Canadian government were deemed more important than the protests of 10,000 'half-castes,' as Sir John Macdonald contemptuously called the *Métis.*

The long negotiations carried on by Cartier and Macdonald with the Hudson's Bay Company finally came to an end. The company's deed of surrender of November 19, 1869, was to take effect with the transfer of the North-West Territories to Canada on December 1, when the latter was to pay £300,000, in addition to making land grants and other privileges to extinguish the company's claim. Under the Act for the Temporary Government of Rupert's Land, passed in June 1869 without consultation of the Red River people, Canada was to have both federal and provincial powers in the Territories, since the proposed governmental organization provided only for an appointed governor and council, whose members did not have to be residents. This was a backward step politically, for the old Council of Assiniboia had included local representation (on a roughly equal French and English basis since 1855); and further popular agitation against absentee control arose.

William McDougall, already unpopular with the colonists for his heavyhanded expansionist activities, was appointed lieutenant-governor and dispatched by way of Chicago and St. Paul to the Red River, where he was to take office after the transfer of title on December 1. His council included Joseph - Norbert Provencher, nephew of the pioneer missionary bishop of the Red River and a former editor of *La Minerve,* Cartier's Conservative organ in Montreal; but for the rest was as militantly 'Anglo-Saxon' and Protestant as McDougall could have wished. The new government was frankly despotic, for Macdonald wrote Charles Tupper that McDougall 'will be for the time Paternal despot, as in other small Crown Colonies, his Council being one of advice, he and they, however, being governed by instructions from Headquarters.' Joseph Howe, shortly to become Dominion Secretary of State, paid an unofficial visit to the Red River to assuage the rising unrest there, and found that discontent was general. The company officials felt that they should have received a share of the £300,000; the English were dissatisfied at not being consulted about the transfer; and the French were uneasy because of the appointment as governor of the francophobe imperialist McDougall.

Chester Martin, "The First 'New Province' of the Dominion," *Canadian Historical Review,* Vol. 1, 1920, pp. 366-369. Reprinted by permission of the University of Toronto Press.

## Rights in Jeopardy

It will not be necessary to trace in detail the course of the Riel Insurrection, but the political difficulties at Red River undoubtedly arose from the French and Roman Catholic section of the community; and French obstruction to the Union in 1869-70 has undoubtedly left its mark upon the subsequent political history, not only of Manitoba, but of the whole Dominion.

The policy of building up a smaller Quebec upon the banks of the Red River had been patiently and successfully pursued for more than fifty years. The French *Métis,* the chief charge of a devoted clergy, had not lost the characteristics which [Alexander] Ross [the historian] had attributed to the preceding generation. They were "generous, warm-hearted and brave, and left to themselves, quiet and orderly." Living still largely by the buffalo hunt, their credulous good-nature and their very improvidence left them responsive to clerical control. They were correspondingly dependent upon their clerical guardians for knowledge and counsel. By 1869 they had become thoroughly alarmed by the changing order of the times. *The Nor-' Wester* predicted imminent changes "be-

fore the march of a superior intelligence." The *Métis* sought to "raise some breakwater" against the deluge. They were "uneducated, and only half civilized," said Riel before the Council of Assiniboia on October 25, 1869, "and felt, if a large immigration were to take place, they would probably be crowded out." They had been "sold like so many sheep" and disposed of "like the buffaloes on the prairie." The Canadian Confederation was but two years old, and the French, even of Quebec, were anxiously testing out their provincial rights in the new Dominion. Neither the Roman Catholic clergy nor the primitive people beneath their control at the Red River could be expected to welcome Canadian domination "without safeguards." The *Métis,* suspicious and unenlightened, were easily moved to something more than passive resistance beneath the vainglorious leadership of Louis Riel—a resistance which on more than one occasion passed beyond control and finally degenerated into wanton arrogance and bloodshed. The brains of the movement, however, were not those of Louis Riel; and it would not be unjust perhaps either to the French *Métis* or to their guardians in all that was well-ordered and sustained in the Riel Insurrection, to regard the *Métis* as the secular arm of the Church at Red River.

The ultimate aims of the Roman Catholic clergy were undoubtedly more comprehensive than reserves of land for the *Métis.* Archbishop Taché, on his way to Rome in 1869, wrote bitterly to Sir George Cartier of the "ruin of that which has cost us so dear." "I have always feared," he wrote, "the entrance of the North-West into Confederation, because I have always believed that the French-Canadian element would be sacrificed; but I tell you frankly it had never occurred to me that our rights would be so quickly and so completely forgotten." In Archbishop Taché's absence the French cause was left largely in the hands of Rev. J. N. Ritchot of St. Norbert, and it is not difficult to trace the influence of Père Ritchot's subtle and resourceful mind throughout the Insurrection itself and upon the negotiations culminating in provincial status under the Manitoba Act. . . .

. . . The English-speaking population of Assiniboia long remained in ignorance of the influences which resulted in provincial status under the Manitoba Act.

These influences were undoubtedly French and Roman Catholic in origin, and their cogency is very easily understood. Special terms of union, safeguarding by statute the official use of the French language, separate schools, control of lands by the local legislature, etc., were much more enduring guarantees of French claims than the most explicit declaration of policy. . . .

George F. G. Stanley, *Louis Riel: Patriot or Rebel?* (Ottawa, Canadian Historical Association, 1954), Historical Booklet No. 2, pp. 3, 4-5, 24. Reprinted by permission of the Author.

## Civilization vs. Frontier

In essence the troubles associated with the name of Louis Riel were the manifestation, not of the traditional rivalries of French Catholic Quebec and English Protestant Ontario, but of the traditional problems of cultural conflict, of the clash between primitive and civilized peoples. . . . Both in Manitoba and in Saskatchewan the métis had their own primitive society and their own primitive economy. They hunted the buffalo, they trafficked in furs, they freighted goods for the Hudson's Bay Company, and they indifferently cultivated their long narrow farms along the banks of the rivers. Few of them were equipped by education or experience to compete with the whites, or to share with them the political responsibilities of citizenship. When faced with the invasion of civilization they drew together; they did not want to be civilized; they wanted only to survive. Their fears and bewilderment drove them into resistance which, when reduced to armed conflict, held small chance of success. . . .

The half-breeds of the Hudson's Bay Company Territories were a remarkable people. Children of the fur traders and the Indian women of the plains, they combined many of the best qualities of both races. Physically they excited the admiration of visitors. They were as much at home on the prairie as any Indian tribesmen and in their elaborate organization for the buffalo hunt they had a self-made military organization as efficient for its own purpose as the Boer Commando. Despite their semi-nomadic life and their mixed blood they were not savages. They were religious and reasonably honest; and in the golden days of the Red River Settlement serious crime was unknown. The authority of the Hudson's Bay Company was almost entirely moral; and when left to themselves the métis got on well with the Indians, with each other and with their rulers.

The serpent in this Eden was progress. For a long time the menace came from the south. American settlement proceeded faster than Canadian, and while there was still an empty wilderness between Fort Garry and Western Ontario there were fast growing settlements in the United States. Developments south of the frontier made it difficult if not impossible to enforce the fur monopoly; and developments south of the frontier meant the end of the buffalo and the demoralization of the Indians.

The newly created federation of Canada, fearful—and with ample justification—of American expansion northwards and of the intrigues of Senator Alexander Ramsey and the Minnesota party, finally concluded an agreement with the Hudson's Bay Company for the transfer of the Company's territories to Canada. To Canada and to the Canadians the acquisition of the North-West was a logical and necessary corollary to confederation; but to the people of Red River it meant their transfer to a "foreign" government whose interests were very different from their own.

Evidence of these differences was soon afforded by the arrival in Red River of a party of Canadian surveyors who proceeded to lay out the land in symmetrical pattern, taking little or no heed of the irregularities of the métis holdings, and precursing, in any event, close settlement, the destruction of the buffalo and the end of the wandering life of the prairie. The sons of Isaac were advancing on the lands of the sons of Ishmael. A clash was inevitable. . . .

Louis Riel was not a great man; he was not even what Carlyle would call a near great. Nevertheless he became, in death, one of the decisive figures of our history. By historical accident rather than by design he became the symbol of divisions as old as the Franco-British struggle for the control of northern North America. It is this historical accident which has obscured the fundamental character of the two risings which bear Riel's name; for the Riel "rebellions" were not what the politicians argued and what the people believed, a continuation on the banks of the Red and the Saskatchewan of the traditional hostilities of old Canada. They were, instead, the typical, even inevitable results of the advance of the frontier, the last organized attempts on the part of Canada's primitive peoples to withstand what, for want of a better word, may be termed progress, and to preserve their culture and their identity against the encroachments of civilization. To present-day Canadians Riel appears, no longer as the wilful "rebel" or "murderer" of Thomas Scott, but as a sad, pathetic, unstable man, who led his followers in a suicidal crusade and whose brief glory rests upon a distortion of history. To the métis, the people whom he loved, he will always be, mad or sane, the voice of an inarticulate race and the prophet of a doomed cause.

Joseph Kinsey Howard, *Strange Empire, a Narrative of the Northwest,* (New York, William Morrow & Co., 1952), pp. 14-17. © 1952 by Joseph Kinsey Howard. Reprinted by permission of William Morrow & Co. Inc.

## White Man vs. Red

This book is about the period of transition in the North American West—Red River to the Rockies, in Canada and the United States. Some of the incidents with which it deals are familiar, others have been almost forgotten; a few, I think, have never before been put into a book. But that does not matter much; what does matter—at least to me—is that incidents heretofore reported as isolated, and perhaps of only local or regional significance or of no significance at all, can be shown to have been related to each other and to the whole: the War for the West.

I believe it also can be shown that the West was a social and economic entity; that this war, though it took differing forms, raged on both sides of that "imaginary line," the forty-ninth parallel, at the same time; that the boundary, in fact, made very little sense to anybody on either side of it, and its elimination motivated some who were caught up in the bigger struggle of native against invader.

Philippe Régis de Trobriand, one of the most brilliant of the many intellectuals who were drawn to the far Western frontier, noted in his journal in 1867, "The destiny of the white race in America is to destroy the red race." Yet the native cause was not quite so hopeless as our histories have led us to believe. There were times when Manifest Destiny slid off the trail and bogged down. There were times when the defenders, given a little more skill, could have wrested a better bargain from white civilization. . . .

American and Canadian military commanders knew that their task of subjugating or destroying the primitive peoples of the West would be hopeless, at least for many years, if the native races should unite. This idea came to Sitting Bull—too late; it came still later to the leaders of another but related people in Canada. Had there been time for them to act upon it there might have been independent, semiprimitive tribal societies in North America such as still exist on other continents as near neighbors to modern states.

Most of the crucial events on both sides of the boundary occurred within a span of fifteen years after 1870. It was a tortured time—a time of war, famine, disease, moral dissolution. It was a time when smallpox, whiskey, prostitution and the slaughter of the buffalo did more to win an empire than bullets could; and perhaps the bullets could never have done it alone.

The native defenders of the West in this period were for the most part Sioux, Cree and Blackfeet Indians and their "cousins," the Métis or "half-breeds." Their "empire" was the great mid-continent buffalo range now designated the Northern Great Plains; as the Indians doggedly retreated from it, the Métis and whites moved in. But the Métis inherited all of the Indians' problems while the whites gained strength and cunning. The Métis therefore were the worst sufferers, and this book concerns itself chiefly with their nation because their tragedy climaxed and epitomized the whole struggle of red man, or brown, against white.

That nation evolved from what had gone before; like many others it was conceived quickly and crudely; in a sudden urgency of history; it was born of violence and despair in the hearts of a wordless people, and reared to brief glory in the souls of two great men.

One of these men, perhaps against his conscious will, became a dictator, and there is interest in the study of dichotomy in the human soul—for this dictator, who adored God and feared bloodshed, defied his priests to lead the people he loved into a suicidal crusade. It was said, of course, that he was mad; but mad or sane he grew to full stature as protagonist and symbol, personification, voice, and brain of a doomed race. He was supremely conscious of his historic role.

The comrade who shared his leadership [Gabriel Dumont] was not concerned about God's justice or racial destiny or his own standing with posterity; he simply liked to fight. He was a practical man harnessed to an idealist and sometimes pulled hard against the traces. In this contest the practical man, for once, lost. But the war was lost, too.

When the Métis sought to achieve nationhood in the strange empire of the West, white men called it treason, the greatest of crimes.

More men went to trial for treason after World War II than ever before in history, and some were condemned for betrayal of their national allegiance on a law written in the Middle Ages, the same law that doomed the central figure in this book. Others died for an offence new to jurisprudence, for which a word had to be coined—genocide, destruction of a race, treason against the human spirit. The victors defined the crime, but victors and vanquished both knew that in the future there might be other trials, other culprits, and other judges.

The crime of genocide is older than its name, older than the judicial retribution now visited upon its practitioners. The races with which we are concerned in this book were martyred in the name of Manifest Destiny or Canada First or an Anglo-Saxon God. There were no gas chambers then, but there was malevolent intention; and there were guns and hunger, smallpox and syphilis. And "backward" peoples, then as now, could be used as puppets in the power politics of dynamic "civilized" states. . . .

Those with whom this book deals clung to the old loyalties, defied science and the machine—and perished. Of course they were an illiterate people, primitive and unstable, not even white. And their spokesman and symbol, who believed the old values to be good, became thereby a traitor.

He died on the gallows and his nation with him—his nation, and the dream of a strange empire in the West.

W. L. Morton (ed.), *Alexander Begg's Red River Journal and Other Papers Relative to the Red River Resistance of 1869-1870,* (Toronto, The Champlain Society), 1956, pp. 1-3, 14-16. Reprinted by permission of the Champlain Society.

# Red River, a Civilized Community

[The] Resistance of the *métis* was an event of major significance at the time, and its consequences were momentous for the future. Involved in its course and outcome were the relations of half-breed and Indian with the white immigrant in the North-West, and the relations between French and English, their language and institutions, in one-third of Canada, and this affected also their political relations in Old Canada. Involved also was the question as to whether the North-West was to be Canadian or American; and within that was the more important question whether, in the face of a United States stretching from Alaska to Florida, old Canada would be able to maintain its independence. Red River was the key to the North-West, the North-West to the future of the new Dominion; and in October, 1869, Louis Riel and his followers seized and held that key to win for themselves and the people of the North-West guaranteed rights as civilized men. Their error was not so much that they risked rebellion, as that they used this great lever

to exact what in due course would have been generously given.

If they used means disproportionate to their ends, however, the ends were neither ignoble nor mistaken. The half-breeds claimed as their birthright the civil and political rights of British subjects. This they were entitled to do, for they were civilized men, their leaders educated, the main body of the people simple and honest folk, intelligent, if illiterate. That the majority of the *métis* of Red River were hunters and freighters did not make them nomads. The long contest between nomadism and settlement was being ended on the whole in favour of the latter. The colony was their settled abode, and in the farther North-West were new Red River Settlements in the making. To describe Red River as a frontier is to use a term of such general application and of so little local relevance as to possess slight scientific value.* By 1869 Red River had had a government, courts, churches and schools for nearly fifty years. It had become a civilized society, largely of mixed white and Indian blood, it is true, but civilized by every test except that of self-government; and that test in no forced sense of the word it could also meet. Red River was not a frontier, but an island of civilization in the wilderness. It was the offspring of the fur frontier, which was not, as was the agricultural frontier, a

* The disagreement with G. F. G. Stanley's Introduction to *The Birth of Western Canada* (London, 1936) expressed here is based on the belief that it is an error to treat the fur frontier of Canada as identical with an agricultural or pastoral frontier. What the *métis* chiefly feared in 1869 was not the entrance of the agricultural frontier of Ontario into Red River—and they would have welcomed that of Quebec—but the sudden influx of immigrants of English speech and Protestant faith.

conflict of civilization and barbarism, but a partnership of trader and native. Of this partnership, the *métis,* or French half-breeds, were the offspring; and the colony of Red River was, in virtue of its part in the extended fur-trade of the North-West, a community unique both in history and character. The *métis,* one half of its people, were unique also in that they thought of themselves as a "new nation", a "peculiar people", as Riel termed it. Neither French nor Indian, but intermediate, they claimed to unite the civilization of their fathers' with the rights of their mothers' people in a new nationality of the North-West. The "new nation" was a unique ethnic and political reality, sprung from the continental fur-trade; and it was not unaware both of its uniqueness and of its dependence on the old way of life, and also of its need to adapt itself to the changes which had been foreseen for at least a decade before 1869.

It is in this sense of nationhood of the *métis* that an understanding of the Resistance of 1869 is to be found. They sought guaranteed rights as a community of civilized people. The Canadian government was entirely ready to grant the normal rights of British subjects to all civilized individuals in the North-West, without respect to race. But it had no idea that it was dealing with a corporate entity, a "nation" by sentiment and by their own claim. It is in this conflict between the half-articulated demand for *corporate* rights by the *métis,* and the intention of the Canadian authorities to grant *individual* rights in due course, that the true character of the Resistance is to be found. . . .

As a natural concomitant of the continental fur-trade, the Red River Settlement had developed its peculiar character of a civilized community in the wilderness;

a community civilized indeed, but dependent upon, and in constant contact with, the wilderness through hunt and trip. Even farming had its seasonal links with the uncultivated wastes, for the agriculture of Red River depended upon an unlimited supply of wild hay and the possibility of "wintering" cattle in the woods. Thus any fundamental change in the order of life which had developed during the régime of the fur-trade would have profound repercussions on the Red River Settlement. This was true of all elements in the Settlement to some degree, even of the Scots of Kildonan, who had pursued agriculture exclusively and kept themselves apart in great measure from the mixture of blood which was rapidly making all Red River a half-caste society. But it was especially true of the French element, of whom the great majority were *métis*.

The Red River Settlement was an Anglo-French colony, united by a substratum of Indian blood drawn from the fur-trade. As it was dual in composition, so had it been dual in origin. . . . [The] larger part of the French community of Red River derived from the lowest ranks of the fur trade, from the Company which had been absorbed in the union of 1821, and from a Canadian, not a British, source. It had also been far more deeply immersed in the sea of Indian blood and Indian custom, partly because of the low rank of its white progenitors, partly from the French gift of intimacy with the savage mind and savage customs. From all these accidents and qualities sprang that readiness to identify themselves with the North-West which the North West Company had fostered in the *métis,* in an effort to use them against Selkirk's colony and the Hudson's Bay Company. It had encouraged them to claim title to the lands of the North-West as a birthright from their

Indian mothers and to think of themselves as a "new nation." The *nation métisse* had never lost this original sense of identity; and even after being reconciled to the colony of which it had been the scourge, and to the Company that its old *bourgeois* had fought, the "new nation" of the half-breeds remained a community apart in the larger community of Red River. This sense of community had been kept alive by the great annual buffalo hunts, the all but exclusive occupation of the *métis*, and the recurrent conflicts with the Sioux. It had been kept alive by Canadian leaders, amongst whom the elder Riel may be noted, and by the conflict with the Company over free trade in 1844-1849. After the reconciliation with the Company which followed 1849, it was confirmed by the use of the *métis* as the bulwark of the colony against the Sioux, and their consequent realization that they were, in the absence of regular troops after 1861, the one organized armed force in the Settle-ment. Nor did the dependence of the Company on the *métis* to man the boat and cart brigades, and the dependence of the Settlement on the buffalo hunts for provisions and robes, do anything to diminish this corporate consciousness.

The French community as a whole, it is true, had developed beyond the simple and essentially nomadic society and economy of the *métis*. It now included elements other than hunters and voyageurs. There was a small group of Canadians in St. Boniface, mostly craftsmen, and educated, settled folk. There were French and *métis* traders and farmers. . . . But no professional middle class had developed: the *métis* had given no priest to the church, no lawyer to the courts of Assiniboia, no doctor to practise among his people. . . . Thus the "new nation", even more than Red River as a whole, was ill equipped to fit itself into any new order which might follow union with Canada. . . .

Lionel Groulx, *Histoire du Canada français depuis la découverte,* (Montreal, L'Action Nationale, 1952), Vol. 4, pp. 114-118. Reprinted by permission of Editions Fides.

# Canadian Duality

Would one really have to be such a great prophet to foresee these coming disasters? It was not in vain that we insisted on the artificial character of the federation of 1867. The brilliant facade failed to conceal the precarious adjustments hastily improvised without spontaneity. Had the roles of bilingualism, equal rights and privileges between the two contracting races been determined, without possible controversy, in the federal state and the federal services, particularly the civil services? Were the principle and legal establishment of the two cultures and equal respect for [religious] beliefs accepted on all sides in the same spirit, with the same loyalty over the whole of the country? Around 1867 noble illusions were fostered by words and deeds. Lord Carnarvon, in the imperial parliament, exceeded the text and the guarantees of Article 93 to promise freedom in education to all Canadian minorities, whatever they were, present or future, *in esse* or *in posse*. And at first this spirit of generous liberalism was indeed inspiring. In 1870, when Manitoba entered Confederation, Article 133 of the Canadian constitution on the official use of the two languages was inserted in its en-

tirety in the constitution of the new province. Freedom in education also received supplementary guarantees. The protection of Article 93, used in 1867 to affirm rights already legally established, was extended in Manitoba to rights established only by custom. In 1875 the federal parliament proceeded to organize politically the North West Territories, with the same evidence of a liberal spirit. Each minority was granted its right to separate schools. And the use of the two official languages of the country was here defined by the same terms as in Article 133 of the federal constitution. It seemed that the central government was determined to maintain national and religious duality right to the Rockies. It appeared that certain utterances in the Parliament at Ottawa during the debates of 1875 dispelled any possibility of equivocation. Edward Blake, then Minister of Justice in the Liberal cabinet of Alexander Mackenzie [*sic*], said: "In my opinion, we must not allow in these regions the animosities and the difficulties which have afflicted other parts of Canada, as well as other countries." Alexander Campbell, Conservative, "Father" of Confederation, and at that time leader of the opposition in the Canadian Senate, deigned to add: "The intention of the Act is to establish and maintain in the North West Territories the same school systems as those which exist in the provinces of Ontario and Quebec, and which have been functioning so well to further peace and harmony between the different populations of these provinces."

Nevertheless, to the perspicacious there were many disquieting symptoms and warning signs. It is a well-known fact of history that there is a built-in tendency in federations to turn their disparate or diverse elements into a uniform whole. In 1875 speeches like those of Blake and

Campbell and some others sounded agreeably to the ear. Were they expressing the unanimous opinion of English Canadians? One willingly speaks of the generous liberal spirit of 1867. And with reason. But was this generosity and liberalism without alloy? We recall the acrimonious debates of 1865 and 1866 over minimal concessions to the Catholic minority of Upper Canada; concessions clearly just but which nevertheless nearly precipitated a ministerial crisis, after having unleashed an historic tempest in the press and in the parliament of the united Canadas. Who does not still remember, on the very eve of 1867, the fierce opposition of Charles Tupper to the principle of separate schools in his province of Nova Scotia, a legal recognition which, by the terms of Article 93, would have secured the rights of confessional schools? But other events of the same period take on an even more worrying significance. The federal state was hardly inaugurated before the Red River Affair erupted violently in the west. An objective evaluation of the events of 1869-70 can cause stupefaction. What disparity there was between the simple and natural reaction of a small group of people who did not want to be pushed into Confederation without having any say, and the terrible tempest unleashed across the country by this completely legitimate act. A wave of bitter polemic swept the provinces of Ontario and Quebec. Opinion was divided along that electrically charged line which is the racial frontier. The French Canadians en bloc took the part of the people of Red River and their young leader Louis Riel; English Canadian opinion was ranged on the opposite side and with equal unanimity. To attempt to explain this phenomenon is to risk taking the wrong path, as so many historians have done. Some say that it was because the

provisional government of Red River was illegitimate; others that the execution of Thomas Scott by this same government was ill-advised. But was there material in all this for a quarrel of national proportions? Illegitimate government? Nevertheless Ottawa had agreed to negotiate with it. Perhaps the execution of Scott was impolitic, but it was the execution of an obscure agitator—*with no claim to fame* —according to A. R. M. Lower. On both sides responsibilities were too divided for sound judgment. "I do not want to incriminate anyone," Mgr. Taché wrote to the governor general, Sir John Young, "but if the most culpable and rebellious must be punished, the punishment could well be inflicted on some of those who are esteemed as champions of loyalty, duty and honour." It is difficult to have illusions about the indiscreet, even ostentatious plots of those who formed the "Canadian Party" as it was called in Red River, emigrants from Ontario, surveyors, adventurers, determined to carve out for themselves feudal domains on the Prairies, *to secure as much of the country to themselves as possible,* as we are told by the historian Alexander Begg in the *Creation of Manitoba*. They were snatchers of the land, who, to attain their ends, were prepared to go to the lengths of plotting the physical expulsion of the original occupants, ready to destroy or to remove "from their native soil," according to the Archbishop of Saint-Boniface, the "serfs," "the black dependents of Bishop Taché, the poor French Canadians of the North West." But at the hour of crisis the conduct of the government at Ottawa was indeed strange. Strange also was the poorly disguised disdain of certain ministers for the "miserable Métis" of the North-West. And most strange of all was the body of politicians and administrators, composed almost entirely of those who spoke English, sent to the Red River region where the majority were French. It is impossible to avoid the impression that at the heart of this conflict there was a confrontation in the West, brought about by the equivocations of Ottawa, of divergent interpretations of the Canadian reality, on one side the natives, wanting to see in the future of Manitoba and all the Territories a loyal extension of the Canadian duality of culture and religion; and on the other side those, determined to build there an annex to Ontario. Deplorable events. And if they are related to what was happening at the same time in New Brunswick, where the first conflict over the school question was breaking out, are they not to be regarded as the tragedy at the cradle of Confederation?

W. L. Morton, "Manitoba's Historic Role," *Papers Read Before the Historical and Scientific Society of Manitoba,* Series III, No. 19, 1964, pp. 51-55. Reprinted by permission of The Historical and Scientific Society of Manitoba.

# A Working Duality at Red River

The beginning of all Canadian history is, of course, that at the planting of European civilization in America this country, every bit of it from the Bay of Fundy to the Saskatchewan valley, was French.

The second thing is that first Nova Scotia—Acadia, we should say—and then Canada were conquered and annexed by the Crown of England. All that was demanded of their people, however, was allegiance; French they might remain in speech and Catholic in religion. The Canadians, indeed, were allowed their own civil law.

The third thing is that in the lands that became Canada the French outnumbered the English in all parts of British America until the decade 1841-1851. In short, the French have been a minority of the population in Canada only a little over a hundred years.

These are most powerful reasons, then, for the French to claim the right, both historical and constitutional, to remain French in speech and culture. The same reasons entitle them to claim equality with the English; indeed, no one, not even the earliest English immigrants, has so good a claim to "equality" as the French have. If this is so, then, that the French ought of historic and legal right be equal with the English in Canada, why should French Canadians feel that they are not, and why should there in fact be grave limitations on those rights in every province of Canada other than Quebec? Why in particular should there be such limitations in the Province of Manitoba, a province peculiarly of French creation?

An answer is to be found, I think, in two things. The first is that historically the French of Canada have been identified, at the time of Confederation were identified, and still themselves when Quebeckers tend to identify themselves, with the Province of Quebec, the original Canada. Note for example what Hector Louis Langevin, Father of Confederation and with George Etienne Cartier the only French Canadians at the Westminster Conference that made final the terms of Confederation, note what he wrote in the utmost secrecy to his trusted wife Justine—with Mrs. George Brown one of the two women to whom all students of Confederation must be grateful, for their husbands entrusted them with the most important news—note, I say, what Langevin wrote when the details of the Bill that became the B.N.A. Act were settled. (Surely there could be no better evidence of what a French Canadian really thought of Confederation.)

"You can easily believe how proud I am of the result. I am convinced that our position as people speaking the French language is assured as much as human things can be assured . . .

"As for separate or dissident schools, the right and privileges of minorities, those of schools existing now or may be acquired hereafter, are guaranteed, as a right of appeal lies to the central power. In other words, we grant to the Protestants of Lower Canada the protection they ought to have and in consideration of that we extend our protection to 700,000 to 800,000 Catholics of Upper Canada and the Maritime Provinces."

Note also that to Langevin Confederation was a "treaty", as Macdonald had described it in the Canadian Parliament, and as Carnarvon, the Colonial Secretary who introduced the B.N.A. Bill, described it in the House of Lords a few days after Langevin's letter. Note also that it was a treaty designed to preserve the culture and nationality of the French. The B.N.A. Act, we must remember, was a summing up of British American history, and in that summing up were the historic rights of the French to grow as a distinct nationality within the new political order of Confederation. But those rights were confined to the Province of Quebec and the federal parliament and courts; they were not made Canada wide.

The second matter which suggests why limitations exist on French Canadian rights is not an easy matter to state briefly. But in substance it amounts to no more than this that Confederation, except in New Brunswick, was carried by the British American legislatures and the British Parliament alone, without any reference to the colonial electorates in general election, constitutional convention, or plebiscite. Confederation rested on the exercise of parliamentary sovereignty alone. One might almost say that there was a definite refusal to consider the alternative sovereignty of the people. The demands of the Rouge leader, A. A. Dorion, and of Joseph Howe, the great opponent of Confederation in Nova Scotia, were ignored in a way that would be wholly impossible

in our days, but that was quite possible then.

The result was that the treaty rights of the French rested on parliamentary sovereignty and not on declared popular approval. Within a generation, however, the doctrine of popular sovereignty, the belief of a minority in 1867, had become a generally accepted doctrine a generation later, particularly in Ontario, and in the Province of Manitoba and the Territories it was populating to the westward: this was most significant, for if political power was to rest on numbers, power would reside with the majority. And that, in every province but Quebec, and in Canada as a whole, was English and Protestant.

The rights of French Canada, then, to be a distinct nationality within Confederation rested on history and the constitution. But those rights were limited by the constitution, as well as established. They were not regarded by English Canadians as an historic right embodied in a treaty, and capable of growth with the growth of French numbers. They were thought of as a political concession written into an Act of Parliament and limited to the Province of Quebec and the federal parliament and courts.

Out of this difference of view, a difference between French and English Canadians overcome at Confederation only by a few leading statesmen, and out of the misunderstanding that resulted sprang the Province of Manitoba. This province came into being only because of the differing views of English and French with respect to Confederation. This is why its role is so strongly historic; this is why Manitoba cannot escape history.

You will recall that the lands now Manitoba were discovered and first exploited by both English and French. The English were first on Hudson Bay, the

French first on Red River. The first Europeans in this province owed allegiance either to the Stuarts of England or the Bourbons of France. And French and English remained together in the exploitations of the fur trade of the Northwest even after the cession of Canada. (If nearly all the *bourgeois* were Scots, that after all is something normal for the English proper, and they don't like it any more than the French!)

In consequence of the common exploitation of the Northwest, the population that grew up in Red River and elsewhere in the Northwest after connection with Canada practically ended in 1821, was and remained about half-and-half French and English. It is true, of course, that there was a strong and increasing diffusion of Indian blood, except among the Selkirk settlers and a few Canadian families at St. Boniface. This was particularly true among the French. But the common enterprise of the fur trade and the work of the missionaries produced a society that, while it had two distinct halves, was none the less a true community, a working duality. It was especially so after the assertion in the Sayer outbreak of 1849 of the French right to full participation in the commerce and government of the colony. The result was a working partnership that quite reconciled the French to the prevailing order by 1857.

In that year, however, came the great inquiry into the conduct of the Hudson's Bay Company prior to a renewal or discontinuance of its licence to trade. A party of old Hudson's Bay Company servants and a group of Toronto businessmen combined to demand the annexation of the Northwest to Canada. They revived the old French claim to the Northwest the North West Company had used against the Hudson's Bay Company and Selkirk's

colony in 1815 and 1816. So successful were they that the acquisition became an object of Canadian policy, and so remained until it was accomplished in 1870.

There were to be, however, certain checks to the carrying out of the Canadian policy. One was the legal difficulties caused by the Hudson's Bay Company's charter and its actual possession. A second was that the Canadian government was by no means ready to assume the government of the Northwest. Still a third, the most intangible, but the most significant historically, was that the Canada of 1857 was a union of two sections, Lower Canada (correctly Canada East) and Upper Canada (Canada West). Each section had an equal number of representatives in the Canadian Parliament. But, since the publications of the first Canadian Census in 1851, it had been revealed that Upper Canada had a greater population than that of Lower Canada. George Brown of *The Globe,* the spokesman of the same interests who were to demand the annexation of the Northwest, began to agitate for representation by population in the sections of Canada. This threatened to reduce Lower Canada to a minority in Parliament. If the Northwest were simply to be annexed to Upper Canada and then populated with representation, Lower Canada would become a minority indeed.

It is my belief, therefore, that Cartier, when he went to London in 1858 with a Canadian delegation to urge the Confederation of British North America, made it clear to the British government that Lower Canada could never agree that Upper Canada should itself gain the Northwest. If the Northwest were annexed to Canada, it must be as a province or territory of all Canada. While I have failed to find any explicit statement of Cartier, or of the colonial office, or of Sir Edward Bulwer

Lytton, Colonial Secretary, that this was so, I know Lytton, Cartier and A. K. Isbister discussed this matter of Confederation together. I am therefore prepared to accept Isbister's statement of Cartier's views published in *The Nor'Wester* on January 14, 1860, as being an authentic summary of his thought.

Such a view in fact became incorporated into the inter-locking set of changes each necessary to all the others, the federation of all British America, the building of the Intercolonial Railway, the separation of Lower and Upper Canada, the annexation of the Northwest, the set of changes on which the coalition of 1864 was founded, and which became the basis of the Quebec Resolutions of that year. The Northwest must be brought into a federal union as a distinct area.

There remained, in the hustle and the tremendous effort involved in defeating the Fenian attacks and bringing New Brunswick and Nova Scotia into the Union, the matter of what kind of area the Northwest was to be and how it was to be governed. It was still unsettled when in 1869 the terms of the transfer from the Hudson's Bay Company to Canada were agreed upon. The Canadian government had been much too busy to decide how it would handle the delicate issue of bringing new territories into union. It therefore decided to take its time, give the Northwest a temporary government and have it make inquiries as to how the Northwest was to be governed. It was quite a sensible decision, but it overlooked the people of the Northwest and particularly a very difficult young man, a Westerner born who had not been too successful a student in Montreal, the second Louis Riel.

The Red River Resistance had many causes, but the root one was the same as that of the rising of 1849, to force recog-nition of the rights of the half-breed to participation in the trade and government of Red River. Because of the relatively backward conditions of the *métis,* or French half-breeds, and because of the background of their leaders, the two Riel's, it became a struggle to obtain recognition of the rights of the French to equality in the government of Red River and the Northwest. Thus the issue raised by the entrance of the Northwest in Confederation was, on what terms should it enter, and what particular terms should the French have. Out of this issue came the Province of Manitoba with both French and English as official languages and with a dual and confessional school system. The same rights were entrusted to the Territories in 1875.

Thus the Northwest entered Confederation on the basis of duality and equality. That duality and equality rested on the realities of population. Had that equality of numbers been continued, how different Canada would be today. But few French came to Manitoba and the Northwest; many English Canadians, many British, some Europeans did. The balance of numbers tilted against the French.

Then came the Saskatchewan Rebellion and the return of Riel. The Rebellion was crushed and Riel was hanged. The results were grave. Already in Quebec the Red River troubles had provoked an ultramontane, nationalist reaction that had defeated Cartier in Montreal East in 1872. Now the hanging of Riel precipitated the first great nationalist explosion in Quebec, that which brought Honoré Mercier to office in 1888 [sic]. He pursued a defiant, nationalist course. Ontario in reaction struck out at French nationalist pretensions, as many of its people thought them. The attack found a favourable hearing in Manitoba, where an overwhelmingly English and Protestant population were weary of the dual and confessional system of 1870. Both the use of French and the dual school system were abolished in 1890. In the Territories the abolition of French and a modification of the dual school system followed. The constitutions of Manitoba and the Northwest had by 1901 changed from what the federal Parliament had made them, and changed at the instance of popular majorities acting under the provincial and territorial constitutions. The Laurier-Greenway Compromise of 1897 only modified this basic change by restoring bilingual teaching and a mode of religious instruction in the schools. . . .

# Part II

# 1869-70: Causes and "Characters"

In the spring of 1869 in London Sir George Etienne Cartier and William Mc-Dougall negotiated with the Imperial government and the Hudson's Bay Company the final terms of the transfer of the Company's territories to the two-year old Dominion of Canada. The date of the transfer was initially fixed for October of 1869, then changed to December, and McDougall chosen as the first Lieutenant-Governor of Rupert's Land and the North West Territories. In October the first act of resistance to the new order in the west occurred when a group of *métis* led by Louis Riel prevented Canadian surveyors from running their lines in the Red River Settlement. In defence of his action Riel stated that the Canadian government had no right to make surveys without the permission of the people. The same month McDougall, travelling via the United States, reached Pembina at the border between the United States and the Settlement. There he was met by a delegation of *métis* who handed him an order prohibiting him from entering the North West Territories without permission of the recently organized *Comité National des Métis.*

The Council of Assiniboia, the body appointed by the Hudson's Bay Company to govern the Red River Settlement, expressed its indignation at what it termed these "outrageous proceedings" and called on representatives of the *Comité* to explain. In response, Riel, Secretary of the *Comité,* stated to the Council that the *métis* objected to a Governor coming from Canada without their being consulted. The Council, having no police or military force to support its authority, was powerless to take any action other than to advise McDougall to remain at the border outside the territory.

Early in November, Riel seized Fort Garry, arguing that it was necessary to do so to forestall similar action by hostile Canadians in the Settlement. He then invited the

English-speaking parts of the community to send representatives to participate in a Convention for the purpose of considering the political state of the country. To this Convention Riel proposed the establishment of a Provisional Government. In the meantime, the Canadian government, on learning of the resistance to McDougall, advised its agent in London to withhold payment to the Hudson's Bay Company and informed the Imperial government that Canada could not accept the transfer until "quiet possession" could be given. Nevertheless, on December 1st McDougall, not knowing that the transfer had been postponed, stepped across the frontier, read a Proclamation establishing the authority of the Crown in the North West Territories, and returned to American soil. On the same date he issued a commission to J. S. Dennis of the Canadian survey party authorizing him to organize and arm a force sufficient to disperse the armed men in the Settlement "unlawfully assembled and disturbing the public peace." A week later Riel issued a "Declaration of the People of Rupert's Land and the North-West" establishing a Provisional Government. On December 18th McDougall left the village of Pembina and returned to Canada. Before his departure the Canadian government had requested Donald A. Smith of the Hudson's Bay Company to proceed to the Red River Settlement to act as a commissioner to inquire and report on the causes of the disturbances and to explain to the inhabitants of the territory the principles on which Canada intended to govern the country. At public meetings held within the walls of Fort Garry on January 19, 20, 1870 Smith was partially successful in allaying many fears as to the nature of the new regime. The outcome of Smith's pacification mission was the drafting of a Bill of Rights and the appointment of delegates to negotiate with the Canadian government the terms of the terri-

tory's entry into Confederation.

The readings in this section deal with the Red River disturbances of 1869-70 and have been arranged according to a "Cast of Characters" for the purpose of setting forth both the alleged causes of the uprising and the role of various elements directly involved in the events.

There is, it will be seen, general agreement between contemporary and later observers in respect to two elements in the situation—the Canadians in the Red River Settlement, and the Canadian government. The Canadians in the Settlement have been charged with creating in *métis* minds a damaging image of Canada, the Canadian government with failing to recognize and assess discontent in the Settlement. Even John A. Macdonald admitted that his Lieutenant-Governor designate, William McDougall, had blundered and that Canadian agents had "not helped at all to smooth matters."

Macdonald, as ever, suspected American influences and had little faith in the good will of Riel. Some of the comments in his correspondence reflect attitudes on which the *métis* fear of annexation and of Canadian expansionists in 1869 was based. The Toronto *Globe*, an early exponent of westward expansion, indulged in its favourite pastime of attacking both Macdonald and the French, and was ready to pin the label of "Villain" on the Roman Catholic clergy. George Stanley and W. L. Morton present a more balanced appraisal of American and clerical influence.

The comments of Sir Stafford Northcote, Governor of the Hudson's Bay Company, who was in Ottawa while the delegates from Red River were treating with the Canadian government, and the editorials from Le Nouveau Monde and the Globe are contemporary opinions which were later developed in the interpretation of the events of 1869-70 as racial and religious rivalry.

# Some Canadians and the Canadian Government

Robert Rumilly, *Histoire du Canada,* (Paris, La Clé d'Or, 1951), pp. 390-392 Reprinted by permission of the Author.

## Sold Like Cattle

The annexation of the North West was a bargain made without any consultation with the population concerned. The Métis of the West, descendants of the "voyageurs" of the Hudson's Bay Company or of the North West Company, were angry at being sold like heads of cattle. The federal government named William McDougall, former lieutenant of George Brown, who remained in the coalition after the departure of his leader, Lieutenant-Governor of the North West Territories. He packed the administration of the Territories with English-speaking officials who acted as if they were conquerors of the country. He sent surveyors to carve out territorial divisions along the lines they were accustomed to, which differed from the local custom. The Métis, fearing they would be dispossessed, showed the surveyors out. Monseigneur Alexandre Taché, Bishop of Saint Boniface, warned the federal authorities but with little success.

One of the Métis, Louis Riel, suddenly assumed their leadership. He was, in fact, a French Canadian with some Indian blood from his mother's side. Riel and his Métis wanted to belong to the Canadian Confederation, but on condition that they were able to negotiate their entry as free men and to see their rights guaranteed. They formed a "National Committee of Defense" which forbade entry into the Territories of the Lieutenant-Governor nominated by Ottawa. Faced with the determined stand taken by the Métis, McDougall retreated. Riel seized Fort Garry, the main station of the Hudson's Bay Company.

United States intervention would destroy the dream of a Canada stretching from the Atlantic to the Pacific. There were new threats of a Fenian invasion at the frontiers of Quebec and Ontario. The acquisition of the North West Territories and the construction of the railway at a cost of millions received a bad press in Quebec. Emigration from Canada to the United States was at its height. There was a latent desire for annexation in many parts of the country. Macdonald and Cartier were prepared to use every means, diplomatic and military, to hold on to the North West.

It should be said in parenthesis that in all countries, legend prevails over history. Canadians believe in a Confederation born of enthusiasm and an almost spontaneous coming together of all the provinces. But Newfoundland had rejected Confederation, Nova Scotia had nearly rebelled, Prince Edward Island and British Columbia took a long time to be persuaded, and it will be seen that Confederation was imposed on the future provinces of the Prairies by force.

Ottawa entered into negotiations with the provisional government which assumed it was then recognized *ipso facto*. Donald Smith, ambitious and cunning, and a member of the Hudson's Bay Company, was a member of the federal delegation. The Métis sent a delegation bearing a "Declaration of Rights" to negotiate the conditions for the entry of the North West into Confederation.

One incident spoiled things. Some loyalists, adversaries of Riel, attempted a coup against the provisional government of Fort Garry. The attack failed, and they left some prisoners behind. One of these, the Orangeman Thomas Scott, stirred up a rising amongst his companions. The provisional government condemned him to death and had him shot.

A howl of protest went up from all Orangemen. All Ontario demanded the head of Riel in exchange for the shooting of Scott. The federal government stopped negotiating with the provisional government. The federal government sent out Colonel Garnet Wolseley, who seized Fort Garry and treated the Métis brutally. Riel fled to the United States. Ontario demanded vigorous reprisals. In Quebec, a sentiment of brotherhood swung opinion in favour of the Métis.

John A. Macdonald to John Rose, November 23, 1869. From Joseph Pope, *Correspondence of Sir John A. Macdonald*, (Toronto, Oxford University Press), 1921, p. 106.

## John A. Faces the Fiasco

You see we have commenced the extension of our sovereignty with a war! of which I informed you by cable. It appears that the half-breeds have been soured by all kinds of stories as to the intention of Canada to deprive them of their lands and to govern them without any reference to the residents. These stories have been industriously propagated, and *entre nous,* I fear that the people that McDougall sent up there— Snow and Mair and Stoughton Dennis have not helped at all to smooth matters.

These French half-breeds have always been truly loyal to the Hudson's Bay Company, and greatly dislike Schultz and that small section who published the *Nor-Wester* and are opposed to the Company. I am afraid that Snow and Dennis fraternized too much with that fellow, who is a clever sort of man but exceedingly *cantankerous* and ill-conditioned. To make matters worse, Governor McTavish [*sic*] is dying and unable to arrange matters with a firm hand. However, we must possess our souls in patience, and deal with these refractory people as best we may. Unfortunately the majority of priests up there are from Old France, and their sympathies are not with us. And to add to our troubles, Cartier rather snubbed Bishop Taché when he was here on his way to Rome. Langevin thought he had made it all right, but it appears now that the Bishop has conveyed his feelings of irritation to his representative—a person from Old France. . . .

John A. Macdonald to William McDougall, November 27, 1869. From Joseph Pope, *Memoirs of the Right Honourable Sir John Alexander Macdonald.* (Ottawa, J. Durie & Son, 1894), vol. 2, pp. 54-55.

You speak of crossing the line and being sworn in the moment that you receive official notice of the transfer of the Territory. Now, it occurs to us that that step cannot well be taken. You ought not to swear that you will perform duties that you are, by the action of the insurgents, prevented from performing. By assuming the government, you relieve the Hudson's Bay authorities from all responsibility in the matter. As things stand, they are responsible for the peace and good government of the country, and ought to be held to that responsibility until they are in a position to give peaceable possession. A proclamation, such as you suggest, calling upon the people, in your capacity as Lieut. Governor, to unite to support the law, and calling upon the insurgents to disperse, would be very well if it were sure to be obeyed. If, however, it were disobeyed, your weakness and inability to enforce the authority of the Dominion would be painfully exhibited, not only to the people of Red River, but to the people and Government of the United States. An assumption of the government by you, of course, puts an end to that of the Hudson's Bay Company's authorities, and Governor

McTavish and his Council would be deprived even of the semblance of legal right to interfere. There would then be, if you were not admitted into the country, no legal government existing and anarchy must follow. In such a case, no matter how the anarchy is produced, it is quite open by the law of nations for the inhabitants to form a government *ex necessitate* for the protection of life and property, and such a government has certain sovereign rights by the *jus gentium*, which might be very convenient for the United States, but exceedingly inconvenient to you. The temptation to an acknowledgment of such a government by the United States would be very great, and ought not to be lightly risked. We have formally notified the Colonial Office by cable of the situation of affairs, and stated the helplessness and inaction of the Hudson's Bay authorities. We have thrown the responsibility on the Imperial Government, and they will doubtless urge the Hudson's Bay people by cable to take active and vigorous steps. Meanwhile, your course has been altogether right. By staying at Pembina you will be at an easy distance from the territory, and can, it is hoped, open communication, singly or otherwise, with the insurgent leaders.

John A. Macdonald to John Rose, December 31, 1869. From Joseph Pope, *Memoirs of the Right Honourable Sir John Alexander Macdonald,* (Ottawa, J. Durie & Son, 1894), Vol. 2, pp. 59-61.

I have yours of the 13th. McDougall has made a most inglorious *fiasco* at Red River. When he left here he fully understood that he was to go as a private individual to report on the state of affairs at Red River, but to assume no authority until officially notified from here that Rupert's Land was united to Canada. He wrote to that effect to Governor McTavish [*sic*] immediately on his arrival at Pembina, stating that he would take no action until officially notified.

Notwithstanding this, from mere impatience at his uncomfortable position at Pembina, and before he could possibly have received instructions in answer to his report of being stopped on the way, he chose to assume that, on the 1st of December, the surrender was made by the Company and the Order in Council passed by the Queen, and that the Order in Council was to appoint the day of its issue as the day of the Union. He issued a proclamation under the Great Seal of the new province, formally adding it to the Dominion. He then entered into a series of inglorious intrigues, particulars of which I do not yet know, with the Swamp Indians near Red River, and with the Sioux Indians at Portage la Prairie, and sent the irrepressible Stoughton Dennis, in his capacity of 'Conservator of the Peace,' as he dubbed him, to surprise the Stone Fort. Dennis took possession of the fort, and held it for a little while, and then, as I understand it, after having first summoned all the loyal residents to join him, published a proclamation declaring the inexpediency of their organizing themselves on the rumour that Riel was going to send a deputation to treat with McDougall. What has become of Dennis I do not know, but it is said that he has abandoned the Stone Fort, and is lurking somewhere. All these movements aroused Riel, who collected his forces, and has a large band at Fort Garry, estimated variously at from 300 to 700 men.

By the way, I forgot to mention that Col. Dennis, while at Fort Garry, consulted the Recorder, Black, as to the advisability of declaring martial law. Did you ever hear such frenzy?

Riel, in order to starve McDougall out, took possession of the Hudson's Bay post, two miles from Pembina, and McDougall thereupon retreated to St. Paul, where I understand he will be today.

All this has been done in the direct teeth of instructions, and he has ingeniously contrived to humiliate himself and Canada, to arouse the hopes and pretensions of the insurgents, and to leave them in undisputed possession until next spring. He has, in fact, done all in his power to prevent the success of our emissaries, who were to arrive at Pembina on Xmas Day, and who would, I think, if things had been kept quiet, have been able to reconcile matters without any difficulty. As it is now, it is more than doubtful that they will be allowed access to the Territory or intercourse with the insurgents.

If my fears should be realized, the only thing left is the preparation of an expedition in the spring, *via* Thunder Bay. All this I tell you, of course, in confidence.

McDougall has weakened our case enormously with the Imperial Government, but we must put the best face possible on matters. We have undoubted information that the insurgents have been in communication with the Fenian body in New York, and letters have been interchanged. O'Donoghue, the young priest, has thrown off the ecclesiastical garb, and avowed himself a Fenian. The governing body at New York will send neither men nor money, but have been most liberal with promises. They have, I believe, sent an agent to stir them up. It is said that General Spear, one of the U.S. Generals of the last war, and whom you may remember to have been in command at St. Albans in '66, is the man who has gone.

By the middle of January we may expect to hear from Donald Smith, the Hudson's Bay man, and from Mr. Thibault; but, as I fear they will be unsuccessful, we must at once address ourselves to preparations for the spring. In this view, we must know what Her Majesty's Government will do, and most likely we shall next week address a despatch to Lord Granville on the subject. Our Council will re-assemble on Monday, the 3rd of January, and I shall endeavour to get the result of our deliberations off by the first Allan steamer afterwards. . . .

John A Macdonald to John Rose, February 23, 1870. From Joseph Pope, *Correspondence of Sir John Macdonald*, (Toronto, Oxford University Press, 1921), pp. 127-129.

Bishop Taché has been here and has left for the Red River, after exceedingly full and unreserved communication with him as to our policy and requirements, of all of which he approves. He is strongly opposed to the idea of an Imperial Commission, believing, as indeed, we all do, that to send out an overwashed Englishman, utterly ignorant of the country and full of crotchets, as all Englishmen are, would be a mistake. He would be certain to make propositions and consent to arrangements which Canada could not possibly accept.

Everything looks well for a delegation coming to Ottawa including the redoubtable Riel. If we once get him here, as you must know pretty well by this time, he is a gone coon. There is no place in the ministry for him to sit next to Howe, but perhaps we may make him a senator for the Territory!

I received yesterday your cable to the effect that Her Majesty's Government will co-operate in the expedition. I am very glad of this. Even if the force does not go, the agreement of England to co-operate with us will be immensely satisfactory to us, and show that England has no intention of abandoning her colonies. You will, long ere this reaches you, have received our Minute as to the proposed expeditionary force, which I hope you will approve of.

I am exceedingly glad that General Lindsay is coming out. He knows something of the country, and is a good soldier and a frank and ready man of business.

The reason why I telegraphed for the organization of the Irish constabulary is that we propose to organize a mounted Police Force under the command of Captain Cameron for Red River purposes.

We must never subject the Government there to the humiliations offered to McTavish. These impulsive half-breeds have got spoilt by this *émeute*, and must be kept down by a strong hand until they are swamped by the influx of settlers. . . .

McDougall is behaving with an utter want of judgment and proper feeling, but he has been hitherto spared, inasmuch as considerable sympathy is felt for the accumulated political misfortunes which have befallen him. Had he come back and borne his failure with dignity and reticence, we would have sustained him to the utmost extent. He has made so many enemies for himself by his folly, that I fancy he must go by the board. How he is to live, I do not know.

John A. Macdonald to John Rose, March 11, 1870. From Joseph Pope, *Memoirs of the Right Honourable Sir John Alexander Macdonald,* (Ottawa, J. Durie & Son, 1894), Vol. 2, pp. 62-63.

The propositions adopted at the Red River conference are, most of them, reasonable enough, and can easily be disposed of with their delegates. Things look well enough, were we only assured of Riel's good faith. But the unpleasant suspicion remains that he is only wasting time by sending this delegation, until the approach of summer enables him to get material support from the United States. It is believed by many that he is in the pay of the U.S. We may settle upon the terms of the constitution to be granted to the North-West with the delegates, when they arrive here, and pass an Act for the purpose, but that will not prevent Riel from refusing to ratify the arrangement, if he pleases. Meanwhile, he is in possession of the country, and is consolidating his Government. The foolish and criminal attempt of —— and —— to renew the fight has added greatly to Riel's strength. He has put down two distinct attempts to upset his Government, and American sympathizers will begin to argue that his Government has acquired a legal status, and he will be readily persuaded of that fact himself. Besides, the longer he remains in power, the more unwilling will he be to resign it, and I have, therefore, no great confidence in his ratifying any arrangements made here with the delegates. Under these circumstances the preparations for the expeditionary force must not be delayed. We shall receive the delegation with all kindness, and, I think, beyond a doubt, make an arrangement with them; but we shall, at the same time, prepare for the expedition to leave by the end of April or beginning of May.

Louis Riel, *L'Amnistie,* (Montreal, Le Nouveau Monde, 1874), pp. 3-5, 12.

## The Causes According to Riel

The North West Territories was transferred to Canada only on July 15, 1870. But in 1868-69, Canada started some public works in its name in Rupert's Land and the North West without the authorization of the Hudson's Bay Company.

The arrival of the Canadian agents in the country was remarkable by the disdain which they affected for the authority of the Company and for the original settlers. They attempted to seize the best properties of the Métis, particularly at Oak Point, a parish established about 30 miles east of Fort Garry. They pretended that they had bought these properties from the Indians. And in order to brace themselves for the coming struggle with us, they attempted to conclude an alliance with the Indians, and in order to attract them, sold them intoxicating liquor, which was contrary to the law.

In addition, the superintendent of the Canadian works at Oak Point, Mr. Snow, and his subordinates behaved very badly: they very nearly murdered each other on certain occasions. One of the employees, Th. Scott, who was later executed, held a pistol to the head of his master, and in company with some men as unruly as himself, dragged him to the river to kill him.

Some of the Métis saved the superintendent from the hands of his employees who were mostly from Ontario. It can be imagined that behaviour such as this by these foreigners did not impress the inhabitants of the country very favourably.

The Hudson's Bay Company authorities were obliged to object strongly against these disorders. And they protested to the Canadian government, less on account of the bad behaviour of their employees than because they had undertaken public works on their territory without their sanction. After Mr. Snow had begun work on the Dawson Road between Lake of the Woods and Oak Point in 1868, in the name of Canada, Canada committed another intrusion in the summer of 1869 by surveying the public and private lands around Fort Garry with a new system of measurement, thus disturbing, without any explanation, the established order and unscrupulously upsetting the original settlers in the peaceful and legal possession of their land.

The objections of the Hudson's Bay Company government were soon followed by those of the settlers who greatly objected to the fact that people thus suspected should open public roads and survey their [the settlers'] own lands, in the name of a foreign government, and with no guarantees.

At the same time, Mr. McDougall appeared on the frontier at Pembina. Everyone said he was sent by Canada to govern us. In fact, he brought with him a Council entirely composed of men whom we did not know. But his principal claim to our respect was that a considerable number of rifles were following him close behind.

The alarmed Métis formed a National Committee, advanced to meet Mr. McDougall, and sent ahead couriers to him to warn him not to enter the country. Mr. McDougall's reply was disdainful and insulting. Many of the adventurers who had attached themselves to the leadership of Mr. Snow and Colonel Dennis, then would-be surveyor general, and who were likewise compromised either by opening a Canadian road at Oak Point or by making surveys in the rest of the country, had already announced that they had come from Ontario in advance of Mr. McDougall as soldiers to help him use force against us, and that they were determined to have Mr. McDougall enter and be installed as their Governor, by force if necessary. And no sooner had Mr. McDougall arrived at Pembina than these adventurers talked publicly of seizing Fort Garry, the seat of our public affairs.

Besides, neither the English government nor the government of the Hudson's Bay Company had announced any change to us. Neither spoke to us about Mr. McDougall or his Council. Therefore Mr. McDougall was an invader. We repulsed him on November 1, 1869. And on the 3rd, we entered Fort Garry and set ourselves to guard it against the attacks by which it was menaced.

Only then did the government retreat before the disturbance caused by its trespasses and the misdeeds of its employees. It asked England to change the time of transfer, declaring that the Hudson's Bay Company had not acted correctly towards it because it had not warned the government of the troubles which disturbed the territory when it sold its charter rights to Canada.

But Lord Granville was well aware of the premature role the Canadian government had been playing in the North West. In a despatch of November 30, 1869, he said to the Governor General that the troubles which had arisen in the Territories were the result of the Canadian government's conduct.

As a result of all this, and since the Imperial authorities had seen fit to reprimand the cabinet at Ottawa, it has always seemed strange to the people of Assiniboia to hear themselves spoken of in official and other documents in Canada as a rebellious and misguided population, because we did not want to submit to the arbitrary procedures of the Canadian government.

On November 17, 1869, and on subsequent days, the so-called friends of Canada in Winnipeg wrote to Mr. McDougall who was staying at Pembina, to cause him to proclaim without delay the transfer of the North West Territories to the Canadian government. They did not worry whether the Queen's Proclamation was in effect or not. What they wanted was to overthrow at the earliest possible moment the Hudson's Bay Company government, and the establishment, by whatever means, of that of Mr. McDougall. . . .

This simple account of the principal events during our troubles from the autumn of 1868 up to the last part of February 1870, together with the testimony of Lord Granville, prove (1) that the Canadian government provoked the troubles which broke out in the North West Territories over the transfer of these territories to its power, consequently the government should bear the sole responsibility for these troubles.

(2) That it was the employees of Canada who, by destroying little by little the Hudson's Bay Company government

in 1869, forced the inhabitants of these territories to provide themselves with a provisional government whose legality was thus not in doubt, firstly because it was based on the rights of the people; secondly because it was admitted by the Honourable Privy Council for Canada in an official document of December 10, 1869; thirdly because the provisional government had received the support of the whole country of which it had become, after the Crown, the principal safeguard in view of exceptional circumstances; fourthly because this same provisional government received official recognition from the three Canadian commissioners whom I have the honour to mention: Mr. D. A. Smith, Rev. J. B. Thibault, and Colonel de Salaberry; and fifthly because this provisional government was officially invited by Canada to treat with its government to arrange amicable conditions of our entry into Confederation.

Evidence of Rev. N. J. Ritchot, "Report of the Select Committee on the Causes of the Difficulties in the North-West Territory in 1869-70," *Journals of the House of Commons 1874,* Vol. 8, Appendix 6.

# The People had no Notice

I am the parish priest of St. Norbert, in the Diocese of St. Boniface, in the Province of Manitoba. I was in the North-West before 1869, and during 1869 and 1870. I arrived there in the spring of 1862, and remained there up to my coming here on the delegation. I always resided there. The causes of the trouble arose chiefly so far as I could see from the fact that the people had no notice whatsoever of the transactions which seemed to be treated on between the Imperial Government, the Hudson's Bay Company, and the Government of Canada, with reference to the transfer of the North-West Territory to Canada. The nature of these transactions was completely unknown in the North-West, and the people were dissatisfied from the first at being left in that position. That, so far as I could see, was the chief cause of discontent.

The dissatisfaction was increased at first by the conduct of a certain "Canadian" party settled in Manitoba. That was in the autumn of 1868. It arose chiefly because that party treated the people with contempt in correspondence in the newspapers. They were few in number, and it was chiefly due to the action of their newspaper and a few individuals whose names were published. Only a few names were known. I do not know the probable number of the party. The newspaper was the "North Wester" [*sic*]. The troubles were increased in the autumn of 1868 by the arrival of a party of Canadian employees. Difficulties commenced in the course of the winter. The principal cause of the difficulty then was the rumour that these employees had made a treaty with the Indians for a certain tract of land, part of which the people of the country had claimed for themselves. I became aware of this through evidence in the Court, at the sitting of which I was present, in a case against Mr. Snow. On the occasion of that suit, the witnesses stated that on such a day Mr. Snow treated with the Indians, and gave them flour, pork and drink in exchange for the lands. I was present when that was said by the witnesses against Mr. Snow. This testimony corroborated the rumours I had heard with reference to the treaty. This was in the month of March, 1869. Subsequently to that date I had no knowledge of any special difficulty till the month of July. In the month of July, on the 29th of that month, a meeting was held at the Court House. I think it was a meeting at which all the people of the country were expected. From all I could learn of the object of the meeting, it was for the purpose of demanding the money, or a portion of the money, the Hudson's Bay Company were to receive from Canada for the country, and moreover, to overthrow the Government of the Hudson's Bay Company. I state word for word what was told me at the time. I was not at the meeting. This was told me before the meeting by the party who was to be the chairman—Mr. William Dease. I heard this on the 24th July (Saturday), and on the Sunday I warned my people to be on their guard, as to the object of the meeting, as I considered it of a dangerous character. I cannot positively state who originated the meeting; however, names were put forward. Mr. Dease is a half-breed. The chief names were Paschal Breland, W. Hallet and Joseph Genton. It was rumoured that Dr. Schultz was the prime mover in the matter. After this meeting, which failed in its object, came the discontent on the occasion of the survey by Canada. From and after the month of June, until the autumn, there were repeated difficulties with reference to the surveyors. The inhabitants demanded of the surveyors on what authority they came to survey the lands of the country. The surveyors never produced any paper or gave any satisfactory answer. The inhabitants also made enquiry of the Council of Assiniboia as to who had authorized the surveying of the lands, and were unable to get any satisfactory answer. Contrary to what usually happens, this movement originated with the people themselves—the agricultural classes. They did not consult me on that matter, and I took no part whatever in political matters at the time. These were the first causes of the difficulties to my knowledge. The discontent was increased by the news that Mr. McDougall had left Canada with an escort and a quantity of arms for the purpose of taking possession of the country. . . .

*The Globe,* Toronto, December 31, 1869.

# The Government's Errors

### The North-West

It is no pleasant task to pass in review the recent policy of the Dominion of Canada towards the North-West Territory; yet under the circumstances it cannot be avoided. The original fundamental error of the Government lay in ignoring altogether the opinions and feelings of the inhabitants of the Selkirk Settlement. The people may be divided politically into three classes: the Hudson's Bay Company, officials and adherents; the English and Scottish settlers, with their half-breed connections; and the French, principally half-breeds. The Hudson's Bay Company were naturally inclined to view with jealousy the introduction of a new order of things forced upon them by Imperial authority. The other two classes, although in the main, favourable to Canadian Annexation, were jealously on the watch lest the new system should fail to give them the perfect right of self-government which they had been hitherto denied; and for the attainment of which they had gladly welcomed the change. The French were doubly jealous, however, inasmuch as some of them feared to be over-run by British Canadians, alien to them in race and religion.

It is impossible to say whether the Ottawa authorities had any sinister motives for so acting; whether they desired to parcel out the lands of the Territory to suit their own purposes, without interference from its old occupants; but certain it is that they ignored the people of Selkirk altogether in the formation of the first Government. In spite of the warnings of the Opposition in the House of Commons and of this journal, they refused to introduce at once a representative system of Government and left the control of the affairs of the Territory for an indefinite period to a Governor and Council. In the selection of a Governor they were guided by motives of temporary political expediency; Mr. McDougall had answered all the purposes for which he was retained in the Cabinet, after the retirement of Mr. Brown; the elections of 1867 were carried by the Conservative party; Mr. McDougall had no friends in the House of Commons, and he not only was troublesome in matters of policy with the Cabinet, but his presence caused jealousy and ill-will among the Conservative followers of the Premier in Parliament. The time had arrived for getting rid of Mr. McDougall, and he was shunted off to the North-West, without consideration for the feelings of the people there. No one can deny that Mr. McDougall has some qualities of head which, under favourable circumstances, would render him a fair Governor; but one more unsuitable for the crisis could hardly have been selected. There is a considerable body of Reformers in the Settlement, who are the true friends of Canada there; but no enthusiasm was excited among them by the presence of one whom they were accustomed to regard as a traitor to his party and the principles he formerly professed. As to the Hudson's Bay Company officials, unfriendly as they are to Canadian rule, there was nothing in Mr. McDougall's antecedents, character or position, to recommend him to them; while to the French he was specially obnoxious, on account of the old quarrel about Manitoulin lands. Mr. McDougall's lack of frankness and *bonhommie* was an effectual stop to the removal of any of the prejudices, ill or well founded, which had been formed against him in the Settlement. His appointment was generally received in Canada with the remark, that if the people of the North-West were satisfied to receive him, we could have no objections, since we were about to get rid of him.

In the choice of a Council, the Government were equally unfortunate. They undoubtedly designed at one time to form it by the selection of two representatives from the larger Provinces, two from Selkirk itself, and one each from the smaller Provinces. The Government organ at Ottawa openly defended this scheme when it was assailed by the Reform press. As it was, two members of the Council, the Attorney General and the Secretary, one from Ontario and the other from Quebec, were sent up with Mr. McDougall. Capt. Cameron, Dr. Tupper's son-in-law, went up as a kind of Chief of Police, we believe, and it is to be presumed was intended to represent Nova Scotia. The surveying party, which preceded the Governor and began work, was exclusively composed of Canadians; and evidently it appeared to the people of the Territory that every good thing in the gift of the new Government was to be absorbed by strangers, and that those who had penetrated far from civilization, and lived for forty or fifty years in the hope of attaining the blessings of self-government, were about to be placed under the control of a set of foreign officials, as grasping as those of the Hudson's Bay Company. Let our readers in Ontario put themselves in the place of the people of Selkirk, and say whether they also would not have felt indignant when so treated.

It is unquestionably true that whatever might be the motives of the Government, or the character of their proceedings, the people of Canada would never have tolerated any injustice being inflicted upon the people of Selkirk. The more intelligent people of the Settlement were well aware of this fact, and were willing, in spite of the error of the Government, to receive Mr. McDougall; but their hands were weakened by these errors, and they have been compelled to succumb to the rule of the less intelligent and more headstrong.

The errors which marked the inception of the new Government are, however, less than those of its after progress. Without any intimation to Gov. McTavish [*sic*] of his approach, Mr. McDougall was sent up to the Territory. If he had gone when first appointed in summer, he would have been comparatively well received, the half-breeds being then on the plains; but he waited to air his honours through Ontario, the buffalo-hunters returned, the causes of discontent festered and rankled in the minds of the people, and he was stopped at the frontier. Before he left Toronto, Mr. McDougall was told what would happen if his Council was not better constituted than the Government journals proposed that it should be; but he disregarded the warning. Mr. Howe had been at Red River before him, and surely could not have failed to perceive the extent of the dissatisfaction which existed. There is a characteristic story told of him which shows that at all events some portion had come under his notice. It is said that a resident of Red River declaiming loudly against Confederation, appealed to him as one of the ancient opponents. "Yes," said the member for Hants, "I did oppose it, till I got a fat office, and so, I suppose, will you." The Government did not hold out to the people of Red River even a prospect of the fat offices which have so great an effect upon the opinions of the Howes of politics. . . .

Mr. McDougall faithfully carried out the programme laid down for him. Although he was cooped up in the village of Pembina, unable to enter the promised land; although his subjects were in rebellion against his authority, and his messengers obliged to steal into his seat of Government under disguise, he boldly proclaimed the transference of the Territory to Canada and claimed the loyal obedience of the inhabitants. But what in the meantime had been the course of the Government at Ottawa. While McDougall was issuing his proclamation of the annexation of the territory to Canada, they had put a stop to the annexation altogether; they had prevented the payment of the money in England and indefinitely postponed the issue of the Queen's proclamation. We look upon this act as a wrong to Mr. McDougall; but, what is much more important, a great injury to the Dominion. It has been said by one Government journal that as Canada is purchasing the Territory, it is the duty of the Hudson's Bay Company and the Imperial Government to give peaceable possession: but our claim has always been that the country has belonged to Canada since the Conquest, and that the payment of £300,000 is made to extinguish the claims which the Hudson's Bay Company had acquired by temporary occupation. To ask the Hudson's Bay Company to give us possession of the Territory is to ask an impossibility—they have not men nor money enough at command. To ask the Home Government to put down the insurrection, is to ask what will not be granted. The answer will be, "you did not wait for us to hand over the Territory; you sent in your surveyors and other officials in the most injudicious way you could have chosen, the difficulties which exist you have yourselves created, get out of them the best way you can."

This is the aspect in which the Government have placed us before the Imperial authorities. But in regard to the people of Red River the position they have selected is still more disastrous. . . . The Territory does not belong to Canada, the Hudson's Bay Company has ceased to govern, and Messrs. Bruce and Riel may hoist any flag they please without a special charge of disloyalty being raised against them. A third of the series of letters from a Hudson's Bay Company source, which we publish today, expresses as strongly as ever the absence of any desire for annexation to the United States on the part of the insurgents, and, in fact, the absence of any other desire except for union with Canada on fair terms. But the end of an insurrection cannot be predicted from the views of the actors at the beginning. The first declaration of the American Revolutionists of 1776 was filled with expressions of loyalty to George the Third. We cannot, therefore, view without alarm the present position of affairs. The Ministry, apparently, have entirely abandoned the North-West for the time being. One of their journals in Kingston declares that Canada does not want the Red River Settlement; that the idea of building a Pacific Railroad through British Territory is chimerical; and that the Territory can never be aught else than a bill of expense, with no prospect of future benefit. . . .

The actors in the scenes of the last few months have certainly placed themselves in a position ludicrous enough, but we cannot find it in our hearts to laugh at folly which has endangered the future of this country. Mr. McDougall's position may furnish many a merry jest for boon companions at Ottawa; but the people of Ontario cannot view without indignation and alarm the fair hopes of securing the North-West Territory for themselves and their children blasted by the recklessness and incapacity of their rulers.

The policy of abandonment, of relinquishment of the Territory for an indefinite period, will not satisfy public opinion. The Government selected a bad Governor and a bad Council to carry out a bad system. A portion of the people of Red River have committed grave errors, but the Ottawa Government were the first to do wrong, and ought to be the first to acknowledge it, and make restitution. . . .

*Le Nouveau Monde,* Montreal, November 26, 1869.

## A Question of Nationality and Religion

We learn from information received this morning from the Hudson's Bay territory that Mr. McDougall has decided to spend the winter at Pembina, a small American town situated at the confluence of the Red and Pembina rivers, on the Canadian frontier and marking the boundary between the State of Minnesota and the territory of Dakota. There the future governor of the province of Winnipeg will await events and a solution of the difficulties which have stopped him at the gates of the colony.

The opposition of the inhabitants of Red River to the new regime has been discussed and commented on in various ways by the whole of the Canadian press.

Some, like the *Evening Telegraph,* have already gone to war, drums beating, powder ready; others, and these are the greater number, have no illusions about the gravity of the insurrection. War with the Métis would mean war with the savage tribes of the West, and the example of the United States, which has spent millions upon millions for a century to subdue these tribes, rightly horrifies them. They advise prudence, discretion, delay and concessions. This has been the view of the *Nouveau Monde* for more than a year, and it seems to us that if attention had been paid to our warnings, the government would not have the deplorable fiasco of Mr. McDougall on its hands.

At the bottom of the whole affair is the question of nationality and religion, and the Métis seem about to repeat the dark pages which mark certain periods in the history of the Acadians and the Canadiens, their ancestors. Who can blame them for demanding guarantees from a regime which seems to have been at pains for more than a year to present itself to them under the most suspicious guise?

Certainly, we could not approve of the character which the Métis opposition could assume if it ever surpassed the limits which appear to have been assigned to it; nevertheless, we know who would suffer if it should happen. We expect great things of the government at Ottawa in this difficult situation, and we firmly hope that it will do justice to all rights; but the language of some of its spokesmen is not calculated to help its efforts.

Sir Stafford Northcote, Ottawa, to Benjamin Disraeli, April 28, 1870. Included in W. L. Morton (ed.), *Manitoba: The Birth of a Province,* (Altona, Manitoba Record Society, 1965), pp. xxi-xxii, from an original in the Iddesleigh Papers, British Museum.

## Political Considerations

The situation here is curious and interesting. Macdonald and Cartier, so long as they hold together, and so long as Cartier commands the French vote, are very strong. Ontario, however, is the dominant element in the Dominion and tends to become more and more so, and Macdonald is not supreme in Ontario, even if he has a majority there. Quebec, on the other hand, is alarmed at the power of Ontario, and desires to neutralize it by creating a French Catholic province in the North West. This had a great deal to do with the origins of the present diffculties, which have been fomented by the French priest, Bishop Taché, it is supposed, throwing the first brand after a personal quarrel with Cartier, though he did not mean to do quite as much mischief. The result has been the almost open raising of a national struggle between French and English, the former openly advocating Riel's cause until he made the stupid blunder of shooting Scott, and setting themselves strongly against an Expedition that it seemed very doubtful at one time whether Cartier would be able to retain his command of them. Ontario on the other hand has been for war and forcible measures from the first, and when Scott's death was known there was an outburst of fury, and a band of filibusters would have gone off had the Expedition been checked. Upon a division that might have taken place the opposition would have gone with Macdonald in this question. But it would have been a division between French and English *(eo nomine),* not between Catholics and Protestants (for the Irish would have all gone against the French) and the result would have been either to make a split between Macdonald and Cartier, or to destroy the influence of the latter with his own party—either of which results must soon have destroyed the present combination and would probably have produced permanent hostility between the two races. The two leaders have shown great skill and tact in avoiding the catastrophe.

# The Canadians in the Red River Settlement

W. L. Morton, (ed.), *Alexander Begg's Red River Journal and Other Papers Relative to the Red River Resistance of 1869-1870,* (Toronto, The Champlain Society, 1956), pp. 12-14, 23-24, 40-41. Reprinted by permission of The Champlain Society.

## The Unpopular Canadians

There was . . . little active sentiment for union with Canada. No official or semi-official action had been taken to create any; and in the circumstances of the colony and its government by the Hudson's Bay Company, it would have been difficult, if not impossible, to do so. What had been done had been done by the [Toronto] *Globe,* which had its subscribers in the Settlement, and by English Canadian immigrants to Red River. The first of these had come after 1857, the year in which Upper Canadian interest in the annexation of the North-West became active with the despatch of the exploring expeditions led by S. J. Dawson and H. Y. Hind. Some of these immigrants were farmers in search of land. . . . A few drifted in year by year, nearly all going to the upper Assiniboine parishes. . . . This infiltration of land seekers, though highly significant of what would follow when access to the prairie lands became easier, was quiet and hardly noted. It was other Canadians, who settled in Winnipeg to practise professions and enter the free trade, who attained notoriety. This small handful of men, led by Dr. John Schultz, were advocates of Canada's manifest destiny to acquire the North-West. When in 1864 Schultz had acquired an interest in the *Nor'Wester* he had made it a reckless advocate of Canadian annexation and an embittered critic of the Hudson's Bay Company's "monopoly" and government. In 1865 Schultz became full proprietor, and in 1868 sold out to his partner W. R. Bown; but both only succeeded in alienating the Company and the authorities of the Settlement without winning any noticeable popular support. They and the "Canadian party", as their followers were called, succeeded indeed in making the name of Canada unpopular amongst the great majority of the Settlement, and this fact largely accounts for the hostility or indifference with which the transfer was viewed. In the spring and summer of 1869, however, the Canadian party was strengthened by a steady trickle of English Canadian immigrants into the Settlement. With its numbers thus increased and with its prestige enhanced, the Canadian party and its leader, Dr. Schultz, bade fair to become a considerable power under the new order, and indeed to be its principal beneficiaries. It is this likelihood of the small and intensely unpopular Canadian party becoming the chief power and established favourite in the new order that more than anything else explains the Resistance of the *métis* to the transfer in 1869. . . .

It is difficult to avoid the conclusion that the feeling aroused against [John A.] Snow and [Charles] Mair was aggravated by their intimate association with [John C.] Schultz, an error other Canadians later committed. The feeling was also augmented by William McDougall, who apparently took no pains to see that a single French Canadian was a member of Snow's

[road-building] party or of the survey party which was to follow. All this seemed to confirm a growing suspicion amongst clergy and *métis* that English, Protestant, Orange *Ontario,* not the Dominion of Canada, was to annex the North-West and swamp its people with a rush of rough lumber-jacks from the Ottawa Valley and hard-handed backwoods farmers from Bruce and Huron counties. The fear was not unjustified. It was the expectation both of McDougall, who represented in the Dominion Cabinet the "Clear Grit" wing of Canadian Liberalism—anti-clerical, democratic and uncompromisingly Anglo-Saxon— and also of the youthful conspirators of the nascent "Canada First" party, who had hailed Schultz as a fellow soul, that the North-West would in fact become an extension of Ontario. . . .

During September [1869] the fears of Riel and of the clergy that the transfer was going to mean in fact the immediate occupation of the Red River valley by a flood of Protestant Upper Canadians, under a régime of their own making, were intensified by reports that the new governor was to be William McDougall. These reports were verified by McDougall's appointment to that post on September 28. It was a natural appointment. McDougall represented that element in Canada (the agrarian "Clear Grits" of western Upper Canada) which for over ten years had been demanding the annexation of the North-West as an area of Canadian colonization. He had publicly urged the annexation for years. Since 1867 he had fought a bitter battle against Lower Canadian and Maritime interests in the federal cabinet to bring about the implementation of Section 146 of the British North America Act, which provided for the acquisition of Rupert's Land and the North West Territory by the new

Confederation. McDougall's appointment also solved certain of the Prime Minister's difficulties in a re-organization of the cabinet which had been delayed for some months. But it showed the disposition of Macdonald and his colleagues to use the annexation of the North-West as a sop to McDougall and western Upper Canada. To the watchful eye of St. Boniface and the *métis* of Red River it could only seem the final proof of their suspicion that the North-West was to be delivered uncondi- tionally to Protestant Upper Canada. . . . Red River and the North-West would pass under the control, or at least the influence, of the long derided, long suspected, Canadian party; and the "Canadas", as the *métis* called the Upper Canadians, would be in the saddle. Some of the latter, it seems, had been rash enough to boast that such would be the case, and that they would make the country their own, pushing the *métis* westward to the Saskatchewan.

George F. G. Stanley, *Louis Riel,* (Toronto, The Ryerson Press, 1963), pp. 43-45, 48, 52, 55. Reprinted by permission of The Ryerson Press.

## The Advance Guard of a New Order

It was not until after the passage of the British North America Act in 1867 and the formation of the first federal cabinet that the North-West question was taken up seriously. In April, 1868, negotiations with the Colonial office were resumed. The Canadians, although still disposed to be difficult, were more disposed to yield to British pressure and accept the principle of compensation. The Company, too, yielded to pressure from the same source and reluctantly agreed to dispose of its rights and privileges, under the famous charter of Charles II, for a token cash payment of £300,000 . . ., a land allocation equal to one-twentieth of the land in the area to be opened for colonization, a promise not to impose restrictions against the Company's trade and the purchase of the materials for the neglected telegraph line. It was a victory for Canada; certainly the compensation was pitifully small for an area extending from the Great Lakes to the Rockies and from the 49th parallel to the Arctic.

Nevertheless, the niggardly attitude of the Canadian government, its determination to take as much as possible and give as little as practicable, left a legacy of ill-will among Company servants in Great Britain and the Territories alike. There was little that Canada could expect from them in the way of co-operation and assistance in facilitating the transfer when it should take place.

Nor was there any reason why Canada should expect help from the people of Red River. In the discussions in London the latter had played no part. Their views had never been considered; even their existence had scarcely been recognized either by Canada, Great Britain or the Hudson's Bay Company. As far as the Dominion was concerned, the government continued to maintain the fiction that the North-West had belonged by right to Canada since the days of the Ancien Régime. The people who lived there were therefore Canadians. How could there be any question of consulting them about their future when they were merely returning to their original allegiance? As far as the Indians were concerned, their title could be extinguished by some treaty arrangements; but the Selkirk settlers, the French métis and the Scotch half-breeds were forgotten or rather simply ignored. So Canada went ahead with its plans for the transfer without attempting to ascertain the climate of opinion in Red River, or even informing, officially, the Governor and Council of Assiniboia of what was being planned in Ottawa for the little colony on the banks of the Red and Assiniboine Rivers. . . .

In 1869 the Red River Settlement was ripe for a change of administration. It had ceased to be what it had been twelve years before, when the Company's overlordship had been discussed by the

Select Committee in London. It was no longer a community that could, with any justice, be described as one in which the people were "without the vexations and the heart-burning of active politics"; one in which "the rivalries that existed were in keeping with their simple life, and had nothing of that fierce element of competition into which the newer civilization was to hurl them", or one in which the contests of life turned on the speed of horses "especially if they were owned in different parts of the colony," or who could be first with the seeding and the harvest, or who could carry the greatest number of bags of wheat, or who could survive longest in the almost endless rounds of the Red River jig. It is true that the people had challenged the Hudson' Bay Company on the question of the Company's trade policy, but they had never tried to replace the Company rule with some other form of administration. They had accepted the Council of Assiniboia without worrying very much about whether it was an elective or appointed body, or whether the Company was really behind the throne of the governor of Assiniboia. . . . The local government had seldom had a military force to back up its decrees, but it had seldom needed one. It had succeeded in maintaining its authority largely because the people were prepared to accept it.

The newcomers who had entered the colony within the last ten years felt no sense of loyalty to the Hudson's Bay Company or to the local government in the Settlement. On the contrary, many of them regarded themselves as the advance guard of a new economic and political order. All of them brought in their trunks and valises the political ideas and prejudices of the part of Canada from which they had come. Almost to a man they had come from Canada West or Ontario. They

challenged the Company régime, they ridiculed it, they refused to obey its orders, they tore the trappings of dignity from it, bared its nakedness and revealed its puny muscles. The years between 1857 and 1869 were the years of decline in the old order in the Red River Settlement, the years of chaos, and finally the years of the collapse of the local administration.

The most serious challenge to the Hudson's Bay Company rule came from the newspaper, the *Nor'Wester*. The paper's first issue had spoken of "assisting in the work of governmental organization," as if there was no question whatsoever of the need of some new organization. At the outset, editorial comment in the paper was comparatively mild, but after 1860, when James Ross began to write the leading articles, there was a noticeable sharpening in the tone of the editorials. Ross, although he had been born in Red River, had been educated in Canada. He had seen the outside world and had picked up new political ideas. If not really a very able man, he did possess considerable facility with his pen, and under his direction the *Nor'Wester* began to advocate closer trade relations and more intimate ties with Canada. Ross even began to talk about the end of Hudson's Bay Company rule in the North-West, and the possibility of a crown colony being established in the Company's territories. "It requires neither acuteness nor hostility on our part," he wrote, to see that for things to continue as they were was *"simply impossible."* . . .

However, from 1864, when John Schultz took over control of the *Nor'-Wester,* the agitation and the agitators became more positive, more provocative, more emphatically Canadian. Schultz's aim was annexation to Canada, and to that end he worked unremittingly. And he had the material with which to work, since Ross had prepared the way. It did not need Schultz to expose the weakness of Company rule, to stir the dormant waters of political thought, to raise doubts about the security of the Company's land titles or to create a general feeling of discontent within the Settlement. All that Schultz had to do was to take advantage of what Ross had done and to keep pressing forward to the overthrow of the Company régime. It should be remembered that Schultz and the Canadian Party, of which he became the acknowledged head, were not taking an unreasonable stand when they contended that the existing régime had ceased to meet the needs of the Settlement. A commercial company could not hope to govern indefinitely a colony in an age that was becoming increasingly democratic. It could offer no defence against American infiltration; the fate of Oregon was proof of that. . . .

To compound this aggravation, [Charles] Mair wrote a series of letters to his brother in Perth describing his journey and the beauties of the Red River valley. Ostensibly they were private letters; but there seems little doubt but that Mair expected them to be printed. And printed they were, first in the *Perth Courier* and then in the Toronto *Globe*. It was unfortunate that, while talking in glowing terms about the land and its fertility, Mair should have made slighting remarks about the morals of the women of the colony, the half-breed women. He suggested that the real explanation for the destitution in the colony was the fact that the half-breeds were on "their beam ends" simply because they "will hunt buffaloes, drive ox-carts . . . do anything but farm." Mair suffered for his rude and distasteful remarks when he was horse-whipped by Mrs. Bannatyne; but the damage had been done, and the growing animosity of the métis spilled over on everyone who came from Canada. Even

then Mair might have been forgiven: after all, he had come to the Settlement with letters of introduction to Bishop Taché. But he sought no advice from those who could have helped him most, and he continued to send communications to the newspaper stressing the attractiveness of the country for Canadian immigrants—"Minnesota is *sand* compared to this." The Canadian farmer, dissatisfied with the tree-grown or rocky land in Ontario, was urged to come to Red River at once. He should: "bring with him provisions to subsist his family for at least one year. He should also bring his seed grain (spring wheat), a Pittsburgh plough with movable point, harrow teeth, and a combined mower and reaper, or, better still, one of Marsh's Harvesters, and a separate mower." On arrival in Red River: "he could find Canadian friends to advise and assist him, in Dr. Schultz and others, and he would have no difficulty in selecting a farm. There is no Hobson's choice about it—'this or none.' The cake is 700 miles long and 400 miles wide with plenty of elbow room."

Statements such as these seemed to give colour to the mutterings that were growing in volume throughout the Settlement. They implied that the Canadians wanted to swamp the old settlers with immigrants, with democratic, anti-clerical, anti-French, anti-half-breed immigrants. What would happen to the old settlers, to their lands, to their simple economy, to their easy-going live and let-live bi-culturalism? At least Schultz knew what to expect from the anticipated explosion of immigration. "I shall buy heavily in Montreal and ship at once and still hope to be back in time," he wrote from Toronto in March, 1869. . . .

The Canadians not only had their eyes on the political jobs, they had their eyes on the vacant lands too. There was good land in the Settlement—Mair had written frequently on this subject—and it was to be had for the taking. Certainly men like Schultz and Mair were not likely to lose any opportunity to turn an honest or dishonest dollar when the Canadian immigrants would come pouring into the country. Good land close to the river and the centres of population would demand good prices. There is evidence that not only did Schultz and Mair speculate in lands, but that [John A.] Snow and other government employees did likewise. The staking of land-claims, even if the claims did not infringe upon existing rights of ownership, was enough to nourish the cancer of suspicion that was growing throughout the body of the population of Red River.

It was the staking of lands that, in fact, led the métis to take the first steps in their resistance to Canada.

# Some Inhabitants of the Red River Settlement

*Canada Sessional Papers 1870*, Vol. 5, No. 12.

## A Government is Organized

DECLARATION OF THE PEOPLE OF RUPERT'S LAND AND THE NORTH-WEST

Whereas, it is admitted by all men, as a fundamental principle, that the public authority commands the obedience and respect of its subjects. It is also admitted, that a people, when it has no Government, is free to adopt one form of Government, in preference to another, to give or to refuse allegiance to that which is proposed. In accordance with the above first principle, the people of this country had obeyed and respected the authority to which the circumstances surrounded its infancy compelled it to be subject.

A company of adventurers known as the "Hudson Bay Company," and invested with certain powers, granted by His Majesty (Charles II), established itself in Rupert's Land, and in the North-West Territory, for trading purposes only. This company, consisting of many persons, required a certain constitution. But as there was a question of commerce only, their constitution was framed in reference thereto. Yet, since there was at that time no

Government to see to the interests of a people already existing in the country, it became necessary for judicial affairs to have recourse to the officers of the Hudson Bay Company. This inaugurated that species of government which, slightly modified by subsequent circumstances, ruled this country up to a recent date.

Whereas, that Government, thus accepted, was far from answering to the wants of the people, and became more and more so, as the population increased in numbers, and as the country was developed, and commerce extended, until the present day, when it commands a place amongst the colonies; and this people, ever actuated by the above-mentioned principles, had generously supported the aforesaid Government, and gave to it a faithful allegiance, when, contrary to the law of nations, in March, 1869, that said Government surrendered and transferred to Canada all the rights which it had, or pretended to have, in this Territory, by transactions with which the people were considered unworthy to be made acquainted.

And, whereas, it is also generally admitted that a people is at liberty to establish any form of government it may consider suited to its wants, as soon as the power to which it was subject abandons it, or attempts to subjugate it, without its consent to a foreign power; and maintain, that no right can be transferred to such foreign power. Now, therefore, first, we, the representatives of the people, in Council assembled in Upper Fort Garry, on the 24th day of November, 1869, after having invoked the God of Nations, relying on these fundamental moral principles, solemnly declare, in the name of our constituents, and in our own names, before God and man, that, from the day on which the Government we had always

respected abandoned us, by transferring to a strange power the sacred authority confided to it, the people of Rupert's Land and the North-West became free and exempt from all allegiance to the said Government. Second. That we refuse to recognize the authority of Canada, which pretends to have a right to coerce us, and impose upon us a despotic form of government still more contrary to our rights and interests as British subjects, than was that Government to which we had subjected ourselves, through necessity, up to a recent date. Thirdly. That, by sending an expedition on the 1st of November, ult., charged to drive back Mr. William McDougall and his companions, coming in the name of Canada, to rule us with the rod of despotism, without previous notification to that effect, we have acted conformably to that sacred right which commands every citizen to offer energetic opposition to prevent this country from being enslaved. Fourth. That we continue, and shall continue, to oppose, with all our strength, the establishing of the Canadian authority in our country, under the announced form; and, in case of persistence on the part of the Canadian Government to enforce its obnoxious policy upon us by force of arms, we protest beforehand against such an unjust and unlawful course; and we declare the said Canadian Government responsible, before God and men, for the innumerable evils which may be caused by so unwarrantable a course. Be it known, therefore, to the world in general, and to the Canadian Government in particular, that, as we have always heretofore successfully defended our country in frequent wars with the neighbouring tribes of Indians, who are now on friendly relations with us, we are firmly resolved in future, not less than in the past, to repel all invasions from whatsoever quarter they may come; and, furthermore, we do declare and proclaim, in the name of the people of Rupert's Land and the North-West, that we have, on the said 24th day of November, 1869, above mentioned, established a Provisional Government, and hold it to be the only and lawful authority now in existence in Rupert's Land and the North-West which claims the obedience and respect of the people; that, meanwhile, we hold ourselves in readiness to enter in such negociations with the Canadian Government as may be favourable for the good government and prosperity of this people. In support of this declaration, relying on the protection of Divine Providence, we mutually pledge ourselves, on oath, our lives, our fortunes, and our sacred honor, to each other.

Issued at Fort Garry, this Eighth day of December, in the year of our Lord One thousand eight hundred and sixty-nine.

JOHN BRUCE, Pres.
LOUIS RIEL, Sec.

*Canada Sessional Papers 1870*, Vol. 5, No. 12.

## Some Demands Made

LIST OF RIGHTS

1. That the people have the right to elect their own Legislature.

2. That the Legislature have the power to pass all laws local to the Territory over the veto of the Executive by a two-thirds vote.

3. That no Act of the Dominion Parliament (local to the Territory) be binding on the people until sanctioned by the Legislature of the Territory.

4. That all Sheriffs, Magistrates, Constables, School Commissioners, &c., be elected by the people.

5. A free homestead and pre-emption land law.

6. That a portion of the public lands be appropriated to the benefit of schools, the building of bridges, roads, and public buildings.

7. That it be guaranteed to connect Winnipeg by rail with the nearest line of railroad, within a term of five years; the land grant to be subject to the Local Legislature.

8. That, for the term of four years, all military, civil, and municipal expenses be paid out of the Dominion funds.

9. That the military be composed of the inhabitants now existing in the Territory.

10. That the English and French languages be common in the Legislature and Courts, and that all public documents and Acts of the Legislature be published in both languages.

11. That the Judge of the Supreme Court speak the English and French languages.

12. That treaties be concluded and ratified between the Dominion Government and the several tribes of Indians in the Territory, to ensure peace on the frontier.

13. That we have a fair and full representation in the Canadian Parliament.

14. That all privileges, customs, and usages existing at the time of the transfer, be respected.

All the above articles have been severally discussed and adopted by the French and English Representatives without a dissenting voice, as the conditions upon which the people of Rupert's Land enter into confederation.

The French Representatives then proposed, in order to secure the above rights, that a Delegation be appointed and sent to Pembina to see Mr. McDougall, and ask him if he could guarantee these rights by virtue of his commission; and, if he could do so, that then the French people would join to a man to escort Mr. McDougall into his Government seat. But, on the contrary, if Mr. McDougall could not guarantee such rights, that the Delegates request him to remain where he is, or return, till the rights be guaranteed by Act of the Canadian Parliament.

The English Representatives refused to appoint delegates to go to Pembina to consult with Mr. McDougall, stating they had no authority to do so from their constituents, upon which the Council was dissolved.

The meeting at which the above resolutions were adopted, was held at Fort Garry, on Wednesday, December 1st, 1869.

Winnipeg, December 9th, 1869.

W. L. Morton (ed.), *Alexander Begg's Red River Journal and Other Papers Relative to the Red River Resistance of 1869-1870,* (Toronto, The Champlain Society, 1956), pp. 6-8, 12. Reprinted by permission of the Champlain Society.

# The Hudson's Bay Men

# and Others

If the Roman Catholic clergy on the whole followed discreetly where the *métis* dared to tread, the resident officers of the Hudson's Bay Company were at least tempted to do the same. Like the missionaries, the local officers of the Company had come to fear the major adjustments which would be necessary in the conduct, and indeed in the character, of the Company's operation once the North-West was opened to settlement. Not only would the Company cease to be the government of the country, and become one of the governed, its officers citizens among the citizens; but also the new government would be one of Canadians, perhaps under the influence of the years of propaganda against the Company. With settlement would come an increase in the number of competitors in the fur-trade, and great and unpredictable changes in the distribution of wild life and in the regulation of relations with the Indians, on which the conduct of the fur-trade depended.

In addition to these general causes for misgiving, the officers of the Company resident in Rupert's Land and the North-West Territory had a definite grievance of their own. This was the failure of the Governor and Committee, and the General Court of the Company, to consult them with respect to the terms on which the Company had surrendered its rights in the North-West to the Crown for transfer to Canada, or to acknowledge explicitly the right of the commissioned officers of the Company to share in the sum of £300,000 to be paid by Canada in compensation for that surrender. A further aggravation of their uncertainty and discontent was that the officers at Fort Garry, and in particular William Mactavish, who was Governor both of Rupert's Land and Assiniboia, had not been informed of the time or manner of the transfer by the Governor and Committee of the Company, the Imperial Government, or the Canadian Government. There is good reason to think that the perplexity and discontent of Mactavish and his subordinates was communicated to the *métis*. There is, however, no evidence, and no reason to think that any officer of the Company, with the exception of John H. McTavish, Chief Accountant at Fort Garry, either inspired the Resistance of the *métis* to the transfer, or attempted to use that Resistance for any purpose of the Company.

If the resident officers viewed the transfer of the North-West to Canada with misgivings, they also accepted it with resignation, for they had no alternative to desire or advocate. Any disposition that individual officers may have shown in favour of annexation to the United States was owing to one or all of three factors. First, there was disbelief in the ability of Canada to maintain the union with the North-West. Second, there was resentment at English indifference to the fate of the North-West. Finally, there were the agreeable relations established with American businessmen and publicists, which influenced sentiment but did not create any positive wish for political union with the United States. . . . All [the English-speaking colonists] were prepared to accept the transfer, but a few thought terms should be demanded of Canada before the transfer was completed. At the other extreme, some saw it as a matter of simple loyalty, and were ardently in favour of union with Canada as a means of confirming the British allegiance of Red River. These were settlers with Canadian connections, or pensioners manifesting a soldier's unquestioning loyalty. The great majority, however, were passive, if not apathetic. Most of them disliked the failure to consult the people or the authorities of the colony in any way, but were confident either that Canada would do the right thing, or that the Imperial Government would ensure that it was done. Amongst the half-breeds, however, were many who disliked the Canadians in the Settlement, and to whom Canada was unknown; and these were worried as to how they would fare in the new order. Thus the English-speaking population was divided by its two extremes, one in favour of the demanding of terms, the other in favour of unquestioning acceptance; while the great central body of sentiment was inclined to risk nothing for Canada, and was at first not unsympathetic with the cause, if critical of the acts, of the *métis*, with whom they possessed ties of blood and of long association on hunt and trip.

## The Clergy

━━━━━━━━━━━━━━━━━━━━

*The Globe,* Toronto, December 9, 1869.

### *The Globe* Discovers the Villains

THE RED RIVER ROW

We have some further information from a gentleman just arrived from Red River in reference to the troubles there. It appears that Father Richot [*sic*] is the head and front of the whole movement by the French half-breeds. He is a parish priest at Stinking River, and a man apparently of strong passions. He is said to have declared, striking his hand upon his breast, that Governor McDougall should only enter the Settlement over his dead body. The sooner his ecclesiastical superiors deal with this gentleman the better. It is believed in the Settlement that Bishop Taché, who held a correspondence with Sir George Cartier some months ago, but who is now in Rome, is partly responsible for the movement. Possibly he wrote a letter which was misconstrued by some of his subordinates in the Territory; we do not believe that he contemplated the outrages which have since occurred. There seems to have been some idea on the part of the French, that they were about to be overrun by Protestants from Canada, but it is only charitable to believe that few of them could have conceived the idea that they could withhold from settlement the fourth part of a continent, in order to keep them from the contamination of Protestantism.

The French race on this continent is wonderfully exclusive in its ideas; but this is a touch beyond what even a Lower Canadian Frenchman ever conceived.

Our informant believes that the sending in of surveyors before the transfer of the Territory to Canada, and the supercilious manner of some of the Canadian Government officials, have been the great causes of the dissatisfaction among the British part of the population. He has not the slightest doubt that if the Red River people had been conferred with by Government Commissioners, and a proper share given to them in the management of the affairs of the Territory, there would have been no trouble. . . .

Our informant was unable to give any opinion as to the conclusion of the matter; but he is quite distinct in his denial that there is the slightest desire for annexation among the people of the Territory.

George F. G. Stanley, *The Birth of Western Canada, a History of the Riel Rebellions,* (London, Longmans, Green, 1936; Toronto, University of Toronto Press, 1960), pp. 60-61. Reprinted by permission of the University of Toronto Press.

# The Church Supports the Métis

The French half-breeds could never have carried out their successful resistance had they not had the advice and tacit support of their clergy. The part played by the Roman Catholic clergy in the Red River Rebellion has often been misunderstood and sometimes misrepresented. Dr. George Bryce, [a Presbyterian minister and historian] with an obvious bias, speaks of them as "ecclesiastics from old France," with "no love for Canada, no love for any country, no love for society, no love for peace!" To understand the rôle that they played in the rising, we have only to turn to the history of Canada. From the fall of Quebec to the present day, the French Canadian, with the assistance of his curé, has clung strenuously to his laws, his language, his religion and his institutions. Cut off from France, the French Canadians have, nevertheless, maintained inviolate their separate identity; wherever we may go in Canada we find communities of French Canadians maintaining the nationality of their fathers, true to the watchword of old Quebec, "Je me Sou-

viens." Anyone who is acquainted with the French Canadian in Western Canada is struck by the tenacity with which he holds to his language and his nationality in the face of overwhelming odds and difficulties. One of the greatest forces which has assisted this tenacious survival has been the influence exercised by the Roman Catholic Church. From the time of the Conquest it has been the curé who has held the citadel of French Canadian nationalism against the assaults of the Anglo-Saxon. The Church realized that the French Canadian who has lost his language might also lose his faith. It was the strong organization of the Catholic parish which saved the French Canadian as such after 1670, and which maintains him to this day in the midst of the English-speaking provinces of Canada.

This same influence was exercised by the Church in Red River. The Roman Catholic clergy saw that unless some definite guarantee was secured from the Canadian Government, unless some breakwater could be raised against the tide of Protestant English immigration, the French Catholic *métis* would suffer the same fate as the French Catholic Louisianian. Bishop Taché had returned from Canada in 1857 full of apprehension for the future of his race and his religion in the North-West, and expressed his fear in a letter to Sir George Cartier:

*"J'ai toujours redouté l'entrée du Nord-Ouest dans la Confédération parce que j'ai toujours cru que l'élément français catholique serait sacrifié. . . . Le nouveau système me semble de nature à amener la ruine de ce qui nous a coûté si cher."*

Accordingly, certain members of the French Canadian Catholic clergy, particularly the Abbé Ritchot, identifying the cause of the *métis* with that of the French Canadian, threw the weight of their influence on the side of the half-breeds rather than upon that of Canada. Thus the Red River Rebellion, which was fundamentally the revolt of a semi-primitive society against the imposition of a more progressive, alien culture, assumed a religious and racial aspect which was to have unfortunate repercussions in Eastern Canada.

W. L. Morton (ed), *Alexander Begg's Red River Journal and Other Papers Relative to the Red River Resistance of 1869-1870,* (Toronto, The Champlain Society, 1956), pp. 8-9, 85-86. Reprinted by permission of The Champlain Society.

# American Influences at Red River

By the early sixties the Americans, some of German or Irish descent and of the Catholic faith, were a considerable element in the little village of Winnipeg, the seat of the free traders in competition with the Hudson's Bay Company. In the main, the Americans did not engage in the fur-trade itself, but were saloon-keepers, particularly the Germans and Irish, and merchants retailing goods imported from St. Paul. As such, they were able to maintain good relations with the Company and with all other elements in the community, and as a group were well liked.

The Americans were, however, naturally and inevitably annexationists. Some of them had come to Red River in the expectation that the pull of continental economic forces would draw the North-West into the Republic. In nursing this expectation they were only the local representatives of those ambitious citizens of St. Paul who saw their city becoming the metropolis of the North-West of America and irresistibly drawing the Canadian North-West to it by the golden bonds of commerce and the supposed attraction of republican institutions. These hopes were the result of a naive and unaggressive belief in the power of natural economic forces and of the continental destiny of the United States. That such a belief was out of date in 1869, in consequence of the rise of economic nationalism in the United States and of political nationalism in Canada, had not yet been realized. Because of this amiable and expectant attitude, the Americans of Winnipeg did nothing overt to inspire or stiffen the Resistance of the *métis* to the transfer. Their attitude was outwardly correct, non-committal and yet sympathetic. As they confidently expected the Resistance to end in annexation, they were at first content to wait upon events, giving advice when asked, and even, it was said, some supplies; not hiding their desire for annexation, but not otherwise actively pushing the cause.

This passive attitude was not shared, however, by certain Americans at Pembina [who] from the first endeavoured to give the Resistance an annexationist visage; and, as they were the only channel of news to the outside world, they succeeded only too well. When the Resistance was made effective in December, these active annexationists were joined by certain Americans of Winnipeg . . . who then endeavoured to bring Riel and the *métis* to choose annexation. . . .

The question of American influence on the Resistance is an obscure and subtle subject. Riel himself was not anti-American in feeling, and seems to have had some admiration of American institutions. This probably was the general attitude of the *métis.* Many of them made freighting trips to St. Paul, and most had American relatives and friends at Pembina, St. Joseph's, and St. Paul. On the other hand they had reservations with respect to union with the United States. One cause of this was the failure of the Pembina Indian Treaty of 1851; another was the refusal of the American Government to recognize half-breeds as a group intermediate between Indian and white; and perhaps the American school system was a third. But there was no hostility, and American influence upon the course of the Resistance had no deep-seated aversion to American institutions to overcome. Riel's statement to Donald A. Smith that he was for annexation "only if the people wished it", meant that he did not expect them to do so, but would not oppose them if they did.

American attempts to influence Riel and his councillors—the distorted news concocted in Pembina; the visits of ⌊Enos⌋ Stutsman, Joseph Rolette, Jr., and Joseph Lemay to Fort Garry; the open hope of the Americans in Winnipeg for annexation; and finally, the frankly annexationist tone of the *New Nation*—were all obvious enough. It seems clear, however, that these factors did not inspire the Resistance or to any degree affect its course. The rising of the *métis* was spontaneous and autonomous, and the Americans simply attempted to use it for their own ends. . . . What these American activities did in fact produce was a readiness on the part of the Canadian Government to conciliate and finally to negotiate with the people of Red River. Riel presumably anticipated this result. He knew also that, if negotiations with Canada failed, then the alternative of annexation to the United States lay ready to hand. Riel, in short, could not quarrel with the Americans until he was sure of terms with Canada.

Rev. George Bryce, *The Remarkable History of the Hudson's Bay Company*, (London, Sampson Low, Marston & Co., 1900), pp. 459-460.

## A Dangerous Element

Two other most important forces in this complicated state of things cannot be left out. The first of these is a matter which requires careful statement, but yet it is a most potential factor in the rebellion. This is the attitude of certain persons in the United States. For twenty years and more the trade of the Red River settlement had been largely carried on by way of St. Paul, in the State of Minnesota. The Hudson Bay route and York boat brigade were unable to compete with the facilities offered by the approach of the railway to the Mississippi River. Accordingly long lines of Red River carts took loads of furs to St. Paul and brought back freight for the Company. The Red River trade was a recognized source of profit in St. Paul. Familiarity in trade led to an interest on the part of the Americans in the public affairs of Red River. Hot-headed and sordid people in Red River settlement had actually spoken of the settlement being connected with the United States.

Now that irritation was manifested at Red River, steps were taken by private parties from the United States to fan the flame. At Pembina, on the border between Rupert's Land and the United States, lived a nest of desperadoes willing to take any steps to accomplish their purposes. They had access to all the mails which came from England to Canada marked "Via Pembina." Pembina was an outpost refuge for law-breakers and outcasts from the United States. Its people used all their power to disturb the peace of Red River settlement. In addition, a considerable number of Americans had come to the little village of Winnipeg, now being begun near the walls of Fort Garry. These men held their private meetings, all looking to the creation of trouble and the provocation of feeling that might lead to change of allegiance. Furthermore, the writer is able to state, on the information of a man high in the service of Canada, and a man not unknown in Manitoba, that there was a large sum of money, of which an amount was named as high as one million dollars, which was available in St. Paul for the purpose of securing a hold by the Americans on the fertile plains of Rupert's Land.

Here, then, was an agency of most dangerous proportions, an element in the village of Winnipeg able to control the election of the first delegate to the convention, a desperate body of men on the border, who with Machiavellian persistence fanned the flame of discontent, and a reserve of power in St. Paul ready to take advantage of any emergency.

# Part III

# Thomas Scott and the Amnesty

The attempt under J. S. Dennis to organize an armed force and to employ Indians in opposition to Riel met with little success in the Red River Settlement. Only the Canadians showed any eagerness to enlist. Early in December, 1869, a number of these gathered at Dr. J. C. Schultz's store to prevent Canadian government supplies intended for the Dawson Road and survey parties from falling into Riel's hands. Riel and his *métis* forces surrounded the store, forced the Canadians to surrender and took the group to Fort Garry as prisoners. Some of these were released in January, 1870 on agreeing to leave the Settlement or take an oath of allegiance to the Provisional Government. By the middle of February all had been released. Several of them, however, had earlier escaped, including Dr. J. C. Schultz, Charles Mair, the poet, and Thomas Scott, a labourer employed by the Canadian government on the building of the Dawson Road. Scott was recaptured with a group which had assembled on February 17th at Portage la Prairie some sixty miles west of Fort Garry and was thought by Riel to be preparing an attack. Charles A. Boulton, the leader of the Portage party, was condemned to be shot but was spared. On March 3, 1870 Scott was brought before a court-martial charged with having taken up arms against the Provisional Government and striking one of his guards. The following day he was executed.

Of all the events of 1869-70 none is more inexplicable than the shooting of Thomas Scott and none proved to be of such consequence to the career and reputation of Louis Riel. That Scott was contemptuous of the *métis,* that he was an unruly prisoner, and that he symbolized a threat to Riel's programme can not be denied. But to have shot him was both an irrational and unnecessary counter-action.

In 1874 Riel published his justification

of the execution, claiming that the death of Scott was necessary to the establishment of respect and authority for the Provisional Government. Later writers have suggested that Riel was forced to execute Scott in order to maintain the unity of his *métis* followers.

At the time, however, no explanation would calm religious and racial extremists in Ontario and Quebec. Reaction to the uprising at Red River and particularly to the execution of Scott foreshadowed the later and more ominous tensions of 1885-86. In the 1870's it bedevilled the question of an amnesty.

On August 23, 1870, as Colonel Garnet Wolseley led an armed force into Fort Garry Riel left the Settlement for the United States. On several occasions he returned to the Settlement but always under fear of capture. In October, 1871 he came forward to offer *métis* assistance to Lieutenant-Governor Adams G. Archibald in turning back a Fenian "invasion" of Manitoba. The following year he campaigned for the federal seat of Provencher in the House of Commons but withdrew at the request of the Canadian government in favour of Sir George Etienne Cartier who had been defeated in Montreal East. Following Cartier's death in May, 1873, he won the constituency in a by-election and again in the general election early in 1874. Though he went to Ottawa he never attempted to take his seat in the Commons. A reward had been offered and warrants issued for his arrest. On March 31, 1874 Mackenzie Bowell, a prominent Ontario Orangeman and Conservative, moved Riel's expulsion from the House of Commons. The motion, which carried by an overwhelming majority, reflected a division on racial rather than party lines.

Prior to this motion the House had appointed a Select Committee to inquire both into the causes of the disturbances of 1869-70 and to what extent promises of an amnesty had been made. Archbishop Taché of St. Boniface and Rev. N. J. Ritchot insisted that an amnesty had been promised to the Red River delegates in negotiations with the Canadian government in 1870. Quebec demanded it. Ontario damned it. And the Canadian government, for political reasons, denied it, seeking to shift responsibility in the matter to the Imperial government.

# The Execution of

# Thomas Scott

George F. G. Stanley, *Louis Riel,* (Toronto, The Ryerson Press, 1963), pp 108, 110-113, 115-117. Reprinted by permission of The Ryerson Press.

## A Political Blunder

. . . The one course from which Riel never deviated was building a strong government in the colony to negotiate with Canada. He had wanted to unite, not to split, the Settlement. But here were [Dr. J. C.] Schultz and the Canadians constantly trying to cause trouble and sow the seeds of dissension. They were the trouble makers, these newcomers who had tried to hurry the establishment of Canadian rule, who had backed McDougall and had twice tried to cause rebellion in Red River. They needed to be taught a lesson. Someone should be punished. . . .

The prisoners: what was to be done about them? There was no doubt in [Donald A.] Smith's mind or in Archdeacon [John] McLean's mind that Riel had promised to release them as soon as the new Provisional Government was firmly established. Such a promise would have fitted the pattern of Riel's thinking, and this was what he had done before. Throughout his life Riel tended to follow the same course, especially when it had enjoyed success on a previous occasion. But when he made this promise Riel neglected to take into consideration the attitude of his own followers. Without his soldiery at Fort Garry, he would never have gained or held his position as head of the Provisional Government; in the final analysis, the success of his movement depended upon their loyalty and their continued support. This was one reason why Riel needed a wider basis for his government and why he strove to obtain it. But the métis soldiers were not a disciplined body; they followed their leader not because they had to but because they wanted to. They would forsake him as soon as his actions failed to satisfy them. And so Riel had to keep on the good side of his men or suffer the consequences. During the last days of February, in the excitement and tension of a civil war that always seemed to threaten but never develop, Riel's men were edgy and unruly, and all the more so when Riel was ill in bed. And the new batch of prisoners contained several men who were truculent and aggressive and difficult to handle—particularly after they learned of the reprieve granted to Major [Charles A.] Boulton.

Of the new prisoners, Thomas Scott was unquestionably the leader in the absence of Schultz. . . . Although his militia captain had thought highly of him and referred to him as "gentlemanly," Scott soon revealed other qualities, qualities likely to emerge under frontier conditions, recklessness, stubbornness and lawlessness. Perhaps it would be fairer to say that Scott was a man prepared to stand up for what he believed to be his rights and prepared to flout authority in order to secure them. . . . Out of work, he drifted into Winnipeg where he drank and fought, and where he came under the influence of John Schultz. Here were two men who understood each other; the one was a man

whom Schultz could use, the other a man whom Scott could serve. . . .

Scott and one of his companions, Murdoch McLeod, set out to make life miserable for their captors. . . . [Scott] had nothing but contempt for all mixed-bloods and to his sense of racial superiority he added the narrow bigotry of the Ulster Orangeman. . . . For a man like Riel, who even as a schoolboy had been noted for an inability to brook opposition, Scott's actions were both irritating and provocative: to a man like Scott, narrow, ignorant and lacking in discretion at a time when passions were aroused, Boulton's reprieve and Riel's admonitions were signs of timidity. Both men misunderstood each other, and as Riel yielded to the demands of his followers that Scott must be punished, Scott was crying: "The *métis* are a pack of cowards. They will not dare to shoot me."

It was a dangerous challenge at any time. It was doubly dangerous when feelings were raw and tempers were rising. On March 3 [1870], the *métis* called a court-martial to try Scott for "insubordination." This was the way they handled problems of a similar nature on the prairie. It was the buffalo hunters' method, the formation of an *ad hoc* tribunal. All the men comprising the court-martial were familiar with the law of the prairie. . . .

Probably no action of Louis Riel excited as much controversy and as much strong feeling as the execution of Thomas Scott. No act of his is harder to explain. There are some who argue that it was an impulsive act of vengeance on the part of the *métis*, that Riel was virtually forced to agree to the execution owing to the pressure upon him of his own men. It has been said that Riel himself was threatened unless he agreed to the death of Scott.

There are others who take the view that the execution was a deliberate act of policy. The latter was certainly the explanation offered by Riel himself. And it probably fits the circumstances better than the former, if only because the *métis*, if quickly moved to anger, were not a people given to bloodshed. The division within the court-martial itself suggests that the pressures on Riel were not so irresistible as to force him into an action against his better judgment. Moreover, Riel several times attempted to explain what lay behind his act. In a memorandum which he sent to L. R. Masson in 1872, he said that the shooting was necessary, not because the métis soldiers insisted upon it, but because it was essential "to intimidate the conspirators." Even though the Portage people had, following Boulton's reprieve, agreed to recognize the Provisional Government, they made it clear they were only waiting for another opportunity to overthrow that government "as soon as they were able to do so." It should be remembered that Riel's delegates had not yet left for Ottawa to negotiate the terms of Red River's entry into Confederation, and that Riel was anxious and determined to prevent anything from interfering with this part of his policy. It had been his *idée maîtresse* from the very beginning of the rising. If it was necessary to spill the blood of a malcontent, one who had not only refused to co-operate with the other settlers, but had even appealed to force in an effort to disrupt the arrangements the Provisional Government was making to obtain concessions from Canada, then that blood would be spilled. It was as simple as that. Moreover, there was the desire to impress. Underneath all his assertiveness, Riel suffered from a feeling of insecurity. Neither he nor his government were taken seriously enough by the Canadians in the Red River Settlement, or by those in Canada. Perhaps an execution would show them that he meant business. "We wanted to be sure that our attitude was taken seriously," Riel wrote to Masson.

The execution of Scott was a political act: and, as such, it was a political blunder. It may have been followed, as it assuredly was, by a lessening of tension and by a period of calm, but it was not a healthy calm. The English-speaking parishes were stunned by the news of Scott's death. They would co-operate with the Provisional Government for the sake of the Settlement which they all loved; but there could be no warmth, no sincere affection in their co-operation, no real unity of spirit. Riel gained his immediate end; but in the long run he opened a breach between the French- and English-speaking elements of the population of Red River which has never been entirely closed. If henceforth little love was lost between them, it was because there was little love to lose. Elsewhere in Canada the Scott affair stripped from the underlying bitterness, of race and religion, the veneer of co-operation with which it had been covered by Confederation in 1867. In the years to come, both Scott and Riel ceased to be men, human beings with human frailties; they became political symbols, political slogans, around which men rallied and for which they argued and fought with little knowledge of the real strengths and weaknesses of the men whose names they bandied to and fro.

By one unfortunate error of judgment—this is what the execution of Scott amounted to—and by one unnecessary deed of bloodshed—for the Provisional Government was an accomplished fact— Louis Riel set his foot upon the path which led not to glory but to the gibbet.

W. L. Morton (ed.), *Alexander Begg's Red River Journal and Other Papers Relative to the Red River Resistance of 1869-1870,* (Toronto, The Champlain Society, 1956), pp. 114-116. Reprinted by permission of The Champlain Society.

## A Matter of Discipline

Why [Thomas] Scott should have been shot is still difficult to explain. His death cannot be accepted as a political necessity, as the execution of [C. A.] Boulton might have been; although Riel and his apologists have ever since defended it as such. As Joseph Howe exclaimed, "The man could not have known the line of his policy." In Canada, the effect of the execution was to shock and anger English Canadians, many of whom had been not unsympathetic with the cause of the *métis*. In Red River, the English were shocked and angered also, but had to contain their anger. The *métis*, for their part, from that day to this have never doubted that the death of Scott was just and necessary. But if it was not a political necessity, it was simply a matter of discipline, and for this the punishment was terribly disproportionate. Continued strict confinement was in fact the only reasonable punishment in the circumstances, coupled with punishment of the intractable guards. . . .

Either as a political act or as a means of discipline or even as an example, the execution of Scott is difficult to explain. Why then was he executed? Two reasons may be advanced. One is that Scott had so exasperated his guards that they had threatened to shoot him themselves. This they would almost certainly have done. For Scott belonged to that type of person, of whom Adam Thom was one and Schultz in certain aspects of his character another, who aroused that curious, inflammable hatred which was characteristic of the *métis*. Scott, the Irish Presbyterian, the Orangeman, the militant loyalist, was the antithesis of everything the *métis* were—French yet Indian savage, Catholic yet superstitious, loyal to those they trusted, implacable to those they disliked. The protagonists of the conflict were the two extremes of the Canadian people. Aware of the difference, Scott may have created an impression of conscious superiority, unforgiveable by a sensitive and primitive people. The conflict of the ill and defiant prisoner and the inflamed guards was shaping toward bloodshed, and Riel was forced to hold the court-martial to regularize what was inevitable. The execution of Scott was preferable to his murder. . . .

The second reason for Scott's death, however, is the one later urged by Riel himself in specific terms, but expanded beyond reason by his apologists. At the beginning of March, [1870] Riel was faced with contemptuous defiance amongst the prisoners taken on February 17; with rumours and fears of an Indian attack; with the determination of the people of Portage [la Prairie], as he believed, to repudiate the Provisional Government at the first opportunity, despite the election of delegates to Canada; and with the dawning knowledge that

Schultz and Mair were racing to Ontario to discredit before their arrival the delegates whose departure had been delayed by the rising of February 14. Riel's justification was therefore that he saw a connection between the defiance within Fort Garry and the unrest outside; and he resolved to still both with one decisive act. Scott was condemned by what was, even in the fairest construction, a summary trial; and Riel refused to alter the sentence except for a delay of a few hours for spiritual preparation.

This defence is a political one, earnestly and no doubt honestly urged. But there must be hesitation in accepting it for if the execution of Scott was a political act, it was, by the same token, a political blunder. The shooting of Scott was a final and fatal departure from Riel's original design of union and negotiation. This he was percipient enough to foresee. The Provisional Government had been recognized, but only after threats had been used. It was his duty and right to maintain it, but only with the minimum coercion possible. To use violence was to confess that his government did not rest on union. Nothing had been more striking, during the course of the Resistance up to March 4, than Riel's avoidance of extreme measures. It seems therefore more in accord with the logic of the known facts of the whole situation to argue that Riel's hand was forced by the exasperation of the guards. Their fury, it must be noted, was caused not only by the defiance of Scott, but also by their belief that [William] Gaddy and [William] Dease had been about to burn their homes during the crisis of February, and by their continued fears of an Indian rising.

Thus the two explanations advanced for Scott's death have a common origin in the February rising. Once the rising had been put down, however, it would have been politic to ignore its worst features. But the *métis* were not politic, and Riel could not be because the peace and unity of the Settlement, he persuaded himself, were in danger and must be enforced. Canada must be shown that the *métis* were in earnest. The deed once done, it could only be defended as a political act, necessitated and justified by the whole course of the Resistance.

No further attempt was made to overthrow the Provisional Government. Indeed, the death of Scott appeared to be quickly forgotten in Red River, though that was not really the case. Its swift and vital consequences in Canada, however, were certainly not anticipated in the Settlement.

Report of Donald A. Smith to Joseph Howe, Secretary of State for the Provinces, April 12, 1870. The report, edited for publication, is found in *Canada Sessional Papers 1870*, Vol. 5, No. 12. The excerpt below is from the complete text in Public Archives of Canada, "Papers of the Secretary of State for the Provinces" and printed in W. L. Morton (ed.), *Manitoba: The Birth of a Province,* (Altona, Manitoba Record Society, 1965), pp. 34-36, 38-40.

## Riel Demands Respect

Rumours now began to circulate of a rising at the Portage, and on the night of the 14th and 15th of February [1870] some 80 or 100 men from the district passed down close to Fort Garry, and proceeded to Kildonan, where they were joined by from 300 to 350 men, principally English half-breeds, from the lower parts of the Settlement. . . . The party was entirely un-organized, indifferently armed, unprovided with food even for one meal, and wholly incapable of coping with the French now re-united who, to the number of at least seven hundred were prepared to offer the most determined resistance, which, . . . they . . . could have done most effectually. . . . The attempt was, therefore, to be deplored, as it resulted in placing the whole settlement at the feet of Riel. The great majority of the settlers, English and Scotch, discountenanced the movement and bitterly complained of those who had set it on foot. Forty-seven of the party were captured on their way home, while passing within

a few hundred yards of the Fort; . . . [Charles Arkoll] Bolton [sic] led the party, and he and his friends at the Portage assured me that he exerted himself to the utmost to keep them from rising, and only joined them at the last moment when he saw they were determined to go forward. He was captured on the 17th, tried by "Court Martial," and condemned to be shot at noon on the following day, but at the intercession of the Lord Bishop of Rupert's Land [Robert Machray], Archdeacon [John] McLean, and, in short, every influential man among the English, and I have been told also, at the earnest entreaty of the Catholic Clergy, the execution was delayed till midnight of Saturday, the 19th. Further than this, Riel declared he could not, would not, yield, except, indeed. Dr. Schultz should be captured in the meantime, in which case *he* would be shot instead of Bolton [sic]. . . .

I had no further communication with Riel until Monday, the 4th March, . . . He then said that the conduct of the prisoners was very unsatisfactory, that they were very unruly, insolent to the "soldiers" and their behaviour altogether so very bad, that he was afraid the guards might be forced to retaliate in self defence. I expressed much surprise at the information he gave, as the prisoners, without exception, had promised to Archdeacon McLean and myself, that seeing their helpless condition, they would endeavour to act so as to avoid giving offence to their guards, and we encouraged them to look forward to being speedily released, in fulfillment of the promise made by Mr. Riel. One man, Parker, was mentioned as having made himself particularly obnoxious by his violent conduct, but not one word was said on this occasion regarding [Thomas] Scott, or the slightest intimation given, that he or any other person had been condemned to be shot. . . . [After Scott had been condemned] Père [Jean-Marie] Lestanc consented to accompany me, and we called on Riel. . . . He said in substance that Scott had throughout been a most troublesome character, had been the ringleader in a rising against Mr. [John A.] Snow, who had charge of the party employed by the Canadian Government during the preceding summer in road making; that he had risen against the "Provisional Government" in December last, that his life was then spared; that he escaped, had again been taken in arms, and once more pardoned,—referring no doubt to the promise he had made to me that the lives and liberty of all the prisoners were secured—but that he was incorrigible, and quite incapable of appreciating the clemency with which he had been treated; that he was rough and abusive to the guards, and insulting to him, Mr. Riel; that his example had been productive of the very worse effects on the other prisoners, who had become insubordinate to such an extent, that it was difficult to withhold the guards from retaliating. . . . I pointed out that the one great merit claimed for the insurrection was that, so far, it had been bloodless, except in one sad instance, which all were willing to look upon as an accident, and implored him not now to stain it, to burden it with what would be considered a horrible crime. He exclaimed "we must make Canada respect us."

Louis Riel, *L'Amnistie, Montreal,* Le Nouveau Monde, 1874, pp. 13-15.

## Riel's Version

At the beginning of December, 1869, after Mr. McDougall had declared war on us, Th. Scott was imprisoned at Fort Garry as one of the most dangerous partisans of Dr. Schultz, McDougall and Dennis. Shortly after, Scott escaped and took refuge in Portage Laprairie. In February 1870, at the very moment when a convention of 40 delegates established the Provisional Government in the name of the people, Thomas Scott came down from Portage with a band of men armed for revolt, and for a distance of approximately 40 miles, they forced a number of peaceful citizens to take up arms unwillingly and follow him.

Having thus recruited about a hundred men by the time they reached the parish of Headingley, which is situated 15 to 20 miles west of Fort Garry on the Assiniboine River, they marched along the Assiniboine to Fort Garry. It was not more than two days before that representatives of the whole country had definitely established the Provisional Government when Scott, in revolt against this authority, entered the town of Winnipeg armed for war. Scott, at the head of his troops, attempted to seize the President of the Government by surrounding a house where the President was often to be found.

When they found they had not surprised the President, they went to St. Andrew's to rejoin the disorderly mob of savages and whites under the orders of Dr. Schultz. . . .

On February 17, when Boulton was taken with 47 men, all armed at the walls of Fort Garry, Scott was one of them.

Thus captured for the second time, Scott in prison made himself conspicuous by the violence of his conduct, particularly on March 1. On that day, Th. Scott and Mr. McLeod forced the doors of their prison and hurled themselves on their guards, inviting their companions to do the same. The Métis, who had always treated their prisoners with a great deal of consideration, were so angry at these outrages that they dragged Scott outside and were ready to kill him, when one of the representatives intervened. Everyone demanded that Scott should be brought before a council of war. It had been said that Scott was immediately given a Court Martial. The President of the Provisional Government tried to avoid going to these lengths by having an interview with Scott. The President asked Scott to consider his position, and begged him, whatever his feelings, to behave quietly in prison; in this way, said the President, I shall have a reason for preventing you from having to appear before the Council of the Adjutant General, which is what the Métis soldiers are loudly demanding.

Scott ignored this advice and persisted in his bad conduct.

New troubles were expected to arise at any time; these were likely to put the life of our citizens in danger, and tended to hinder the departure of our delegates. Such delays could not fail to be favourable to Dr. Schultz, who, no longer able to stay at Red River, had gone to Ontario to arouse the people against the Provisional Government, to prevent our delegates from being officially received by the Canadian government, and to try to have a delegation of his own choice from the North West prevail at Ottawa.

On the third of the same month, we had Scott appear before a court martial. He was examined by sworn witnesses, convicted and condemned to death.

The following day, March 4, 1870, we exercised in all severity the governmental authority which had been provisionally entrusted to us to safeguard a colony of England, and which we had not used during three months of desperate struggle except to disarm our enemies. Scott was executed because his execution was necessary to maintain order and to fulfill our duty by making order respected.

And now, not only has Canada no legal say in this execution, but it is not reasonable that an individual should be held responsible for an act of a government, and that Canada should treat as vile adventurers the members and officials of a legal government with which it had been negotiating in full view of all the world for nearly a whole session of parliament.

Dr. James Lynch to Governor-General Sir John Young, April 12, 1870, printed in George T. Denison, *The Struggle for Imperial Unity*, (Toronto, Macmillan and Co., 1909), pp. 30-31. Reprinted by permission of The Macmillan Co. of Canada.

## One of Riel's Prisoners Speaks

Russell's Hotel, Ottawa
*12th April, 1870.*

MAY IT PLEASE YOUR EXCELLENCY,

Representing the loyal inhabitants of Red River both natives and Canadians, and having heard with feelings of profound regret that your Excellency's Government have it in consideration to receive and hear the so-called delegates from Red River, I beg most humbly to approach Your Excellency in order to lay before Your Excellency a statement of the circumstances under which these men were appointed in order that they may not be received or recognized as the true representatives of the people of Red River.

These so-called delegates, Father Richot [sic] and Mr. Alfred H. Scott, were both among the first organisers and promoters of the outbreak, and have been supporters and associates of Mr. Riel and his faction from that time to the present.

When the delegates were appointed at the convention the undersigned, as well as some fifty others of the loyal people, were in prison on account of having obeyed the Queen's proclamation issued by Governor Macdougall [sic]. Riel had

possession of the Fort, and most of the arms, and a reign of terror existed throughout the whole settlement.

When the question came up in the convention, Riel took upon himself to nominate Father Richot [sic] and Mr. Scott, and the convention, unable to resist, overawed by an armed force, tacitly acquiesced.

Some time after their nomination a rising took place to release the prisoners, and seven hundred men gathered in opposition to Riel's government, and, having obtained the release of their prisoners, and declared that they would not recognize Riel's authority, they separated.

In the name and on behalf of the loyal people of Red River, comprising about two-thirds of the whole population, I most humbly but firmly enter the strongest protest against the reception of Father Richot [sic] and Mr. Scott, as representing the inhabitants of Red River, as they are simply the delegates of an armed minority.

I have also the honour to request that Your Excellency will be pleased to direct that, in the event of an audience being granted to these so-called delegates, that I may be confronted with them and given an opportunity of refuting any false representations, and of expressing at the same time the views and wishes of the loyal portion of the inhabitants.

I have also the honour of informing Your Excellency that Thomas Scott, one of our loyal subjects, has been cruelly murdered by Mr. Riel and his associates, and that these so-called delegates were present at the time of the murder, and are now here as the representatives before Your Excellency of the council which confirmed the sentence.

I have also the honour to inform Your Excellency, that should Your Excellency deem it advisable, I am prepared to provide the most ample evidence to confirm the accuracy and truth of all the statements I have here made.

I have the honour to be
Your Excellency's most humble and obedient servant,

JAMES LYNCH.

George T. Denison, *The Struggle for Imperial Unity, Recollections & Experiences,* (Toronto, The Macmillan Co. of Canada, 1909), pp. 9-12, 19-26, 28-29, 33-35, 36-37, 41-45. Reprinted by permission of The Macmillan Co. of Canada.

# Canada Firsters

The effect of confederation on the Canadians was very remarkable. The small Provinces were all merged into a great Dominion. The Provincial idea was gone. Canada was now a country with immense resources and great possibilities. The idea of expansion had seized upon the people, and at once steps were taken looking to the absorption of the Hudson's Bay Territory and union with British Columbia.

With this came visions of a great and powerful country stretching from ocean to ocean, and destined to be one of the dominant powers of the world. . . .

It was at the period when these conditions existed that business took me to Ottawa from the 15th April until the 20th May, 1868. Wm. A. Foster of Toronto, a barrister, afterwards a leading Queen's Counsel, was there at the same time, and through our friend, Henry J. Morgan, we were introduced to Charles Mair, of Lanark, Ontario, and Robert J. [*sic*] Haliburton, of Halifax, oldest son of the celebrated

author of "Sam Slick." We were five young men of about twenty-eight years of age, except Haliburton, who was four or five years older. We very soon became warm friends, and spent most of our evenings together in Morgan's quarters. We must have been congenial spirits, for our friendship has been close and firm all our lives. Foster and Haliburton have passed away, but their work lives. . . .

Those meetings were the origin of the "Canada First" party. Nothing could show more clearly the hold that confederation had taken of the imagination of young Canadians than the fact that, night after night, five young men should give up their time and their thoughts to discussing the higher interests of their country, and it ended in our making a solemn pledge to each other that we would do all we could to advance the interests of our native land; that we would put our country first, before all personal, or political, or party considerations; that we would change our party affiliations as often as the true interests of Canada required it. Some years afterwards we adopted, as I will explain, the name "Canada First," meaning that the true interest of Canada was to be first in our minds on every occasion. Forty years have lapsed and I feel that every one of the five held true to the promise we then made to each other.

One point that we discussed constantly was the necessity, now that we had a great country, of encouraging in every possible way the growth of a strong national spirit. . . .

It was apparent that until there should grow, not only a feeling of unity, but also a national pride and devotion to Canada as a Dominion, no real progress could be made towards building up a strong and powerful community. We therefore considered it to be our first duty to work in that direction and do everything possible to encourage national sentiment. . . .

This idea we were to preach in season and out of season whenever opportunity offered. The next point that attracted our attention was the necessity of securing for the new Dominion the Hudson's Bay Territory and the adhesion of British Columbia. . . .

When the news of [the Red River disturbances] came to Ontario there was a good deal of dissatisfaction, but the distance was so great, and the news so scanty, and so lacking in details, that the public generally were not at first much interested. The Canada First group were of course keenly aroused by the imprisonment and dangerous position of [Charles] Mair and [J. C.] Schultz, and at that time matters looked very serious to those of us who were so keenly anxious for the acquisition of the Hudson's Bay Territory. Lieut.-Governor Macdougall [sic] had been driven out, his deputy had disappeared after his futile and ill-managed attempt to put down the insurrection, Mair and Schultz and the loyal men were in prison, Riel had established his government firmly, and had a large armed force and the possession of the most important stronghold in the country. An unbroken wilderness of hundreds of miles separated the district from Canada, and made a military expedition a difficult and tedious operation. These difficulties, however, we knew were not the most dangerous. There were many influences working against the true interests of Canada, and it is hard for the present generation to appreciate the gravity of the situation.

In the first place the people of Ontario were indifferent, they did not at first seem to feel or understand the great importance of the question, and this indifference was the greatest source of anxiety to us in the councils of our party. By this time Foster and I had gained a number of recruits. Dr. [William] Canniff, J. D. Edgar, Richard Grahame, Hugh Scott, Thomas Walmsley, George Kingsmill, Joseph E. McDougall, and George M. Rae had all joined the executive committee, and we had a number of other adherents ready and willing to assist. Foster and I were constantly conferring and discussing the difficulties, and meetings of the committee were often called to decide upon the best action to adopt.

Governor Macdougall [sic] had returned humiliated and baffled, blaming the Hon. Joseph Howe for having fed the dissatisfaction at Fort Garry. This charge has not been supported by any evidence, and such evidence as there is conveys a very different impression.

Governor McTavish [sic] of the Hudson's Bay Company was believed to be in collusion with Riel, and willing to thwart the aims of Canada. Mr. Macdougall [sic] states in his pamphlet of *Letters to Joseph Howe,* that in September 1868 every member of the Government, except Mr. Tilley and himself, was either indifferent or hostile to the acquisition of the Territories. He also charges the French Catholic priests as being very hostile to Canada, and says that from the moment he was met with armed resistance, until his return to Canada, the policy of the Government was consistent in one direction, namely, to abandon the country. . . .

The Canada First organisation was at this time a strictly secret one, its strength, its aims, even its existence being unknown outside of the ranks of the members. The committee were fully aware of all these difficulties, and felt that the people generally were not impressed with the importance of the issues and were ignorant of the facts. The idea had been quietly circulated through the Government organs that the troubles had been caused mainly through the indiscreet and aggressive spirit shown by the Canadians at Fort Garry, and much aggravated through the ill-advised and hasty conduct of Lieut.-Governor Macdougall. [sic]

The result was that there was little or no sympathy with any of those who had been cast into prison, except among the ranks of the little Canada First group, who understood the question better, and had been directly affected through the imprisonment of two of their leading members.

The news came down in the early spring of 1870 that Schultz and Mair had escaped, and soon afterwards came the information that Thomas Scott, a loyal Ontario man, an Orangeman, had been cruelly put to death by the Rebel Government. Up to this time it had been found difficult to excite any interest in Ontario in the fact that a number of Canadians had been thrown into prison. Foster and I, who had been consulting almost daily, were much depressed at the apathy of the public, but when we heard that Schultz and Mair, as well as Dr. [James] Lynch, were all on the way to Ontario, and that Scott had been murdered, it was seen at once that there was an opportunity, by giving a public reception to the loyal refugees, to draw attention to the matter, and by denouncing the murder of Scott, to arouse the indignation of the people, and foment a public opinion that would force the Government to send up an armed expedition to restore order.

George Kingsmill, the editor of the Toronto *Daily Telegraph,* at that time was one of our committee, and on Foster's suggestion the paper was printed in

mourning with "turned rules" as a mark of respect to the memory of the murdered Scott, and Foster, who had already contributed able articles to the *Westminster Review* in April and October 1865, began a series of articles which were published by Kingsmill as editorials, which at once attracted attention. It was like putting a match to tinder. Foster was accustomed to discuss these articles with me, and to read them to me in manuscript, and I was delighted with the vigour and intense national spirit which breathed in them all. He met the arguments of the official Press with vehement appeals to the patriotism of his fellow countrymen. The Government organs were endeavouring to quiet public opinion, and suggestions were freely made that the loyal Canadians who had taken up arms on behalf of the Queen's authority in obedience to Governor Macdougall's [sic] proclamation had been indiscreet, and had brought upon themselves the imprisonment and hardships they had suffered. . . .

We heard of their arrival [i.e. Schultz and Mair] at St. Paul by telegraph and our committee called a meeting to consider the question of a reception to the refugees. This meeting was not called by advertisement, so much did we dread the indifference of the public and the danger of our efforts being a failure. It was decided that we should invite a number to come privately, being careful to choose only those whom we considered would be sympathetic. This private meeting took place on the 2nd April, 1870. I was delayed, and did not arrive at the meeting until two or three speeches had been made. The late John Macnab, the County Attorney, was speaking when I came in; to my astonishment he was averse to taking any action whatever until further information had been obtained. His argument was that very little information had been received from Fort Garry, and that it would be wiser to wait until the refugees had gone to Ottawa, and had laid their case before the Government, and the Government had expressed their views on the matter, that these men might have been indiscreet, &c. Not knowing that previous speakers had spoken on the same line I sat listening to this, getting more angry every minute. When he sat down I was thoroughly aroused. I knew such a policy as that meant handing over the loyal men to the mercies of a hostile element. I jumped up at once, and in vehement tones denounced the speaker. I said that these refugees had risked their lives in obedience to a proclamation in the Queen's name, calling upon them to take up arms on her behalf; that there were only a few Ontario men, seventy in number, in that remote and inaccessible region, surrounded by half savages, besieged until supplies gave out. When abandoned by the officer who had appealed to them to take up arms, they were obliged to surrender, and suffered for long months in prison. I said these Canadians did this for Canada, and were we at home to be critical as to their method of proving their devotion to our country? I went on to say that they had escaped and were coming to their own province to tell of their wrongs, to ask assistance to relieve the intolerable condition of their comrades in the Red River Settlement, and I asked, Is there any Ontario man who will not hold out a hand of welcome to these men? Any man who hesitates is no true Canadian. I repudiate him as a countryman of mine. Are we to talk about indiscretion when men have risked their lives? We have too little of that indiscretion nowadays and should hail it with enthusiasm. I soon had the whole meeting with me.

When I sat down James D. Edgar, afterwards Sir J. D. Edgar, moved that we should ask the Mayor to call a public meeting. This was at once agreed to, and a requisition made out and signed, and the Mayor was waited upon, and asked to call a meeting for the 6th. This was agreed to, Mr. Macnab coming to me and saying I was right, and that he would do all he could to help, which he loyally did.

From the 2nd until the 6th we were busily engaged in asking our friends to attend the meeting. The Mayor and Corporation were requested to make the refugees the guests of the City during their stay in Toronto, and quarters were taken for them at the Queen's Hotel. Foster's articles in the *Telegraph* were beginning to have their influence, and when Schultz, Lynch, [Joseph] Monkman, and [William] Dreever, [*sic*] arrived at the station on the evening of the 6th April, a crowd of about one thousand people met them and escorted them to the Queen's. The meeting was to be held in the St. Lawrence Hall that evening, but when we arrived there with the party, we found the hall crowded and nearly ten thousand people outside. The meeting was therefore adjourned to the Market Square, and the speakers stood on the roof of the porch of the old City Hall.

The resolutions carried covered three points. Firstly, a welcome to the refugees, and an endorsation of their action in fearlessly, and at the sacrifice of their liberty and property, resisting the usurpation of power by the murderer Riel; secondly, advocating the adoption of decisive measures to suppress the revolt, and to afford speedy protection to the loyal subjects in the North-West, and thirdly, declaring that "It would be a gross injustice to the loyal inhabitants of Red River, humiliating to our national honour, and contrary to all

British traditions for our Government to receive, negotiate, or treat with the emissaries of those who have robbed, imprisoned, and murdered loyal Canadians, whose only fault was zeal for British institutions, whose only crime was devotion to the old flag." This last resolution, which was carried with great enthusiasm, was moved by Capt. James Bennett and seconded by myself.

Foster and I had conferences with Schultz, Mair, and Lynch that evening and next day, and it was decided that I should go to Ottawa with the party, to assist them in furthering their views before the Government. In the meantime Dr. Canniff and other members of the party had sent word to friends at Cobourg, Belleville, Prescott, etc., to organise demonstrations of welcome to the loyalists at the different points. . . .

On our arrival in Ottawa we found that the Government were not at all friendly to the loyal men, and were not desirous of doing anything that we had been advocating. The first urgent matter was the expected arrival of Richot [sic] and [Alfred H.] Scott, the rebel emissaries, who were on the way down from St. Paul. I went to see Sir John A Macdonald at the earliest moment. I had been one of his supporters and had worked hard for him and the party for the previous eight or nine years—in fact since I had been old enough to take an active part in politics; and he knew me well. I asked him at once if he intended to receive Richot and Scott, in view of the fact that since Sir John had invited Riel to send down representatives, Thomas Scott had been murdered. To my astonishment he said he would have to receive them. I urged him vehemently not to do so, to send someone to meet them and to advise them to return. I told him he [sic] had a

copy of their Bill of Rights and knew exactly what they wanted, and I said he could make a most liberal settlement of the difficulties and give them everything that was reasonable, and so weaken Riel by taking away the grievances that gave him his strength. That then a relief expedition could be sent up, and the leading rebels finding their followers leaving them, would decamp, and the trouble would be over. I pointed out to him that the meetings being held all over Ontario should strengthen his hands, and those of the British section of the Cabinet, and that the French Canadians should be satisfied if full justice was done to the half-breeds, and should not humiliate our national honour. Sir John did not seem able to answer my arguments, and only repeated that he could not help himself, and that the British Government were favourable to their reception. I think Sir Stafford Northcote was at the time in Ottawa representing the Home Government, or the Hudson's Bay Company.

Finding that Sir John was determined to receive them I said, "Well, Sir John, I have always supported you, but from the day that you receive Richot [sic] and Scott, you must look upon me as a strong and vigorous opponent." He patted me on the shoulder and said, "Oh, no, you will not oppose me, you must never do that." I replied, "I am very sorry, Sir John. I never thought for a moment that you would humiliate us. . . ."

. . . Feeling much disheartened I left him, and worked against him, and did not support him again, until many years afterwards, when the leaders of the party I had been attached to foolishly began to coquette with commercial union, and some even with veiled treason, while Sir John came out boldly for the Empire, and on the side of loyalty, under the well-known cry, "A British subject I was born, a British subject I will die." . . .

During the spring of 1870 there had been an agitation in favour of sending an expedition of troops to the Red River Settlement, to restore the Queen's authority, to protect the loyal people still there, and to give security to the exiles who desired to return to their homes. The Canada First group had taken an active part in this agitation, and had urged strongly that Colonel Wolseley (now Field-Marshal Viscount Wolseley) should be sent in command. We knew that under his directions the expedition would be successfully conducted, and that not only would he have no sympathy with the enemy, but that he would not be a party to any dishonest methods or underhand plotting. . . .

The expedition was soon organised under Colonel Wolseley's skilful leadership, and he started for Port Arthur from Toronto on the 21st May, 1870. The Hon. George Brown had asked me to go up with the expedition as correspondent for the *Globe,* and Colonel Wolseley had urged me strongly to accept the offer and go with him. I should have liked immensely to have taken part in the expedition, but we were doubtful of the good faith of the Government, on account of the great influence of Sir George Cartier and the French Canadian party, and the decided feeling which they had shown in favour of the rebels. We feared very much that there would be intrigues to betray or delay the expedition. I was confident that Colonel Wolseley's real difficulty would be in his rear, and not in front of him, and therefore I was determined to remain at home to guard the rear. . . .

. . . Sir John A. Macdonald was taken with a very severe and dangerous illness, so that during this important period the control of affairs passed into the hands of Sir George Cartier and the French Canadian party. This caused great anxiety in Ontario, for we could not tell what might happen. Our committee were very watchful, and from rumours we heard, we thought it well to be prepared, and on the 13th July, Foster, Grahame and I prepared a requisition to the Mayor to call a public meeting, to protest against any amnesty being granted to the rebels; and getting it well signed by a number of the foremost men in the city, we held it over, to be ready to have the meeting called on the first sign of treachery.

. . . If the expedition had been withdrawn, what security would the loyalist leaders have had as to their safety, after the murder of Scott, and the recognition and endorsation of the murderers? It was essential that the expedition should go on. On the first suspicion of difficulty, I had written to Colonel Wolseley and warned him of the danger, and urged him to push on, and not encourage any messages from the rear. Letters were written to officers on the expedition to impede and delay any messengers who might be sent up, and in case the troops were ordered home, the idea was conveyed to the Ontario men to let the regulars go back, but for them to take their boats and provisions and go on at all hazards. . . . .

Hearing on the 19th that Cartier and Taché were coming through Toronto the next night on their way to Niagara, our committee planned a hostile demonstration and were arranging to burn Cartier's effigy at the station. Something of this leaked out and Lieutenant-Colonel Durie, District Adjutant-General commanding in Toronto, attempted to arrange for a guard of honour to meet Cartier, who was Minister of Militia, in order to protect him. . . .

I was at that time out of the force,

but I went to Lt.-Colonel Durie . . . and told him I had heard of the guard of honour business, and asked him if he thought he could intimidate us and I told him if we heard any more of it, we would take possession of the armoury that night, and that we would have ten men to his one, and if anyone in Toronto wanted to fight it out, we were ready to fight it out on the streets. He told me I was threatening revolution. I said, "Yes, I know I am, and we can make it one. A half continent is at stake, and it is a stake worth fighting for." . . .

The meeting for which, as has been said, a requisition had been prepared, was called for the 22nd July, and in addition to the formal posters issued by the acting Mayor on our requisition, Foster and I had prepared a series of inflammatory placards in big type on large sheets, which were posted on the fences and bill boards all over the city. There were a large number of these placards; some of them read, "Is Manitoba to be reached through British Territory? Then let our volunteers find a road or make one." "Shall French rebels rule our Dominion?" "Orangemen! is Brother Scott forgotten already?" "Shall our Queen's Representative go a thousand miles through a foreign country, to demean himself to a thief and a murderer?" "Will the volunteers accept defeat at the hands of the Minister of Militia?" "Men of Ontario! Shall Scott's blood cry in vain for vengeance?"

The public meeting was most enthusiastic, and St. Lawrence Hall was crowded to its utmost limit. The Hon. Wm. Macdougall [sic] moved the first resolution in a vigorous and eloquent speech; it was as follows:

Resolved, that the proposal to recall at the request of the Rebel Government the military expedition, now on its way to Fort Garry to establish law and order, would be an act of supreme folly, an abdication of authority, destructive of all confidence in the protection afforded to loyal subjects by a constitutional Government—a death-blow to our national honour, and calls for a prompt and indignant condemnation by the people of this Dominion. . . .

The second resolution called for the prompt punishment of the rebels. It was moved by James D. Edgar (afterwards Sir James D. Edgar, K.C.M.G.) and seconded by Capt. James Bennett, both members of the Canada First group.

The third resolution read:

Resolved, in view of the proposed amnesty to Riel and withdrawal of the expedition, this meeting declares: That the Dominion must and shall have the North-West Territory in fact as well as in name, and if our Government, through weakness or treachery, cannot or will not protect our citizens in it, and recalls our Volunteers, it will then become the duty of the people of Ontario to organise a scheme of armed emigration in order that these Canadians who have been driven from their homes may be reinstated, and that, with the many who desire to settle in new fields, they may have a sure guarantee against the repetition of such outrages as have disgraced our country in the past; that the majesty of the law may be vindicated against all criminals, no matter by whom instigated or by whom protected; and that we may never again see the flag of our ancestors trampled in the dust or a foreign emblem flaunting itself in any part of our broad Dominion.

In moving this resolution, I said, as reported in the Toronto *Telegraph:*

The indignation meeting held three months since has shown the Government the sentiments of Ontario. The expedition has been sent because of these grand and patriotic outbreaks of indignation. Bishop Taché had offered to place the Governor-General in possession of British territory. Was our Governor-General to receive possession of the North-West Territory from him? No! there were young men from Ontario under that splendid officer Colonel Wolseley who would place the Queen's Representative in power in that country in spite of Bishop Taché and without his assistance (loud cheers). We will have that territory in spite of traitors in the Cabinet, and in spite of a rebel Minister of Militia (applause). He had said there were traitors in the Cabinet. Cartier was a traitor in 1837. He was often called a loyal man, but we could buy all their loyalty at the same price of putting our necks under their heels and petting them continually. Why when he was offered only a C.B. his rebel spirit showed out again; he whined, and protested, and threatened and talked of the slight to a million Frenchmen, and the Government yielded to the threat, gave him a baronetcy, patted him on the back, and now he is loyal again for a spell (laughter and cheers).

I also pointed out how, if the expedition were recalled, we could, by grants from municipalities, &c., and by public subscription, easily organise a body of armed emigrants who could soon put down the rebels. This resolution was seconded by Mr. Andrew Fleming and carried with enthusiasm.

Mr. Kenneth McKenzie, Q.C., afterwards Judge of the County Court, moved, and W. A. Foster seconded, the last resolution:

Resolved that it is the duty of our Government to recognise the importance of the obligation cast upon us as a people; to strive in the infancy of our confederation to build up by every possible means a national sentiment such as will give a common end and aim to our actions; to make Canadians feel that they have a country which can avenge those of her sons who suffer and die for her, and to let our fellow Britons know that a Canadian shall not without protest be branded before the world as the only subject whose allegiance brings with it no protection, whose patriotism wins no praise.

The result of this meeting, with the comments of the Ontario Press, had their influence, and Sir George Cartier was obliged to change his policy. The Governor-General, it was said, took the ground that the expedition was composed partly of Imperial troops, and was under the command of an Imperial officer, and could not be withdrawn without the consent of the Home Government.

*The Globe,* Toronto, April 6, 1870.

## A Bloody and Brutal Execution

### The Murder of Scott

From the first outbreak of rebellion at Red River, we have been told that the Roman Catholic clergy were at the head and front of the trouble. We were slow to believe that men who wore the garb of religion and peace had resorted to such measures, but it is impossible to resist the accumulated evidence which forces itself upon our attention. Some years ago, when Mr. [S. J.] Dawson paid his first visit to Winnipeg, he had an interview with Bishop Taché, and drew from him expressions of dissatisfaction with the idea of the country being opened up for settlement. When the same Bishop Taché visited Canada last year, we were told that he carried on a correspondence with Sir George Cartier, in which he opposed with all his force the projected occupation of the country by Canada. A portion of Sir George Cartier's reply to one of the Bishop's missives was published, in which the French Canadian leader gave it very decidedly to be understood that whatever were the consequences, he intended that the Territory should be opened up. Following this, we had Father Richot [*sic*] joining the people in putting up the first barrier against McDougall, and declaring that the Canadian Governor should pass it only after his blood was shed. We had Father Lestange [*sic*], the administrator of Bishop Taché's Diocese, expressing his belief that the country belonged to French Canadians and should be retained for French Canadians. In all this it is impossible to avoid seeing a determination on the part of the French Catholic clergy in the North West Territory to resist the entrance of British Canadians. What their ultimate object may be is not so apparent. We can hardly conceive it possible that men of intelligence can believe that they can prevent the inroads of people from abroad into their fertile Territory. If they could keep out Canadians, Americans would come in, and far more rapidly destroy what Bishop Taché considers valuable than her rivals. It is to be presumed that by this time the clergy have made up their minds as to what they want, and that they have informed the authorities at Ottawa what their objective point is, and have made it plain by what means their consent to Canadians entering the Territory can be secured. Bishop Taché has gone to the Settlement after having held an interview with the Ottawa authorities. Sir George Cartier and Sir John A. Macdonald must be in possession of the ideas of that prelate, and the public will be very glad to know whether he intends to use his influence to secure the attainment of peace. According to our last advices from Red River, the clergy were still fully engaged in supporting Riel. They had not withdrawn one tittle of their support in spite of the bloody and brutal execution of Scott. . . . It is possible—we give all the benefit of the doubt—that Riel has been placed in a position where he is able to dominate over those who give it [sic] to him, and that the clergy would have been glad to have prevented the murder of Scott, while at the same time they feel themselves forced to make the best of it now that it has been committed. We cannot permit, however, the apologies for the deed of blood to pass uncontradicted. The assertion that Scott was unruly in gaol is denied by his fellow-prisoners. The allegation that his death was necessary to the preservation of order is quite untrue, since Riel is in possession of all the arms and ammunition in the Settlement and is safe from attack until the entrance of a British force. The allegation that Scott was of no religion is also untrue. He belonged to the Presbyterian Church, as did all his family, and there is a letter in the possession of his brother, from the Rev. Mr. Young, which states that he showed a penitent spirit towards his Maker, and died in the Christian faith. The elaborate attempt . . . to cast obliquity upon the character of the poor victim of a vile plot is as base as it is futile. . . . Scott was executed, not for insubordination in prison—no sane man could consider that a reason for shooting him—nor for threats against the so-called President, but because it was necessary that Riel should raise up a wall between his party and the people of Canada for the better carrying out of his ultimate designs.

We do not believe that either the Hudson Bay Company's employees or the French clergy are desirous of the annexation of the Territory to the United States; but they have been outwitted by [Enos] Stutsman and other Americans, who have more influence over Riel than they have. It is not the first time that men have engaged in a revolution which has carried them far beyond their original designs. It remains to be seen whether the French clergy who have followed Riel so far will continue to follow him; but, whatever they do can make no difference in the course of the Canadian Government. The rebellion must be put down, whoever are the promoters.

*The Globe,* Toronto, April 16, 1870.

# Riel's Tyranny Must End

### French and English

We observe with regret that the French Canadian press is endeavouring to make the North-West question one of hostility between Ontario and Quebec. We may except *La Minerve* and *Le Pays,* which are singular in the moderation of their tone. The remainder have determined that the question at issue is whether or not French Canadians shall be obliterated from the North West Territory. . . . Against that assumption we protest. It is not founded on truth. To say that Ontario would force the Government into war for the purpose of removing French Canadians from the Territory is not justified by anything contained in the press of this Province, nor in the speeches of her public men; and the assertion that Ontario desires to visit the younger Colony with "fire and bloodshed" because of one man's fault, is at variance with all that the leading newspapers of Upper Canada have uttered on the subject. These authorities have always held—and now find themselves supported by the best abused man of the Quebec press, Dr. Schultz— that the following of Riel compromises only a portion of the French half-breeds. They have always said that the loyal English and Scotch, who were opposed to the acts of Riel, possessed the sympathy of a portion of the French, and from first to last the Reform press, at least, has advocated the immediate extension of perfect freedom and constitutional government to the settlers of Red River. Not until Canadians were unlawfully held in prison did any one talk of coercing Riel and his followers, and not until the murder of Scott did the idea of vengeance enter into the minds of the people of Ontario. The cry against Riel was doubtless intensified by the circumstances attending his crimes. Viewed even as a political execution, it was unnecessary, but it was known to be the result of a vindicative hatred against Scott, and Riel's refusal to listen to the intervention of the clergy and other settlers, and his haste to complete his revenge before the arrival of Bishop Taché, to whom he would have been compelled to submit, demonstrated the nature of the deed. No man really fails to see that Riel and his temporary and illegal power to gratify a personal spite by the murder of his enemy. . . . There is not the least occasion for drawing any dividing lines between English and French Canadians. Riel has taken the life of a Canadian, and we intend to put the law of Great Britain in force against him. We should do so if he were an Englishman or a Scotsman, perhaps with greater anger than we now feel. We look upon the immediate followers of Riel as mistaken men, misled through their ignorance; but we have no very irate feeling against any, except the immediate accomplices of Riel in the murder of Scott. The people of

Ontario desire and are determined that Canada shall possess the North-West. They do not want it for themselves alone, but for all Canada. They look upon a large immigration from Lower Canada as certain and as desirable. Mixed communities always thrive better than those which are homogeneous, and there is no wish to do a particle of injustice to French Canadians, half-breeds now in the Territory, nor to put obstacles in the way of French Canadians entering it.

Matters have arrived at that pass which makes it necessary to occupy Fort Garry with British troops; but we sincerely trust that this may be done without a shot being fired. Ontario desires to see Red River with the same popular institutions as she herself possesses. She would have compelled this before Riel was heard of, had not her Reform representatives at Ottawa been opposed by those who had the support of Lower Canada; and she purposes to fight very hard to prevent anything like favouritism or class legislation for any section of the inhabitants, be they English or French, Catholics or Orangemen. The idea of anything like unfair treatment to the French half-breeds is a phantom of Quebec's own imagina-

tion. Ontario desires nothing better than to see a peaceful occupation of Fort Garry by the troops, the formal trial of Riel and Lepine, the re-assertion of the Queen's authority, and the immediate rush into the Territory of as many Canadians, French and English, as may be disposed to try their fortunes there. For Riel we have, of course, no sympathy, and we charge the Lower Canadian press with creating discord, retarding peace, and distorting the true view of the question by attempting to shield him and draw indignation upon his accusers. They should lend their voice to the cause of law and order, to the support of the Queen and the defence of a flag which has given them a civil and religious freedom possessed by no other French speaking people in the world, to the overthrow of tyranny and the restoration of security, and to mollifying the differences which arise from the contiguity of two religions and two languages. They may aid in the re-establishment of peace, and it will be greatly to be regretted if they continue in a course calculated to widen an opening breach and turn those against one another who should and must work side by side in the cause of liberty and order.

John Hillyard Cameron, M.P. for Peel, Speech in the House of Commons, April 6, 1870.

## A Dominion Agitated

Hon. Mr. Cameron (Peel) said I am exceedingly anxious to know from the Government whether they have had any additional intelligence from Fort Garry, and whether they are in a position to give to the House any further information in respect to the barbarous murder which has so short a time since taken place there. I am also desirous of knowing whether the first Minister is in a position to inform the House what the Government intend to do in reference to that matter, as there has been no subject since Confederation, or for many years before, which has so agitated the whole of the Dominion, and more particularly that portion of it from which I come, than the whole question of the North West, particularly connected with the great tragedy so recently enacted. I am quite aware that the Government of the Dominion must necessarily have certain difficulties in reference to the question, and there must be probably a certain amount of reticence connected with it. That we can all understand and appreciate, but there are certain things which the Government must be enabled to tell this House, and which I shall expect and the country will expect they will tell this House. It is clear that the country still belongs to Great Britain in an Imperial sense, and has not been ceded over to us in the manner, which, at one time, it was supposed it would be ceded. It is therefore clear that the British Government are in the first instance the parties who are interested in bringing to a close any revolutionary movement, which may have taken place there, and therefore we can naturally understand why it would be that this Government should desire that the Imperial Government would in the first place explain very clearly and distinctly what it intends to do before the Dominion Government should state in the most explicit manner what its views would be in reference to the question; but although that is the case, and although we know that the territory belongs to the Imperial Government there are certain responsibilities which attach to our Government, and which Government cannot by any possibility ignore, and which we, the representatives of the people of the Dominion, demand that they shall not ignore in which we are all interested as Canadians, and which require that we should adopt a certain and determined course (hear, hear). There can be no doubt whatever, there can be but one feeling, not merely amongst all members of this House, but amongst all the inhabitants of this country, that a barbarous murder has taken place in that territory (hear, hear). That a man has gone forth from here under the belief, no doubt that he would be as well protected there as in any other part of Her Majesty's Dominions, has suffered with his life, because he has been loyal and true to the flag of his country, and we cannot help feeling that whatever the connection may be between the British Government and the Dominion Government in relation to the manner in which what has taken place here shall be accounted for, that we ourselves and the Government have resting upon us, the responsibility which the people of this country must require at their hands, totally irrespective of any action by the Imperial Government. Not that I would for a single moment interfere with the Imperial authority, but we must all recollect the position which our Government has taken. We must remember that we sent an agent out to that Western Territory, with all the preparations, and with a Commission to take the place, of the Government of that Territory. We must remember that large numbers of persons, knowing perfectly well that that Territory was soon to come under our jurisdiction, went there with the full belief that they would be as safe out in that Western Territory, as they would be in the City of Ottawa, Montreal or Toronto, and that, therefore, our Government and we ourselves did assure to those people certain responsibilities, which by no possibility can we get rid of (hear, hear). Now, Sir, what one desires to know is this—what are the views of our Government in respect to this matter. If the British Government are still possessors of the territory because we have not paid over the three hundred thousand pounds that we contracted to pay, if they are still responsible for the administration of law and the protection of life in that country, if they are the persons to put down insurrectionary movements, then, of course, 'tis quite right that we should have an opportunity of understanding and knowing that. If they require that we should pay the three hundred thousand pounds and that

we should take upon ourselves the responsibility, I say for one that I am prepared to take my portion of the responsibility in saying, that in the dawning birth of this new Dominion that the life of one of our people was worth three hundred thousand pounds (cheers), and that we should not for one moment allow, if it becomes necessary to assert our authority, and if any question arose with reference to our position with regard to that and to whether the expenses were to be borne by the Imperial Government or ourselves, that we should be prepared to show that we are enabled as a people—as we know in the opinion of some people, almost an independent people—that we are ready to take our part in defending not merely the property, but what is of more importance, the lives of our people, against any attempt which may be made by any insurrectionary party which may spring up in any part of the country (hear, hear). And what I think we ought to have, and what I think we may fairly ask for, I and the gentlemen on this side of the House who are in the habit of supporting the Government, believing that they have the interests of the Dominion at heart, what we really require from them is to know whether when these people have gone to that territory under the idea that they were to be protected, whether when these insurrectionists have taken up arms in the manner that they have done, whether when the difficulties have arisen that have culminated in the barbarous murder of this man, when all these things have taken place we would desire to know whether the Government are determined, whatever may occur, to endeavour, so far as in their power, to meet the exigencies of the case and to exercise whatever influence and power the

Dominion may have, in order that they may be so met, and we would desire to know very clearly and distinctly, whether any difficulty whatever is to be thrown in the way, in reference to that; whether these people who have gone out there are to consider themselves as protected; whether Government, if they are in a position to state so, are so ready to assume the responsibility which may be cast upon them; whether they are prepared to follow up what must necessarily take place in reference to this matter, and whether if these self-styled deputies should come down here to treat as if they were the ambassadors of a civilized country, whether they are to be treated after the manner of truculent rebels who have not merely demanded what they call a Bill of Rights, which we as their fellow countrymen would be perfectly willing to give them if they have any grievance under which they suffer, but who have dared to steep their hands in the blood of an unoffending man who came from this country. If these men up there fancy that they have rights in the soil, that they are entitled to have all that property, that they have a right to do with it as they please, and that we are not to go there and that we have no right in it whatever,

and they are sending down people to treat with us, as if they had the right to treat with us, in a manner in which they might say they would have, if they were fairly coming before us with claims which we might meet, but if these men are delegated from those who with a self-styled and so-called court-martial have dared to doom a man to death, and thereby murdered him, I say I hope that our Government will be in a position to say, that although prepared to concede, as we all hope that they will concede, everything honourable and just to the people of that territory, that they will take care not to treat with men who come here with their hands red with blood, red with the blood of an unoffending fellow citizen; a man who went there with the guarantee of the Government, under the belief that everything would be rightly and properly conducted, and who has laid down his life because he believed that the same power which protected the poor captive in Abyssinia, would protect the free man in Red River. Now, I hope that the hon. Minister will give us an answer that will set the feelings of the people at rest, knowing as he does that the feelings of the people of the country is [sic] excited to a red hot heat (cheers).

# The Amnesty

George F. G. Stanley, *Louis Riel,* (Toronto, The Ryerson Press, 1963), pp. 177-181. Reprinted by permission of The Ryerson Press.

## Forced Into Exile

. . . From the day the news of Thomas Scott's execution reached Ontario, Manitoba's politics became the business of both Ontario and Quebec. The agitation that had been directed, if not provoked, by [George T.] Denison and Schultz was never allowed to subside, and feelings against Riel were not permitted to subside. Neither Sir George Cartier nor Sir John A. Macdonald expected that the debate over the events of 1869/70 would be so prolonged and bitter. They had been sincere in their promises to Taché and to Ritchot, and they hoped only that Riel would remain quiet long enough for the recollections of his actions in March, 1870, to be submerged by more immediate and more important political problems.

But it seemed as if neither Riel's enemies nor his friends would allow the Scott affair to be forgotten. To the Liberal Party in Ontario the affair was too important a political issue to be neglected. Accordingly, Edward Blake tried to force through the Ontario legislature a motion demanding that the "murderers" of Scott be brought to justice. It was hardly within the competence of the provincial legislature to adopt a resolution tantamount to a censure of the federal government; and Sandfield Macdonald sought to turn it aside by arguing that the Scott affair was a matter for the federal and not the provincial authorities of Ontario. Blake knew this as well as Macdonald, but he persisted with his resolution, if only to prod the Orangemen into anti-Conservative action by suggesting that the Tories were running Manitoba "in the French and rebel interest." It was also good politics to argue that as long as Sir John A. Macdonald "retained power at Ottawa," Riel and his associates would remain "in the same position in the North-West." Ogle Gowan and D'Arcy Boulton, both leading figures in the Orange Order as well as in the Conservative party, might deplore this attempt to "make political capital out of our Brother's murder by arousing the passions of Orangemen on the eve of a general election against a government that has no power whatever to deal with the crime. . . ." But Blake and Mackenzie knew their people; there is no doubt that Sandfield Macdonald's opposition to Blake's motion played an important part in the defeat of the provincial government in the spring of 1871.

Even after he won his election, Blake would not let the matter rest. He proposed another resolution urging the apprehension and punishment of Scott's "murderers," and he offered a $5,000 reward to any person bringing about their arrest and conviction. If nothing else, this resolution and reward would be a perpetual embarrassment to the Conservatives in Ottawa.

The significance of Blake's manoeuvres was not lost on the astute old gentleman who held the senior cabinet post in the capital of Canada. He had become Prime Minister in 1867. It was now 1871. A few more months and he would have to risk his political future and his party's in a general election. He had no intention, if he could avoid it, of suffering the fate of his namesake Sandfield Macdonald. Everything seemed to point to a Conservative victory: peace had been achieved with the United States, albeit at the sacrifice of the Canadian fisheries; British Columbia had been added to the Canadian federation; there was every chance of starting work on a transcontinental railway that would link the Pacific with the Atlantic provinces of Canada. "I am, as you may fancy," he wrote to Sir John Rose in London, "exceedingly desirous of carrying the elections again. . . . Confederation is only yet in the gristle and it will require five years more before it hardens into bone." . . .

It had been Sir George Cartier's wish, as expressed to Joseph Royal, that Riel should submit to a voluntary exile, not of several months but of several years. To Riel's friends in Manitoba the only just solution seemed to be in the implementation of the promise of amnesty, not in asking Riel to return once more to the United States. In particular Archbishop Taché was hurt and annoyed that no steps had been taken by Cartier or the Ottawa government to carry out the promises that had been made to him and Ritchot during the spring and summer of 1870. He felt he had been placed in an impossible position by the federal authorities. In May, 1871, he wrote to Sir George, "I assure you that I am deeply afflicted. I have spared neither pain, nor fatigue, nor expense, nor humiliation to re-establish order and peace, and it has come to this, that I am to receive from my people the cruel reproach that I have shamefully deceived them." When he received no satisfaction from Cartier, Taché packed his bags and set out once more for Ottawa. Perhaps by personal contact he might obtain a reply that would not only assure Riel's safety but also vindicate the Archbishop's honour.

In Ottawa, Taché soon learned that political considerations had overridden those of simple justice. Sir John A. Macdonald was quite prepared to talk frankly to the Archbishop as a man of the world, to admit that the delays in granting the amnesty were prompted by factors that were political in nature. When Taché talked about the amnesty, the Prime Minister merely pointed out that it was not politically feasible to grant the amnesty. Sir John never denied that he had promised an amnesty; he simply took the view that "No government could stand that would endeavour to procure the amnesty" and that the government should stand, while Confederation was still "in the gristle," was more important to the country than the inconveniences suffered by Louis Riel or the embarrassments experienced by the Archbishop. Instead of an amnesty, Macdonald was prepared to talk about the ways and means of persuading Riel to leave the country "for a while." Taché was quite willing to admit the force of the Prime Minister's arguments, but in conversation with Cartier he could not but point out that it would be "extremely difficult" for him to approach Riel, especially in view of the deception that had been practised on him with regard to the amnesty. But Cartier supported Macdonald's arguments. . . . After

further consultation with Cartier and with the Archbishop, Macdonald wrote privately to Taché, sending him a bank draft for $1,000, "for the individual that we have talked about," suggesting that the money be paid to him periodically rather than in one lump sum, "otherwise the money would be wasted and our embarrassment begin again." He stipulated that the money should be paid over twelve months.

It was no secret why the federal government wanted Riel out of sight. Both Cartier and Macdonald admitted to the Archbishop that, should Riel remain in Manitoba and take an active part in public life, the Liberals would seize upon this and use it to belabour the Conservatives in the forthcoming federal election. Cartier went a step further. He suggested that the voluntary withdrawal of Riel would make it easier for the government to gain "a larger support in the elections, and . . . thus be better able to procure the amnesty."

Lieutenant-Governor Archibald was also anxious to see Riel leave the province. Only a few days after the *métis* leader had fled from Fort Garry, he expressed the view that even if Riel, Lépine and O'Donoghue were amnestied, "they ought not to come in for some considerable time, till the feeling about them blows over. Their presence here would be a continuous temptation to outrage, and nobody could say when a thing of the kind would quit if once begun. Their own interests, therefore, and the interests of the whole Province alike, concur in keeping them away in the meantime." . . .

Thus, when Taché returned to St. Boniface with Cartier's suggestion and Macdonald's bank draft, he found both Riel and Lépine not unwilling to comply with the government's request that they go into exile. It was a bitter pill for Riel to swallow. He had been promised an amnesty; he had administered the country for several months with Cartier's consent; he had rallied his people to support the government in an emergency. For this he was being driven from his home; his name was being reviled; his life threatened; and now he was being asked to accept a voluntary exile for political reasons. . . .

Louis Riel, *L'Amnistie,* (Montreal, Le Nouveau Monde, 1874), pp. 18-22.

## Canadian Perfidy

The first condition proposed by the delegates from the North West was that "after arrangements had been made, a general amnesty would be proclaimed in the North West before Canada took possession of these territories." I do not know whether Canada ever seriously realized that this condition of an amnesty was imposed by our delegates and accepted by the Canadian delegates as a condition *sine qua non.*

It is true that our devotion to Confederation itself rendered it needless for Canada to pay attention to it. But if I may be permitted to say so, justice demands that it be observed.

I have said that the delegates of the Canadian government accepted the condition of the amnesty. In fact Sir John A. and Sir George Etienne said to our delegates that it was because of the friendly nature of the arrangement between our two countries that this amnesty would be proclaimed as they requested. They added that although the proclamation of this amnesty was the royal prerogative, they

were nevertheless in a position to assure the delegates from the North West that it certainly would be proclaimed.

The Honourable Sir John Young, subsequently Lord Lisgar, [and] Sir Clinton Murdoch, a delegate to Ottawa to give information on the Crown's wishes respecting difficulties in the North West, also gave our delegates a firm assurance that this amnesty would be proclaimed to the satisfaction of the inhabitants of the North West.

Nevertheless, our delegates commented to His Excellency that they would be happy to have this promise of an amnesty in writing. His Excellency replied that there would be no difficulty, and that it would take place as soon as parliament had ratified the rest of the arrangements.

The delegates of the Canadian government and those of the Provisional government drew up together the Manitoba Bill.

During this time, the Imperial government considered it advisable to send some regular soldiers into the North West Territories. Such an act was its right and its duty. And we were pleased to see the troops from the metropolis arrive to assume the functions of government.

But imagine our surprise to see Canada arrogate to itself the right to send out also a military expedition during the period of difficulties with us, and without having concluded any arrangement with us.

The President of the Provisional government complained to His Grace, Monseigneur Taché of the unjust conduct and of the pretensions of Canada with regard to us. And he declared to His Grace that since Wolseley's expedition was a Canadian one, it would be shut out of the country until an amicable agreement had been concluded between the Canadian government and the Provisional government, and until we had guarantee of a general amnesty.

Monseigneur used his full authority to condemn our stand. But when we commented to His Grace that we would be defending ourselves justly, Monseigneur replied to us in his capacity as a Canadian commissioner: "Do not do that. I give you my word of honour that a general amnesty will be proclaimed before the Canadian Lieutenant-Governor is installed here."

Besides, the Imperial government had ordered Canada not to send any militia to the North West before the delegates of the country were satisfied.

When the House at Ottawa had passed the Manitoba Act, our delegates insisted that the Canadian government should give them in writing the agreement already made on the amnesty. His Excellency the Governor General replied that he did not think there was anything in the world more certain than the word of a representative of Her Majesty, that he had himself given his word in favour of an amnesty, that the inhabitants of the North West would receive this amnesty and that it would arrive in the North West before the delegates themselves did.

Our delegates returned to Fort Garry on June 17, 1870. On the 24th of the same month, the Provisional Government called together the Chamber of Representatives of the people and had the delegates give an account in public session of the arrangements made with Canada.

The treaty contained two important provisions: (1) A political constitution for a considerable part of the North West Territories as an independent province within the Confederation. This is the actual Manitoba Act. (2) The final settlement of all past difficulties by the immediately pending proclamation of a general amnesty which had been guaranteed to our delegation, as I have just shown.

We had such favourable arrangements with the Canadian government that the Chamber of Representatives of the North West voted without any opposition their consent to our entry into Confederation. And the Provisional Government, through its Secretary of State, Thomas Bunn, accordingly notified the Hon. Joseph Howe, Secretary of State for the Provinces. The document stated that we agreed to confederate with Canada because we had incorporated into the Manitoba Act the principles for which we had been fighting, and because there would be no delay in proclaiming the general amnesty.

His Grace Mgr. Taché took this important official document to the authorities in Ottawa.

It should be pointed out here that the Governor General had already neglected to carry out the assurance which he had given to our delegates that the amnesty would precede their arrival in the North West.

However, on July 15, 1870, Rupert's Land and the North West Territories were transferred to the Canadian government.

To wind up the arrangements, our delegates had warned the delegates of the Canadian government to inform their government that the members and officers of the Provisional government wished to be discharged from their responsibility to govern as soon as the transfer came into effect. But on this point the Honourable Minister of Militia and Defence, Sir George Etienne Cartier, had said insistently to our delegates that Riel and his Council should continue to maintain peace, after the transfer, in Manitoba and the North West, until the arrival of the Lieutenant-Governor, and we accordinglly devoted ourselves to that task. From the 15th of July, 1870 to the 24th of August, we governed the Province of Manitoba and the North West Territories in the interests of Canada. At the end of this period, Colonel Wolsely [*sic*] arrived at Fort Garry. Instead of presenting himself in a friendly fashion, as the rights of the people required, he arrived as an enemy. The Vice President of the Provisional Government, Mr. F. X. Dauphinais, and Mr. F. X. Pagée and Mr. Pierre Poitras, two of the representatives of the people who, on June 24 previously, had voted in favour of our entry into Confederation, were travelling peacefully on the road to their homes. Wolsely had them violently arrested and thrown into prison. One of them, P. Poitras, an old man, was so mistreated by Colonel Wolsely's soldiers that he was gravely wounded.

After taking possession of Fort Garry, which we had left open for the representative of Her Majesty, Wolsely, in a public speech, congratulated himself and his troops on *having put to flight* Riel's bandits. This was the expression he used to designate the President of the Provisional Government and his staff.

A few days later, the Canadian Lieutenant-Governor arrived. But he only took up the reins of government of our country to complete the invidious act of perfidy by which we became the victims of Canada. He was installed without fulfilling the condition *sine qua non* of the amnesty.

Thus from the very beginning the Canadian government broke the solemn treaty which it had made with the Provisional Government.

Furthermore, the Canadian government sent us friendly proposals by the Vicar General, the Reverend J. B. Thibault, and by Colonel de Salaberry; and when we had accepted their amnesty, they laughed at us.

They ignored the public, formal and spontaneous assurances of the amnesty that they gave us in January, 1870, through Mr. D. A. Smith, now superintendent of the honourable Hudson's Bay Company in Manitoba and the North West.

They ignored their word of honour about an amnesty which they had given us without constraint in May, 1870 through His Grace, the Archbishop of Saint Boniface.

Canadian Confederation for Manitoba and the North West is therefore a fraud.

This state of affairs has existed now for three years. But the original inhabitants of Rupert's Land and the North West have never ceased to demand what belongs to them, and which the Canadian government owes them on so many counts. And today more than ever they make their demands forcefully. What we want is the amnesty; the proper execution of the Manitoba Act. Nothing more, but equally nothing less.

Journal of Rev. N. J. Ritchot, March 24-May 28, 1870. From translation printed in W. L. Morton (ed.), *Manitoba: The Birth of a Province,* (Altona, Manitoba Record Society, 1965), pp. 144-146, 153-156. The original French text is found in *La Revue d'Histoire de l'Amérique Française,* March 1964, edited by George F. G. Stanley.

# Assurance from the Governor-General

May 3, [1870] . . .

At four o'clock we presented ourselves to His Excellency the Governor General who had invited us to go to see him at the suggestion of Sir George Cartier.

His Excellency received us very graciously. . . . He asked me if I had ever had knowledge of the proclamation that was based on the telegram of Lord Granville [Secretary of State for the Colonies] and in which he had said that neither the Governor nor the government of Canada wished to mislead the people of the North West, that on the contrary they would always be ready to hear their complaints and to do them justice. I told him that I had known of the telegram and of the proclamation, but that I could not recall the wording of the said proclamation.

His Excellency told me that in the said proclamation he, the Governor General, promised in the name of Her Majesty that no one of those who had taken part in that unfortunate violation of the laws would be troubled, that in effect there would be a general proclamation of amnesty, that Her Majesty asked nothing more than to re-establish peace in the Dominions, that Sir Clinton Murdoch, special representative of Her Majesty to help settle the difficult question, knew fully the intention of Her Majesty on that subject.

Then Sir Clinton Murdoch told us that Her Majesty's government desired only one thing, which was to re-establish peace and to pass the sponge over all the facts and illegal acts which had taken place in the North West and its territories.

We remarked to him once more that we had nothing in writing on a subject so important and that it seemed necessary to have it. He replied to me that at a time when one dealt with men such as those before whom we were, it was not necessary to dot all the *i*'s, that they must have a certain latitude, that it would be more advantageous to have it so, etc.

I thought I should have to yield to these observations, but I observed the people would not be satisfied without having some assurances on this subject.

His Excellency told me that everything would go well, that the settlers of the North West could be reassured, that no one would be troubled. . . .

[May 19, 1870] . . .

His Excellency says that there is nothing to fear for the settlers of Manitoba who have taken part in the movement of last autumn and winter, that Canada has no jurisdiction at Red River, that he is not yet Governor of that part of the British possessions, that when he will be, he will not only make peace prevail, that the English troops have nothing to do before the establishment of the new governor and government, that then the new government will be obliged to follow the orders of His Excellency which are very favourable to the settlers of Manitoba, that the Imperial Government has shown in the telegram of Lord Granville on which he based his proclamation in which he said that those who have taken part in the movement will not be molested so long as they are willing to recognize British authority.

I made the observation to His Excellency that, as I had already said to him, the Manitobans had never resisted England, but that proclamation was only for the past, and other events had happened since that time; that as for me I very much wanted to believe all that His Excellency had told me, but something more was needed to make the people understand. . . .

His Excellency told us that the Proclamation of December 8 is enough to assure us that a general amnesty is going to be proclaimed immediately, that it is not necessary to give another guarantee in writing. I remarked to him again that that proclamation was dated December 6, 1869, and it could happen that it would not be sufficient and not include events that had taken place since. His Excellency assured me that it would suffice, that, moreover, Her Majesty was going to proclaim a general amnesty immediately, that

we could set out for Manitoba, that the amnesty would arrive before us.

I told him this was impossible. His Excellency told me that in any event it would arrive before the lieutenant governor. That meantime he was going to give me assurance in writing the assurance that no one would be molested while awaiting the proclamation of amnesty, that tomorrow he would send me the document. His Excellency told me that he was authorized to do so in virtue of a wholly special commission because he (the governor) had no jurisdiction over the North West, that the government of the Dominion had no jurisdiction in Manitoba. . . .


May 24, [1870]

Sir George Cartier has me informed on behalf of His Excellency the Governor General that we should forward a petition to the Queen, that his Excellency should support it. That would be the best means of obtaining the amnesty immediately. I refused to do so at first and I ended by consenting because it is only a matter of form, I was told, that it was necessary to forward a document to Her Majesty and that the Governor was a little embarrassed at the thought of presenting it himself lest he should compromise himself.

Petition of Rev. N. J. Ritchot and Alfred H. Scott to Queen Victoria, February 8, 1872. Printed in *Report of the Select Committee on the Causes of the Difficulties in the North-West Territory in 1869-70,* Journals of the House of Commons 1874, Vol. 8, Appendix 6, p. 84.

# A Petition to the Queen

"To Her Most Gracious Majesty the "Queen of the United Kingdom of Great "Britain and Ireland, &c., &c., &c.,
"May it please Your Majesty:

"The Petition of the Rev. Abbé "Ritchot and Alfred Scott, Esquire, both "of the Province of Manitoba, Dominion "of Canada, most humbly representeth:—

"That Your Majesty's Petitioners, in "conjunction with the Honorable Judge "John Black, now in Scotland, were "selected as delegates of the North-West; "the subject of their mission being to lay "before Your Majesty's Representative, "the Right Honorable Sir John Young, "Governor General of the Dominion of "Canada, the wishes of the people of the "Red River and of the North-West.

"That the said delegates received "their official mission from the President "of the Provisional Government of the "North-West Territories, in a document "signed by Thomas Bunn, the Secretary "of the said Government, and dated "March 22nd, 1870.

"That it was merely in conformity "with that document that the delegates of "the North-West presented themselves at "Ottawa to negotiate with the Government "of the Dominion.

"That the Cabinet of Ottawa, after "having been informed of the arrival of "the delegates and of the nature of their "mission, notified to them by a letter of "the Honorable Joseph Howe, Secretary "of State for the Provinces, and dated "26th April, that the Honorable Sir John "A. Macdonald and Sir G. E. Cartier had "been appointed to settle with them to "the satisfaction of the people of the Red "River, the difficulties which had arisen "in their midst.

"That on the day and at the hour "appointed, the negotiations were opened, "and that the delegates of the North-West "declared to the Honorable Members of "the Cabinet of Ottawa that in conformity "with their instructions they could not "come to any agreement unless a general "amnesty should be granted for all the "illegal acts which might have been com- "mitted by any of the parties concerned "in the troubles that had occasioned the "actual delegation.

"That the Honorable Sir John A. "Macdonald and Sir G. E. Cartier de- "clared to the delegates that they were in "measure to assure them that such was "the intention of Your Majesty, that they "could consequently proceed with the "negotiations, being satisfied that the "Royal Prerogative of mercy would be "exercised by the grant of a general "amnesty.

"That before closing the negotiations, "that is to say on the 3rd May, 1870, the "delegates of the North-West were hon- "ored by an official invitation from Your "Majesty's Representative Sir John "Young, Governor General of Canada.

"That during that interview, His Excel-
"lency introduced the delegates to Sir
"Clinton Murdoch, stating to them that
"the honorable gentleman was a Com-
"missioner sent by the Government of
"Your Majesty to assist in the settlement
"of the difficulties of the Red River
"people.

"That both the Governor General of
"Canada and Sir Clinton Murdoch enquir-
"ed of the delegates of the North-West if
"they were satisfied with the arrangements
"of the Cabinet of Ottawa, and if not they
"were ready and authorized by the
"Government of Your Majesty to adopt
"such measures as would satisfy them.

"That in reply, the delegates stated
"that the question of the amnesty caused
"them a certain uneasiness, as they had
"no written document to lay before the
"people of Red River as a proof of the
"promise made to them on the same point.

"That the Representatives of Your
"Majesty repeatedly assured the delegates
"that there would be no difficulty on that
"point, and that the amnesty would surely
"be granted in order to do away with all
"the illegalities and irregularities of the
"late troubles.

"That the delegates, entirely confi-
"dent in the assurance given, expressed
"their satisfaction in such a way as to
"enable Sir John Young to telegraph the
"same day to Lord Granville 'negotiations
"with the delegates closed satisfactorily.'

"That in a subsequent interview, on
"the 19th of May, the Governor General
"of Canada renewed to the delegates then
"present, the assurance that the amnesty
"would be granted, and moreover that it
"would reach Manitoba before the arrival
"there of the newly-appointed Lieutenant
"Governor.

"That on the 24th June, 1870, the

"Legislative Assembly, convoked to Fort
"Garry by the President of the Provisional
"Government, were informed by one of
"the delegates that the amnesty had been
"promised by Your Majesty's Representa-
"tive.

"That this very promise and the
"entire confidence it inspired have largely
"contributed to avert new complications.

"That almost two years having
"elapsed without bringing a more explicit
"proof of Your Majesty's intention on this
"point an anxious and regrettable feeling
"exists throughout the Dominion. Some of
"those to whom the amnesty was prom-
"ised, have been the object of personal
"revenge; one was killed; others obliged
"to flee to avoid the same fate, and all
"this from parties who call themselves
"loyal but refuse to believe in the promise
"made at Ottawa.

"That the Legislative Assembly of
"Manitoba, by a motion passed in the
"House on the 5th of the present month,
"is about to present a humble address to
"Your Majesty, praying 'that Your Ma-
"jesty will be pleased to command that the
"same House will be 'made acquainted
"with the action already taken, or which
"it may be Your Majesty's Royal pleasure
"to take, relative to the political move-
"ments of 1869 and '70.'

"Wherefore Your Petitioners dare
"take the liberty to address their humble
"Petition to Your Majesty, convinced that
"the interest Your Majesty bears even to
"the least of Her subjects, will determine
"Her Royal goodwill to take into Her
"favorable consideration their earnest
"prayer, that in order to secure peace and
"tranquillity it will be Your Majesty's
"Royal pleasure to proclaim the amnesty
"which was promised us when negotiating
"at Ottawa.

"And your Petitioners will, as in "duty bound, ever pray and be grateful.
(Signed), "N. J. Ritchot,
"Delegate of the North-West.

(Signed), "Alfred A. [*sic*] Scott,
"Delegate of the North-West.
"Fort Garry, Manitoba,
"8th February, 1872."

Dr. J. S. Lynch to Governor-General Sir John Young, July 1, 1870. Printed in "Report of the Select Committee on the Causes of the Difficulties in the North-West Territory in 1869-70," *Journals of the House of Commons 1874,* Vol. 8, Appendix 6, p. 195.

# No Amnesty to Rebels

I have on several occasions had the honor of addressing Your Excellency on behalf of the loyal portion of the inhabitants of the Red River Settlement and having heard that there is a possibility of the Government favoring the granting of an amnesty for all offences, to the rebels of Red River, including Louis Riel, O'Donoghue, Lepine and others of their leaders, I feel it to be my duty on behalf of the loyal people of the Territory, to protest most strongly against an act that would be unjust to them and at the same time to place on record the reasons which we consider render such clemency not only unfair and cruel but also injudicious, impolitic and dangerous. I therefore beg most humbly and respectfully to lay before Your Excellency on behalf of those whom I represent, the reasons which lead us to protest against the leaders of the rebellion being included in an amnesty, and for which we claim they should be excluded from its effects.

1. A general amnesty would be a serious reflection on the loyal people of Red River Settlement who, throughout this whole affair, have shewn a true spirit of loyalty and devotion to their Sovereign and to British institutions. Months before Mr. McDougall left Canada it was announced that he had been appointed Governor. He had resigned his seat in the Cabinet, and had addressed his constituents prior to his departure. The people of the Settlement had read these announcements, and on the publication of his Proclamation in the Queen's name, with the Royal Arms at its head, they had every reason to consider that the Queen herself called for their services.

These services were given cheerfully, they were enrolled in the Queen's name to put down a rising that was a rebellion that was trampling under foot all law and order and preventing British subjects from entering or passing through British territory. For this they were imprisoned for months, for this they were robbed of all they possessed, and for this—the crime of obeying the call of his Sovereign—one true-hearted loyal Canadian was cruelly and foully murdered. An amnesty to the perpetrators of these outrages by our Government we hold to be a serious reflection on the conduct of the loyal inhabitants and a condemnation of their loyalty.

2. It is an encouragement of rebellion; Riel was guilty of treason when he refused permission to Mr. McDougall, a British subject, to enter British territory, and drove him away by force of arms; he set law at defiance, and committed an open act of rebellion. He also knew that Mr. McDougall had been nominated Governor, knew that he had resigned his seat in the Cabinet, knew that he had bid farewell to his constituents, yet he drove him out by force of arms; and when the

Queen's proclamation was issued—for all he knew by the Queen's authority—he tore it up, scattered the type used in printing it, defied it, and imprisoned, robbed and murdered those whose only crime in his eyes was that they had obeyed it.

It may be said that Riel knew that Mr. McDougall had no authority to issue a proclamation in the Queen's name; a statement of this kind would lead to the inference that it was the result of secret information, and of a conspiracy among some in high positions. This had sometimes been suspected by many, but hitherto has never been believed. An amnesty to Riel and other leaders would be an endorsation of their acts of treason, robbery, and murder, and therefore an encouragement to rebellion.

3. An amnesty is injudicious, impolitic and dangerous if it includes the leaders—some of these who have been robbed and imprisoned, who have seen their comrade and fellow prisoner led out and butchered in cold-blood, seeing the law powerless to protect the innocent and punish the guilty, might in that wild spirit of justice called vengeance, take the life of Riel or some other of the leaders. Should this unfortunately happen, the attempt by means of law to punish the avenger would be attended with serious difficulty, and would not receive the support of the loyal people of the Territory, of the Canadian emigrants who will be pouring in, or of the people of the older Provinces—trouble would arise and further disturbances break out in the settlement. It would be argued with much force that Riel had murdered a loyal man for no crime but his loyalty, and that he was pardoned, and that when a loyal man taking the law into his own hands executed a rebel and a murderer in vengeance for a murder, he would be still more entitled to a pardon, and the result would be that the law could not be carried out when the enforcement of the law would be an outrage to the sense of justice to the community the law would be treated with contempt. A full amnesty will produce this result, and bitter feuds and a legacy of internal discussion entailed upon the country for years to come.

4. It will destroy all confidence in the administration of law and maintenance of order; there could be no feeling of security for life, liberty or property, in a country where treason, murder, robbery, and other crimes had been openly perpetrated, and afterwards condoned and pardoned sweepingly by the highest authorities.

5. The proceedings of the insurgent leaders, previous to the attempt of Mr. McDougall to enter the Territory as well as afterwards, led many to expect that Riel and his associates were in collusion with certain persons holding high official positions, although suspected it would not be believed. An amnesty granted now including every one would confirm these suspicions, preclude the possibility of dissipating them, and leave a lasting distrust in the honor and good faith of the Canadian Government.

In respectfully submitting these arguments for Your Excellency's most favorable consideration, I wish Your Excellency to understand that it is not the object of this protest to stand in the way of an amnesty to the great mass of the rebels, but to provide against the pardon of the ringleaders, those designing men who have inaugurated and kept alive the difficulties and disturbances in the Red River settlement, and who have led on their innocent dupes from one step to another in the commission of crime by false statements and by appealing to their prejudices and passions.

George E. Cartier to Archbishop A. A. Taché, July 5, 1870. Printed in "Report of the Select Committee on the Causes of the Difficulties in the North-West Territory in 1869-70," *Journals of the House of Commons* 1874, Vol. 8, Appendix 6, p. 38.

## A Delicate Question

*Sir George E. Cartier to*
*Archbishop Taché*
*(Private and strictly confidential.)*
                            OTTAWA, 5th July, 1870.
MY LORD,—I must state to you at the outset that I owe your Lordship an apology for not having written to you sooner. The two letters your Lordship did me the honor of writing to me during *last Session* reached me in time, while Father Ritchot and the other *delegates* were in conference with me and my colleagues. If I did not answer you then, do not think, my Lord, that it was through a lack of deference and respect for your Lordship. I feared lest my letters should be intercepted, and I trusted to good Father Ritchot telling you in person after his return what I would not have liked to put on paper. I do not doubt but our friend Father Ritchot must have made to your Lordship a full and detailed report of all the difficulties which accompanied the mission of the delegates and the passing of the Bill for Manitoba. Happily all ended well in spite of the incessant action of prejudices and of all evil passions.

I received your Lordship's letter of the 10th June last, and I have just received your last of the 18th of the same month, accompanied by a letter of good Father Ritchot of the same day. I am grateful to you, my Lord, for all your letters, and say to good Father Ritchot that I thank him for his last, as well as for his two preceding letters, he did me the pleasure of writing to me on his way to Fort Garry.

In one of your letters to Mr. Howe, you stated that you had written to him more than six times and that you had received no answer. Mr. Howe is under the impression that several of your letters must have been intercepted, and that he did not receive so many letters from your Lordship. In one of your letters to Mr. Howe you stated also that I had said in the House that the Government had not had any report from you, although you had written several times to Mr. Howe and to myself. I did not wish to produce and lay before the House your correspondence, consisting only of letters disconnected the one from the other, and which if produced could not constitute a report made in the ordinary form to the Government. Hence it was that I said the Government had received no formal report from your Lordship, and at the time and in the state of minds then, it was better in order to ensure the success of the measure for Manitoba, to lay before the House as few documents as possible.

This letter is written to you, my Lord, with the intention that it is to be strictly confidential, as I have to speak with you of the delicate question of the amnesty. You must be convinced from what you have seen in the newspapers, that Ontario and part of the Province of Quebec and of the Maritime Provinces are keenly opposed to an amnesty. But happily for the people of Red River the question of the amnesty rests with Her Majesty the Queen, and not with the Canadian Government. Father Ritchot must have explained to your Lordship all that relates to this matter, the petition he addressed to the Queen and the interviews he had with Sir John Young. If the amnesty rested with and were the province of the Canadian Government, composed with heterogeneous elements, it would be in great danger. But it is, I repeat, fortunate that it is Her Majesty, aided by the advice of Her Ministers, who will have to decide this question. Her Majesty has already, by the proclamation of the 6th December last, which She caused to be issued by Sir John Young, so to speak, promised an amnesty. This fact was mentioned in Father Ritchot's petition to the Queen. I must now intimate to you that the surest way of securing this amnesty is that the whole population of Red River should accept the new order of things. It would be well that your Lordship, the Anglican Bishop, all those who figured in the Provisional Government, and all the notables of Red River, should offer a hearty welcome to Mr. Archibald, your new Governor, and to the military expedition.

The Queen will perhaps await this result before making known her clemency. The expedition is an expedition of peace, and the Quebec battalion comprises a large number of your friends, amongst others Father Royer. The soldiers will not be instruments of Dr. Schultz or any one else, to arrest or drag to prison any person whomsoever. Remember that your laws and your procedure are not changed, and that it is only in virtue of your laws and of your procedure that any person can be disturbed or interfered with.

I am very glad to see, by your last letter and by Father Ritchot's, that the population seem inclined to receive the Governor well. It would be a great mistake, and show a lack of wisdom if the Canadian half-breeds on the arrival of the Governor and the troops, were to leave all the demonstrations of loyalty to be made by the English and Scotch half-breeds. This would place the Canadian half-breeds in the same false position as the Lower Canadians were formerly placed in after the political troubles.

The Canadian half-breeds must shew themselves more loyal than any. I shall most anxiously await your next letter and that of Father Ritchot, as to the steps you shall have decided to take, in order to give a good reception to your new Governor.

Note the fact that copies of all your letters received here have been sent by Sir John Young to Lord Granville, in order to shew the position of the amnesty question, if it should happen, which I do not apprehend, that opposition were offered on the arrival of the troops and of the new Governor, those who took part in it would incur the risk of finding themselves excluded from the amnesty Her Majesty may have in view, and which She will sooner or later make known. I must state to you that your letter of 9th June last to Mr. Howe, relative to the amnesty, caused a little fear and dismay amongst several of my colleagues, who stand in fear and dread of public opinion in Ontario and other parts of the Dominion on this question.

To dispel these fears, Mr. Howe, yesterday, addressed you an official reply, with a view to set them at rest. This reply explains that the question of amnesty does not rest with the Canadian Government, but with the Queen, and that the responsibility for the assurance you have given must rest on Your Lordship. In order to shew you the excitement of certain minds (and the number of such is very great) on the question of amnesty, I enclose you an extract from the *Globe* and from the *Daily News* of Montreal. You will see that it is fortunate that the exercise of clemency is in the hands of our Gracious Sovereign. Unfortunately, the violent Protestant newspapers renders Your Lordship responsible for every thing that appears or is announced in the *Nouveau Monde.* It would have been better that the amnesty question should not have been discussed, but that it should have been left to be settled between the Queen and the people of Red River.

Excuse this long and hastily written letter. Remember me to good Father Ritchot and Mr. Scott, the delegate, and believe me

My Lord,
Your Lordship's most humble,
Obedient servant and friend,
(Signed,)   GEO. ET. CARTIER.

# Part IV

# The North West Rebellion 1885

In 1875, the year after his expulsion from the House of Commons, Riel was granted an amnesty "conditional on five years' banishment from Her Majesty' Dominions". As an outlaw he wandered aimlessly back and forth between Montreal and French Canadian communities in the United States, subject to fits of extreme mental depression and becoming increasingly obsessed with a religious mission. During 1876-77 he was confined in Quebec asylums, first at Longue Pointe and then at Beauport. On leaving Beauport he returned to the United States and in 1881 settled in Montana. Two years later he became an American citizen. In the summer of 1884, while he was employed as a school teacher at St. Peter's Mission, Montana, a deputation of *métis* from the North West Territories visited him. They asked his assistance in obtaining redress for their grievances against the Canadian government. Riel agreed to return with them to the Saskatchewan, prompted, as he said, by a desire to help his people but stating also his intention of returning to Montana.

As he does in his interpretation of the events of 1869-70, George Stanley writes of the 1885 rebellion within the context of the frontier. He outlines again the problem of conflicting cultures and of reconciling a small primitive society with an advancing and complex agricultural economy. He broadens this analysis, however, in a way which few historians of the west have taken into account. He sees the *métis* uprising as part of the general agrarian protest movement of the 1880's in the Canadian west, noting, for example, that Riel had the support of the white population until he abandoned constitutional methods.

In addition, no other writer has examined the government records of the 1870-1885 period as thoroughly as Professor Stanley. The conclusion he reaches as to the federal government's responsibility in the rebellion parallels the criticisms made by George T. Denison in 1900. Most writers have taken a similar stand, charging the government with delay, inefficiency and neglect, but whether, on the basis of research as extensive as that undertaken by Stanley, they would be as critical must remain a matter of conjecture since no comparable study of the period has been made.

In the House of Commons John A. Macdonald made a spirited defence of his government's policy toward the west. That policy, he said, was based on advice given by Archbishop Taché and the North West Territories Council, and if there had been any maladministration in the west it had taken place under the Liberal government of Alexander Mackenzie. In his defence of July 6, 1885 Macdonald asserted that land speculators had conspired to use Riel to stir up métis grievances for their own selfish ends.

Because of his religious and mental aberrations Riel did not have the sympathy of the Roman Catholic clergy in 1885 to the extent he had had in 1869-70. The poor métis, said members of the clergy, would never had taken up arms against the government had they not been led astray by a "miscreant" who "usurped" the place of the priests for his own purposes.

Similarly Donald Creighton, in his biography of John A. Macdonald, emphasizes the influence of Riel's personality in the events of 1885. The portrait of Riel which emerges is a harsh one. No historian, however, has so clearly outlined the events of 1885 with the framework of Macdonald's transcontinental vision and his search for Canadian unity. For this reason the biography provides a dimension to the story not found in other accounts. Creighton's picture of Macdonald at this time is of a man stunned by the news that Riel appeared willing to accept a bribe—"To Macdonald it was a shattering revelation. It made the whole agitation seem a malevolent sham." The danger in the west, Macdonald believed, lay not in the uprising of a few hundred métis but in the possibility of a general Indian rising. To this danger was added another problem related to Canada's transcontinental destiny. The Canadian Pacific was in financial difficulty and in danger of collapse. "Together these disasters might mean the ruin of everything he had tried to do for the Canadian prairie country. . . . The two disasters—the revolt on the prairie and the collapse of the railway—had come together in time. And together they might destroy him and his Canada." Macdonald could not believe "that a single half-breed megalomaniac could destroy the west as a homeland for British Americans or that the track which was to bind Canada together would be permitted to fail for a few million dollars." The railway was saved. Macdonald used it to defend the west and he used the west to justify its existence. A national army was assembled, the national will was asserted, and Macdonald's fears that the country was breaking to pieces on the rock of sectional discontent proved false.[1]

1. Donald Creighton, *John A. Macdonald, The Old Chieftain*, Toronto, The Macmillan Company of Canada Ltd., 1955, pp. 413-419.

George T. Denison, *Soldiering in Canada, Recollections and Experience,* (Toronto, G. N. Morang, 1900), pp. 261-268.

# Complaints Ignored

The following spring saw the outbreak of the North-West Rebellion. This was caused by a remarkable instance of departmental inefficiency and obstinacy. The department of the Interior was in the charge of Senator Sir David Macpherson, a fine old gentleman, loyal and honourable, but accustomed to being obeyed. A few hundred half-breeds had settled on the south branch of the Saskatchewan River, about twenty-five miles south of Prince Albert, near a point called Batoche's crossing. Some had been in the neighbourhood for many years and others had moved there from the neighbourhood of Fort Garry during the years following the Red River Rebellion. Their farms were laid out and fenced, their houses built and all going on comfortably and prosperously when the Government surveyor came along, insisting on surveying the land on the uniform plan adopted in the unsettled prairies. By this the farms and buildings would have been all mixed up, and great expense and inconvenience caused to the settlers, who had for some years been settled at that point.

Complaints began to be heard and representations were made to the Department at Ottawa, urging them to make special arrangements to leave these poor people undisturbed in their homes. One can easily understand the horror of the officials of the Department of the Interior at the suggestion that their uniform system of survey should be varied in the slightest degree. Such a breach of red tape regulations could not even be considered, so the complaints became more numerous and the department more obstinate. The months went on, nothing was done, and muttering threats were heard.

I happened to be in a position to know something more of what was going on than most people. My friend, Charles Mair, the poet, one of the five originators of the "Canada First" party, had been living for some years in Prince Albert. He had been in prison in Fort Garry in the 1870 insurrection and understood the country thoroughly. He had large interests in Prince Albert, where his wife and family were living with him. For two years or more before the outbreak he had come all the way from Prince Albert to Ottawa, about 2,000 miles (of which 250 miles were travelled by wagon trail), to impress upon the Government the danger. He came about every six months, and was in the habit of staying a day or two with me on his way to Ottawa and on his way back. He told me each time he went down that there would be trouble; each succeeding visit he became more and more alarmed. He begged of the Government to make some concessions, and warned them there would be bloodshed. On one occasion he was one of a deputation of Prince Albert residents who went down and interviewed Sir John Macdonald and Sir David Macpherson. Sir John asked them to put all their points into writing and he would see what could be done.

Mair went back on that occasion more hopeful. Six months passed, and in April, 1884, he came down once more to appeal to the Government to settle the difficulty. When he returned to Toronto from Ottawa he told me most positively that there would be a rebellion, that the officials were absolutely indifferent and immovable, and I could not help laughing at the picture he gave me of Sir David Macpherson, a very large, handsome, erect man of six feet four inches, getting up, leaving his room and walking away down the corridor, while Mair, a short, stout man, had almost to run alongside of him as he made his final appeal to preserve the peace and to prevent bloodshed.

Mair then told me that a rising was inevitable, and that he was determined to remove his family to a place of safety. He left me and went to Windsor, Ontario, bought a house, furnished it, went straight to Prince Albert, and as soon as possible brought his wife and children down to Windsor, installed them there, returned to Prince Albert, wound up his business, fastened up his house and left in September, 1884, to come down to Windsor to await the rebellion, which he, at least, clearly foresaw. So imminent was the danger, even then, that on his way down he would not stop in the Batoche settlement, but drove on ten miles beyond before he would halt for the night. . . .

In December, 1884, he went to Ottawa once more, to impress upon the Government the danger. As he had no interest in the matter in dispute, and was anxious simply that there should be no disturbance, his representations should have received some attention, but I suppose it would have been unconstitutional for a Government to act upon the verbal report of an outsider. There would be nothing to tie up neatly with red tape, and docket and file away in a pigeon hole.

The storm burst on March 26th, 1885. A party of police from Fort Carlton went to Duck Lake to remove some Government stores. With them were a volunteer company from Prince Albert, consisting of forty men. They were met by a largely superior force of half-breeds, an altercation took place, firing began, and in a few minutes eleven of Mair's fellow-villagers and friends were killed, and three wounded, out of forty engaged. The police had to retreat, the news was flashed to Ottawa, and the Government found an expensive and troublesome campaign on their hands. The whole dispute was over some 40,000 or 50,000 acres of land, in a wilderness of tens of millions of acres, for which the Government were crying for settlers. It cost Canada the lives of two hundred of her people, the wounding of many others, the expenditure of about $6,000,000 in cash, and the losses of time and business that cannot be estimated. When it was all over the Government offered, free, to the volunteers 1,800,000 acres of the land if they wanted it to settle on, and yet the whole dispute was mainly about some red tape regulations as to surveying some forty or fifty thousand acres of land on which people were already settled. It is not often a country suffers so severely and so unnecessarily.

George F. G. Stanley, *Louis Riel: Patriot or Rebel?*, (Ottawa, Canadian Historical Association, 1954), Historical Booklet No. 2, pp. 16-17. Reprinted by permission of the Author.

## Civilization Intrudes

Although Riel had achieved many of his objectives during the Manitoba rising, the sad fact was that no legislative safeguards or grants of scrip for lands could really enable the métis to compete with the new settlers who poured into Manitoba after the formation of the province. Within a few years the métis were outnumbered and their homeland remade into something alien to their culture and to their inclination. Sullen, suspicious, embittered over the failure to adapt themselves and estranged from the civilization of the new settlers, many métis sold their scrip for a small portion of its value and sought new homes. Westward they moved, like the bufflalo; and in the valley of the Saskatchewan they founded new settlements: St. Laurent, St. Louis and St. Antoine (Batoche). Here, once more, they were able to live for a few short years the old life of the plains, the semi-primitive existence which they had enjoyed before the arrival of the Canadians in Red River.

But the civilization they feared was close upon their heels. As early as 1873, only three years after the transfer of the North-West to Canada, a bill was introduced into the Canadian House of Commons to found a semi-military police force called the North-West Mounted Police. In 1874 three hundred policemen in scarlet tunics and pill box caps set out across the plains towards the hilly country of what was to become southern Alberta. They were the forerunners of civilization, with its surveyors, its colonization companies and its railway. Civilization meant the end, both for the Indians and the métis, of the old way of life in the North-West; it meant the end of the hunt and the chase, and the end of the buffalo; it meant the establishment of Indian reserves; it meant the filling up of the country with immigrants.

There may have been excuses for Sir John A. Macdonald in 1869; there could be none in 1885. For the problem which faced the Prime Minister was the same one which had faced him earlier; the problem of conflicting cultures, of reconciling a small primitive population with a new complex civilization. But Sir John had other things on his mind—he was building the Canadian Pacific Railway—and the Ministry of the Interior, Sir John's own ministry, starved the Indian services and failed to allay the fears and suspicions of the métis that they would lose their rights as the original holders of the soil. And to add to the bewilderment of the native peoples came the subtle suggestions of those white settlers, who, beggared by early frosts, poor crops and low prices for grain, were prepared to use the métis grievances as a means of belabouring an apparently indifferent government. Thus it was that the settlers of the North Saskatchewan, mixed-blood and white,

English and French-speaking, joined together to invite Louis Riel to take charge of their campaign for the redress of western grievances. . . .

Riel was nervous when he began his agitation in the North Saskatchewan valley in the summer of 1884. He felt unsure of himself when addressing white settlers and the recollections of his past relations with Canadians were not very happy. But as the weeks passed he acquired more confidence. His programme was a moderate one. It was directed towards the white settlers as well as to the half-breeds, and his secretary, Henry Jackson, was Ontario-born. Under Riel's direction a petition was drafted; on December 16th it was sent to Ottawa. This petition embodied the grievances of all the elements then supporting Riel. It demanded more liberal treatment for the Indians, scrip and land patents for the half-breeds; responsible government, representation at Ottawa, reduction in the tariff, modifica-

tion of the homestead laws and construction of a railway to Hudson's Bay for the white settlers. It also contained a lengthy statement of Riel's personal grievances against Ottawa. Receipt of the petition was acknowledged and in January it was announced that a commission would be appointed to investigate and report upon western problems. . . .

That a serious situation was developing in the North-West was by no means unknown to the Canadian government. Police, government officials and private individuals appealed unceasingly to Ottwa. Admittedly the appointment of a commission to look into the complaints from the North-West had been promised, but Macdonald's delays were notorious and the mere promise of a commission of inquiry seemed to hold but small hope of early redress. In any event it was not until March 30th that the government finally decided to name the members. By that time it was too late.

George F. G. Stanley, *Louis Riel,* (Toronto, The Ryerson Press, 1963). pp. 259-260, 264-267. Reprinted by permission of The Ryerson Press.

# Sins of Omission

. . . [The *métis*] had never forgotten the thrill of their successful resistance fifteen years earlier, the sense of isolation that had followed the establishment of Canadian authority, the beatings they had received from the Ontarians, the broken promises regarding the amnesty. The delays and alterations in the half-breed land grant, the pressures exerted by the incoming settlers and the new competitive economy into which they were thrust made the old days and the old ways look even more attractive, when viewed in retrospect. Within several months of the establishment of Lieutenant-Governor Archibald's administration, the Red River métis began to leave the old settlement in small numbers, and the tide of emigration continued with increasing volume, particularly during the eighteen-eighties. Some of the immigrants went to the Missouri—among them was Riel's father-in-law—but the bulk of them went to the Canadian North-West where they could still find their kindred living on the prairie or gathered in small communities like those at Qu'Appelle, or St. Albert near Edmonton, or Duck Lake on the South Saskatchewan. This last community was the outgrowth of a buffalo camp headed by Gabriel Dumont, and it bore the name of St. Laurent.

In their new homes, the métis and half-breeds—for there were English-speaking half-breeds as well as French métis among them—resumed the kind of life to which they had been accustomed on the banks of the Red and the Assiniboine, and on the banks of the Seine in Manitoba. Their farms were long, narrow and running to the river, so that each family would have a frontage on the water. For the first few years they hunted buffalo on the plains, accepting the laws of the hunt and chasing the top-heavy beasts whose existence spelled life to the mixed-blood as well as to the Indian. Unlike the Indians, however, the métis were able to settle down on the land, grub a living out of the soil, growing a few potatoes, a little wheat and a little barley. Farming was the same at St. Albert as it was at St. Laurent and Qu'Appelle, although at Lac la Biche fishing in the cold waters of the lake was a substitute for tilling the soil. In all the settlements the directing figure was the missionary who was anxious to win the métis from nomadism and convert him into a pious agriculturist. But conversion was not easy, and the transition from one economy to the other produced, even among the half-breeds, the same basic uneasiness that it had produced among the Indians. This malaise began to assume more formidable proportions with the development of the neighbouring white settlements at Edmonton, Battleford and Prince Albert. For here were land-hungry farmers, government officials, surveyors and middlemen, with their laws and their magistrates—all of them, even the well-intentioned ones, misunderstanding the métis and treading on their sensitivities. . . .

The agitation of the half-breeds and the métis in the North-West Territories, during the ten years between 1873 and 1883, carried little weight in Ottawa. This may be explained, in part at least, by the hope and belief of the authorities that the native population would soon be outnumbered and submerged in the rising population of white settlers. There is also the fact that the mixed-bloods had no recognized leader and no strategic centre of settlement. St. Laurent, St. Albert and Qu'Appelle were all widely separated from one another, and the local leaders, Charles Nolin, Sam Cunningham and John Fisher were not men of great experience, education or political capacity. Their influence, like their reputation, was largely a matter of local prestige. Yet the material was there, in each locality, to be exploited when the right man should come along. The old feelings of nationalism had not been killed by migration from Red River; they were reviving under the stimulus of indifference and neglect. Bishop [Vital] Grandin of St. Albert saw what was happening and wrote to Sir Hector Langevin in 1884: "the members of the government ought not to ignore the métis. They, as well as the Indians, have their national pride. They like to have attention paid to them and could not be more irritated by the contempt of which they feel themselves, rightly or wrongly, the victims." All they needed now was a leader, a man who would embody this sense of national identity.

The Indians and the métis were not alone when they complained of Ottawa's sins of omission. The English-speaking settlers, white as well as half-breed, were likewise unhappy over the developments in the North-West. Not that they had found themselves unable to adjust to the demands of a new culture imposed on them from outside; rather they had not found conditions as easy or as attractive in the North-West Territories as they had been led to believe. Few of the early white settlers were paupers, men who had left Central Canada owing to their inability to make a living for themselves in the settled parts of the country. Instead they were adventurous types, men with sufficient means to provide themselves with the "outfit" necessary to start upon their homesteads, or better-to-do immigrants proposing to set up as shopkeepers in the towns springing up along the proposed line of the Canadian Pacific Railway. But the reality which they found did not correspond to the hopes they had held on leaving their old homes. The farmers did not know how to combat the problems of early frosts and prolonged drought. These were not everyday problems, but at times they were of a most severe nature. Between 1871 and 1881, conditions were relatively favourable for farming; but between 1881 and 1891, both the frosts and the droughts were devastating. . . .

It did not help matters that the settlers were caught in the fever of land speculation, resulting from the construction of the transcontinental railway, and the influx of immigrants from other parts of Canada. During the early eighties, men were gripped with hopes of rapid developments and early riches—until the boom collapsed. "In almost every locality," reported the Land Commissioner in 1885, "one meets numerous homesteads, once under a fair state of cultivation, but now deserted; the land once tilled being weed grown and less easily cultivated than the virgin prairie; the buildings fast decaying."

There were other factors that caused discontent and disillusionment: the loneliness and the isolation and the hardships that inevitably accompanied unplanned immigration to a new land; debts, poor crops and a perpetual shortage of money. These combined with adverse economic conditions to produce the first of several agrarian protest movements that have been a feature of the history of Western Canada from that day to this. It mattered little that part of the problem was to be found in the settlers' ignorance of the methods of dry farming that were later imported from the western plains of the United States, or in the lack of suitable varieties of quickly maturing wheat, such as were developed in later years. Nor did the farmers always realize that another aspect of their problem was the fact that adequate sources of credit had not been devised for them to obtain the land, the machinery and the stock they needed to make their operations a success. All they could see was the gap between the prices they received at the track and the prices that were obtained by the millers in the east for the produce they had grown. Therefore they laid the blame for their misfortunes on the federal government which tolerated and protected the railway monopoly of the Canadian Pacific, and on the milling companies that amassed the profits.

The farmers drew together for the redress of their grievances. In southern Manitoba, at Manitou, a mass meeting of agriculturists led to the formation of "The Manitoba and North West Farmers' Protective Union," whose declared object was "to urge the repeal of laws militating against their interest" by bringing the railway monopoly to an end, by the institution of cheaper freight rates and by the removal of restrictions on trade. Similar meetings were held in other parts of the province, at Brandon, Pomeroy, Pilot Mound, Ruttanville and elsewhere, and local branches of the Farmers' Union were formed. Finally, in December, [1883] a provincial convention was held in Winnipeg where the representatives of the various farming communities, taking their cue from Louis Riel in 1869/70, drew up a "Bill of Rights" to be presented to the provincial and federal governments. At first supported by men of all parties, the Farmers' Union gradually fell into the hands of the radical elements among its members. The radicals not only talked of taking steps to discourage further immigration to the west until the government remedied their grievances, they even hinted vaguely at taking up arms.

The excitement in Manitoba was a symptom of the times. In the North-West Territories, similar conditions brought about similar reactions, although the remedies suggested were determined by peculiarly local circumstances. Throughout the Territories, regardless of previous party affiliations, the people were dissatisfied both with economic conditions and their position of political tutelage. With the founding of newspapers in various parts of the country—Battleford in 1878 (*Saskatchewan Herald*); Edmonton in 1880 (*Edmonton Bulletin*); Prince Albert in 1882 (*The Prince Albert Times*)—this discontent found means of expression.

Mason Wade, *The French Canadians 1760-1945,* (Toronto, The Macmillan Co., 1955), pp. 405-407. Reprinted by permission of The Macmillan Co. of Canada.

# A Sequel to 1869

The North-West Rebellion of 1885 was largely a sequel and repetition of the Red River troubles of 1869-70, though in the second instance the rising was against unquestioned authority. The French and Scottish *Métis,* who made up most of the population west of the new province of Manitoba, began to petition Governor [David] Laird of the North-West Territories and Ottawa as early as 1874, for their semi-nomadic culture was threatened by the westward advance of agricultural civilization and the decline of the buffalo. An 1877 ordinance restricting the buffalo-hunting upon which *Métis* life was based was followed by the rapid disappearance of the beast from the Saskatchewan country, thanks to the ruthless slaughter of the migratory herds by American hunters seeking buffalo robes. As the telegraph and the Canadian Pacific Railway advanced across the plains, bringing settlers in their wake, the buffalo retreated southward over the frontier and the *Métis* were left in sad straits, prey to land speculators who often robbed them of their homes. Their chief grievances— the government's failure to meet their claims for land scrip and to supply aid in making the transition from semi-nomad to agricultural and commercial life—went unheard in an Ottawa which was preoccupied with vast land-grant schemes devised to lessen the heavy financial burden of railroad construction.

Once more Eastern expansionists were little concerned with the rights of Western pioneers; once more trouble arose out of the government's decision to survey lands after the American square section system, without regard for the Quebec-type riverstrip holdings of the *Métis*. One of the North-West missionaries, Father Vegreville of Saint-Louis-de-Langevin, made urgent representations to Ottawa in 1884 about the need to consider existing land divisions. Captain [E. G.] Deville, the Chief Inspector of Surveys, worked out a compromise between the chosen plan of survey and the *Métis* wishes, but this solution of the difficulty was buried, thanks to red tape in the Ministry of the Interior and to the unwillingness of English-speaking land agents in the West to take extra trouble to meet the wishes of the French-speaking pioneers of the country. With the language difficulty increasing the misunderstanding resulting from the inability of the largely uneducated *Métis* to grasp the complexities of surveying and land regulations drawn up in Ottawa by lawyers unacquainted with the country, new unrest developed.

Its growth was fostered by Ottawa's interminable delay in answering *Métis* petitions. Supporting memoranda from Governor Laird, Archbishop Taché, and the Anglican Bishop [John] McLean in 1878-9 finally were answered in 1881.

Archbishop Taché visited Ottawa in 1882 to intercede for his people without success. In the following year Father [Hyppolite] Leduc and one B. Maloney conveyed the settlers' resolutions to Ottawa, where they won a hearing, though no action was taken on the matters complained of. Finally, in the spring of 1884, a committee was formed by the "people of Saskatchewan," under the presidency of William Cromartie and the secretaryship of Louis Schmidt, to take action. A delegation headed by Gabriel Dumont and composed of Moise Ouellet, James Isbister, and Michel Dumas, was sent 800 miles across the border to seek out Louis Riel in Montana, and to urge him to return to Canada and lead the popular movement. Riel, who was now dreaming of establishing a new half-breed nation in the West, decided to spend the summer in Canada, urging his own Manitoba land claims against the Dominion government, as well as those of the Saskatchewan settlers.

Upon his arrival in the North-West in July, [1884] Riel took the lead in agitation for righting of the settlers' wrongs. According to the account furnished to Governor [Edgar] Dewdney by Father [Alexis] André of Prince Albert, his proceedings at first were quiet and orderly, and he won the support not only of the *Métis,* among whom his prestige was great, but also of most of the whites and Indians. Riel advocated free grants to the *Métis* of the lands they occupied; the elevation of the districts of Saskatchewan, Alberta and Assiniboia into provinces, or at least provision for their representation in parliament; and the amendment of the land laws to further more rapid settlement of the country. Father André warned the government against interfering with Riel as long as he remained quiet, while other informants urged that he should be arrested and the agitation nipped in the bud. Charles Mair, the poetic Canada Firster, who had been a propagandist for the expansionists in the Red River troubles, came East every six months from 1883 to 1885 to warn the government that new trouble was brewing and that action should be taken on the settlers' grievances; but the agitation was nonetheless allowed to run its course.

John A. Macdonald, *House of Commons Debates*, March 26, 1885.

# Half-Breed Claims

. . . We are quite unaware of the approximate cause of the half-breed rising under Riel. Riel came into the country, invited by them, some time ago. I believe he came in for the purpose of attempting to extract money from the public purse, and during this last summer occasionally there were hints—and more than hints, intimations—that if we gave him a sum of money—and a particular sum of five thousand dollars was mentioned—he would depart in peace. Of course that could not be entertained for a moment, and he has remained there, inciting the half-breeds, and attempting to arouse the Indians by stating to them that the country all belonged to them, and that the whites had no rights whatever. As I stated when I last was asked the question about the state of affairs there, it has been alleged that Riel is exceedingly indignant at being told that he was an outlaw—that he was not a British subject—and had no rights there; but such an intimation, so far as I can discover, was never made to him in any way by anybody. He has a great influence over the half-breeds and some over the Indians. From former occurrences in the North-West he is considered a sort of martyr in the cause—a sort of half-breed Mahdi—and they look up to him with a sort of superstitious regard, and from that feeling he is able to act upon these poor people. I do not believe there is the slightest danger from the half-breeds unless they should be joined by the Indians. If the Indians were brought once into the field no one could foresee what the consequence might be, but I am exceedingly glad to state to the House that our information goes to show that the Indians are quite quiet, and there is no danger their joining with the half-breeds. . . . The causes of the rising are what I have expressed. The half-breeds have had a great many claims, some of them, as I have stated, reasonable enough, but some of them are not reasonable. The House knows that at the time the arrangement was made for the settlement of land titles in Manitoba, on the creation of that Province, a large number of Indians settled on the Assiniboine and Red River who had got places, localities, little properties, in possession under the direct sanction, though perhaps not by any other title, of the Hudson Bay Company. Those claims were recognized and a certain quantity of land was appropriated for their satisfaction. Land scrip was issued to those Indians to the value of their holdings. The half-breeds scattered over the plains had no such rights from the Hudson Bay Company or any one, but as they heard that the half-breeds had received certain moneys, or money's worth, within the Red River settlement, they claimed that they all had the same rights. Among those half-breeds that are at Prince Albert and along both banks of the Saskatchewan, there are a number who received their land scrip for their land on the Red River, who have left Manitoba and are on the plains beyond the bounds of Manitoba. They made their claims and they pressed them, thinking they would not be recognized again. They pressed their claims again; they said they were half-breeds, and they tried to enforce a double claim on their behalf. A great many of these have been identified and have been refused. As a whole the half-breeds have been told that if they desire to be considered as Indians there are most liberal reserves that they could go to with the others; but that if they desired to be considered white men they would get 160 acres of land as homesteads. But they are not satisfied with that; they want to get land scrip of equal quantity—I think

upwards of 200 acres—and then get as a matter of course their homesteads as well. Then there was some difficulty about the plots on which these half-breeds had settled along the Saskatchewan. No man has been disturbed in his settlement, and he has been told that he would not be disturbed. Sometimes the half-breeds quarrel amongst themselves, because in the bends of the rivers one man's claim overlaps another. These claims have been very difficult to settle. There have been several reports from different officials for several years, and a great many of these have been settled, but some remain unsettled. Finally there is a commission which we hope will proceed in the spring, or as soon as possible, to settle the few claims that remain unadjusted.

John A. Macdonald, *House of Commons Debates,* July 6, 1885.

# White Man's Conspiracy

. . . Now, every half-breed in the North-West, if he does not claim as an Indian and has not accepted as an Indian, belonging to an Indian band and enjoying all of the advantages of an Indian, and they are great, because the treaties are liberal, the annuities are large, the supply of implements, cattle, seeds, and so on, is very generous, on the whole—and any half-breed who chooses to be an Indian can go with his tribe—but any half-breed who says I will be considered a white man has all the privileges of a white man; he can get his 160 acres, and after three years' cultivation he gets his land. Here is the friend of the half-breeds, Archbishop Taché, who says he shall not get that, but shall only have a claim to land, shall not have the use of it, unless he cultivates it himself, but he shall not be able to alienate it, that he cannot mortgage it or sell it; and who would take the land under these restrictions, when under the more liberal law of the Dominion of Canada, every half-breed can enter himself for 160 acres and get his patent after three years, the same as an emigrant from Ontario and Quebec? So, when the Government took up the question which had been left on their hands unsettled, what was best to do for the half-breeds, they were told by Archbishop Taché that the half-breeds would get no land no matter whether they settled upon it, no matter whether they built a house of marble or a house of clay, that they should have no rights upon it till the third generation. When that was presented to us, do you not think we should consider and pause before we handed over those lands to those people? Archbishop Taché, knowing and believing, having well ascertained that the granting of land to those people would lead to their alienating it for a few dollars, if a man wanted to make a present to his wife of a dress, or if the husband could get the present of a few dollars, or, perhaps, in some cases, a few gallons of whiskey. If we look over the various recommendations of the various bodies, in the North West we get the same result. Bishop MacLean who knew the country well, was not in favour of granting the patent for this land to these men. The bishop of Rupert's Land, who has lately gone there, honestly says he has been too short a time there to judge, and therefore he gives no opinion. But what does the North-West council of 1878 say? The hon. gentleman quoted a portion but not the whole of it. I have not the original document, but I will read it from a letter of Mr. Matthew Ryan, who was a member of the council that passed the order. This was the resolution passed by the North-West council:—

"That in view of the fact that grants of land and issues of scrip were made to the half-breeds of Manitoba towards the extinction of the Indian title for the lands of that Province, there will be dissatisfaction among the half-breeds of the Territories unless they receive some like consideration; that this consideration would most tend to the advantage of the half-breeds were it given in the form of a non-transferable location ticket for, say 160 acres to each half-breed head of a family, and to each half-breed child at the time of the transfer to Canada, the ticket to be issued immediately to any half-breed of eighteen years or over, who furnishes evidence of his claim; that each half-breed obtaining such location ticket should be allowed to locate it upon any unoccupied Dominion lands, but the title of the land so entered should remain in the Crown for ten years."

The recommendation of Archbishop Taché was that the title should be kept away from the half-breeds for three generations. The recommendation of the council was that it should be kept away for ten years. What was the policy of the Government? Go, take your 160 acres; take your pre-emption for 160 acres more, and you shall stand as well as a white man, and shall get your patent after three years, no matter what the Archbishop or the North-West Council have told us. We, the Government of the Dominion of Canada, have more confidence in the half-breeds even than their own Archbishop and their own council. We say: We give you the land; occupy it, cultivate it, live on it, be happy on it, and at the end of three years you will get 160 acres, and you will stand free and independent, a freeholder, a yeoman, a free man in the North-West. You shall not be subject to this paternal Government which has been urged upon you by your own friends in the North-West. Although we are so far away, although we do not know you, although we are charged with dealing unjustly by you, we

have more confidence in you than your own friends. We will not ask you to remain for three generations as slaves of the soil—to remain ten years without your deed. We tell you that in three years you may go and occupy your land, and may God's blessing be with you. Sir, that is the policy of the Government, and that is the policy the hon. gentleman has maligned, that he has condemned, that he would curse. . . . The half-breed had his own lot, he was not cultivating the land that he had. Giving him his land and giving him more land was giving him nothing. The nomadic half-breed, who had been brought up to hunt, having had merely his shanty to repair to in the dead season, when there was no game— what advantage was it to him to give him 160 or 240 acres more? It was of no use to him whatever, but it would have been of great use to the speculators who were working on him and telling him that he was suffering. Oh! How awful he was suffering, ruined, destroyed, starving, because he did not get 240 acres somewhere else, or the scrip for it, that he might sell it for $50! No, Sir; the whole thing is a farce. Now, Mr. Speaker, we, at the last moment, made concessions, and we did it for the sake of peace. The Government knew, my hon. friend, Sir David Macpherson, the Minister of Interior, knew that we were not acting in the interests of the half-breeds in granting them scrip, in granting him the land. We had tried, after consulting man after man, expert after expert, to find what was best for the country, and we found, without one single exception, they were all opposed to granting unlimited scrip and immediate patents to the half-breeds. But, Sir, an agitation arose, and the hon. gentleman has rung the changes on Riel being brought into that country. Who brought him into the country? Not the Indians; not the half-breeds. The half-breeds did not pay the money. The white speculators in Prince Albert gave their money to Gabriel Dumont, and gave it to Lepine, and gave it to others. They had all got their assignments from the half-breeds; they had all got in their pockets the scrip or the assignment, and they sent down to bring Riel in as an agent to be a means of attaining their unhallowed ends. It is to the white men, it is to men of our own race and lineage, and not to the half-breeds, nor yet to the Indians, that we are to attribute the war, the loss of life, the loss of money, and the discredit that this country would have suffered had it not been for the gallant conduct of our volunteers. . . .

We find, in consequence of the continual pressure of the white men, in consequence of the fact that the half-breeds at Prince Albert were the slaves of the white men, of the fact that they held meetings and might rise in arms or might do whatever the white men chose to ask them to do—we made up our mind that although we did not consider it for the interest of the people in the Territories, yet if they would accept nothing else, and we offered them 160 acres of land—if they would place themselves at the mercy of cormorants, who were ruining them and holding them as slaves, and continually keeping up an agitation, we cannot help it; we will give you scrip, although we know it is not in your interest, and it will be thrown away, and will be secured by people who will give you the smallest possible sum for it; but we cannot help it; this matter must be settled. I do not hesitate to say that I did it with the greatest reluctance. I do not easily yield, if there is a better course open; but at the very last moment I yielded, and I said: "Well, for God's sake let them have their scrip; they will either drink it or waste it or sell it; but let us have peace." And my successor, my respected and able successor, Sir David Macpherson, acted upon that decision, which was carried out in January. At that time we knew there was a discontented people; that the white people were making trouble. I say, and I appeal to the judgment of the House to say, if we did not act as we ought to have acted when, in 1879, when we took possession of the Government, when we found that the Government who were behind us had taken not a single step to settle this question; when we found that the Government had denied the right of the half-breed; when the whole thing was thrown upon us—if we did not act wisely, afterwards when we took power, when we went to the chief men of the country, to the men who were known to be friends of the half-breeds, when we went to the hierarchy and the clergy, both Catholic and Protestant; we went to everybody who could give us information, and they were unanimous in saying that it was wrong that this scrip should be used in this way, and that the land could be got possession of for little or nothing. We held out as long as we could, but such was the influence of the half-breeds, who already got a share of their lands in Manitoba, that they went to the North-West, they became dwellers on the plains, they played Indians, and pretended that they had lived in Manitoba; that they were suffering; that their Manitoba friends had got lands and scrip; and nine-tenths of the men claiming it had already got scrip, and were attempting to put up bargains in the North-West. Fourteen out of seventeen petitioners, in one case, were shown to have got lands already in Manitoba. Isidore Dumont, brother of Gabriel Dumont, had land; he applied again, and it was one of his grievances that he did not get more land in the North-West. Gabriel Dumont got not only his 160 acres, as promised, but he had the best house in Batoche; and so it was with very many of these men—they had already got their lands and scrip, but they were greedy to get more. Appetite grew with eating; and though they had got all much more than originally by law they ought to have got, they are clamoring for more. If time would permit, I could prove many such cases, but, perhaps, I may take another occasion, as the hon. gentleman has said we are going to hear from him again on this subject—I may take another occasion to show that the fact of the half-breed not getting, at the moment he wants it, his scrip or his claim for 240 acres, was a mere pretence; yet, Riel, from the beginning, when he went into the country until he left, went there for the purpose of making money. He came there for the most sordid purposes possible, and he told all kinds of lies. Amongst other things, he said that the hon. member for East York, when he was in the Government offered him $20,000, and I offered him $30,000—he remembered perhaps, the old matter, when he got some money on the frontier, in order to clear away. One of the letters read today by the hon. gentleman was that he had been promised a senatorship or a seat in the Cabinet. He came there, and he ruled these men for the most sordid purposes. The white men in Prince Albert and the vicinity, or many of them, subscribed to bring him there, and encouraged him there, for the sake of making a little fuss and drawing attention to Prince Albert and for the sake of threatening the Government into settling the claims of the half-breeds, or, in other words, putting money into their pockets.

Declaration of Roman Catholic priests, June 12, 1885. Printed in Joseph Pope, *Correspondence of Sir John Macdonald,* (Toronto, Oxford University Press, 1921), p. 346.

# A People Led Astray

*Prince Albert, June 12th, 1885.*

We the undersigned, priests of the districts more especially concerned in this Rebellion, viz. St. Laurent, Batoche, and Duck Lake, as it was among our own people here, that the miscreant Louis "David" Riel made his headquarters, and we as residents, and knowing the facts, would draw the attention of our fellow speaking people in Canada and elsewhere to the facts.

That Louis Riel does not deserve the sympathy of thc Roman Catholic Church or its people, as he usurped our places as priests with our flocks, and otherwise deprived our people of the advantages and consolidation of having us among them. All this he did to gain his own selfish ends, and we therefore feel that the Church and people in Canada should sympathize with us and our people, and pity them, rather than blame them for being led astray. A great many of our people are utterly destitute having had their stuff taken by Louis Riel and Council in the first place, and then suffering the usual losses that must follow on an army marching through said districts. General Middleton did all he could to make the losses and suffering of our flocks as light as he could, and deserves our heartfelt thanks. But unless we receive help in some way, our people will starve, and we therefore ask the French speaking people of Canada and others to give their sympathy to us and our flocks,

And to pray with us that the Government may temper justice with mercy in dealing with our people who were led astray.

FATHER ANDRÉ, Superior of the District.

FATHER FOURMOND, Director of O.M.I. St. Laurent.

Ls. TOUSE, O.M.I.

E. LECOQ, PTRE.

V. VÉGRÉVILLE, P.M.A., O.M.I., priest at Batoche.

MOULIN, PTRE., O.M.L., Parish priest of Batoche.

Bishop Vital Grandin to John A. Macdonald, July 11, 1885. Printed in Joseph Pope, *Correspondence of Sir John Macdonald*, (Toronto, Oxford University Press, 1921), pp. 347-348.

## No Sympathy from the Clergy

*Private.     Prince Albert, July 11th, 1885.*
To THE RIGHT HONOURABLE
  SIR JOHN MACDONALD,
    Prime Minister of Canada, Ottawa.
HONOURABLE SIR,

After the sad events from which we have all suffered, both physically and mentally, I undertook to visit that part of my diocese which had been principally the theatre of the disturbance. I cannot think without emotion of the devastation and ruin which I there perceived, nor foresee, without fear and disquiet, the sad consequences of so much misery. What I most dread is the antipathy, the hatred and the desire of revenge which will infallibly arise among the different nationalities and religious denominations of the country. It is also to be feared that a number of excellent and industrious halfbreed families will abandon the country to settle either in the United States or to advance further north into the most destitute parts of the territory, where, living miserably, they will cherish in themselves

and transmit to their descendants, a spirit of hatred and vengeance which poverty and its attendant misery will foster. This fire hidden under the ashes will, sooner or later, burst out and will not be extinguished until it has caused considerable ravages. The more the conditions of the halfbreeds and Indians resemble each other, the more readily will they unite for evil. To prevent these miseries, I have just had a petition signed which I address to the Most Honourable Minister of Justice with a view to obtain all possible indulgence in favour of the halfbreeds who have compromised themselves in the Rebellion, excepting, however, two or three who are in reality the cause of all the evil. These poor halfbreeds would never have taken up arms against the Government had not a miscreant of their own nation, profiting by their discontent, excited them thereto. He gained their confidence by a false and hypocritical piety, and having drawn them from the beneficial influence of their clergy, brought them to look upon himself as a prophet, a man inspired by God and specially charged with a mission in their favour, he forced them to take up arms. So much was he master of them, that no one dared to resist him. If they did not take up arms from enthusiasm, they did so from fear, terrified by his menaces. Captain Moore, who lost his leg in consequence of this deplorable revolt, said to me on signing the petition, that apart from Riel and Gabriel Dumont, he did not know any halfbreed really culpable. He appears, however, to have forgotten a certain Maukuman. When the petition was presented to Mr. Thomas MacKay who had made every possible effort to quell the Rebellion, he expressed his desire that the petition should be made specially in favour of the councillors of Riel; he desired this because he knew that the title of councillor would naturally lead one to suppose that those officers were more culpable, while in reality the men who bore these titles were often only poor blockheads such as in French we would call *de bonnes bêtes,* chosen precisely because they were incapable of saying a word in the assemblies, and very often they did not even know what question was being discussed. I have been assured that only two amongst them are able to write their own names.

I, therefore, beg Your Honour to support this petition with your authority.

The principal inhabitants of the English Colony of Prince Albert, those who have had most to complain of during the Rebellion, are also of my opinion on this point. I do not even except the Government officials nor the military authorities, their official position does not allow them to sign the petition, but they approve of it and express their wishes for its success.

Believe me,
Honourable Sir,
Your humble and devoted servant,
+VITAL J. BISHOP OF ST. ALBERT,
O.M.I.

# Part V

# Riel's Trial

The military campaign of 1885 against the *métis*, under the command of General Frederick Middleton, came to an end with the defeat of Riel's forces at Batoche on May 12, 1885. Three days later Riel surrendered, was taken to the North West Mounted Police Barracks in Regina, and brought to trial on July 20th before magistrate Hugh Richardson. He pleaded not guilty to the charge of treason. His lawyers, François Lemieux and Charles Fitzpatrick, sought to show that Riel was insane and thus not responsible for his actions.

Anyone reading today Riel's statements to the court would not fail to detect evidence of a disturbed mind. On the basis of medical testimony at the time he was judged by the jury to be sane within the legal definition that he knew right from wrong. This conclusion was later upheld in the appeal to the Court of Queen's Bench in Manitoba and by a medical commission appointed by the government.

The medical examination of the prisoner by Dr. James Wallace of Hamilton and Dr. Daniel Clark of Toronto, at the time of Riel's trial, would be considered by present standards a very cursory one. Dr. Clark admitted this in his evidence. Dr. Wallace stated under questioning that he had talked with Riel for only half an hour. On the basis of this talk he was satisfied the prisoner was not insane. The evidence of another doctor, Dr. A. Jukes of the North West Mounted Police, would not be acceptable in a court of law today as "expert" testimony. Only Dr. Francois Roy of Beauport asylum where Riel had been confined in 1877 was in a position to provide evidence based on extensive observation. Dr. Roy did not believe he "was in a condition to be master of his acts."

Two years after the trial Dr. Clark presented a professional paper on Riel's mental condition to the Association of Medical Superintendents of American Institutions for the Insane. A more recent psychiatric opinion of the medico-legal issues in Riel's case is that published in 1965 by Drs. R. E. Turner and E. R. Markson in the Canadian Psychiatrical Association Journal. Students interested in the issue of Riel's mental condition might consult also: C. K. Clarke M.D., "A Critical Study of the Case of Louis Riel" Queen's Quarterly, Vol. 12, No. 4, April 1905 and Vol. 13, No. 1, July 1905; Frank W. Anderson, "Louis Riel's Insanity Reconsidered", Saskatchewan History, Vol. 3, No. 3. Autumn 1950; and Olive Knox, "The Question of Louis Riel's Insanity", Papers of the Historical and Scientific Society of Manitoba, Series III, No. 6, 1951.

The government's case in regard to the conduct of the trial and the decision not to interfere with the verdict was prepared by Alexander Campbell, Minister of Justice. He dealt summarily with the charge that the government's maladministration was responsible for the rebellion. This was a question, he indicated, that would be determined by the representatives of the people in Parliament. Contradicting statements made early in the trial by Riel's lawyers that the trial was unconstitutional, Campbell affirmed that it was legal and fair. He accepted the medical evidence that Riel was sane and defended the government's decision not to interfere with the execution of the "just" sentence of death passed on the prisoner.

Mason Wade, *The French Canadians 1760-1945,* (Toronto, The Macmillan Co., 1955), pp. 412-414. Reprinted by permission of the Macmillan Co. of Canada.

# Trial by Jury

Under the provisions of the North-West Territorial Act of 1880, Riel was tried by an English magistrate with an associated French justice of the peace befor a six-man jury of English settlers and merchants. The Crown counsel had received instructions from the Deputy-Minister of Justice at Ottawa. Only two or three French Canadians were included in the panel of thirty-six jurors selected by the magistrate. . . . The political aspect of the trial was increased by the fact that the prosecution was made up of Conservatives and the defence of Liberals. [Charles] Fitzpatrick [one of Riel's lawyers] first took issue on constitutional grounds with the jurisdiction of the court, seeking to have Riel tried in Ontario or British Columbia, rather than in the aroused Territories. When this plea was rejected, [F.-X] Lemieux and Fitzpatrick obtained an adjournment of a week in order that witnesses for the accused might be obtained. During this adjournment Riel's English secretary, William Henry Jackson, was tried, found insane in half an hour, and committed to an asylum, from which he escaped to the States, seemingly with the connivance of the authorities. Jackson claimed that he shared Riel's responsibility and thus was exposed to the charge of treason. . . .

Riel's request for the presence of the deputy-minister of the Interior, with official documents and the petitions filed by the *Métis,* was denied, as was his request for his papers, which had been seized at Batoche by General Middleton and which were used with telling effect by the Crown. Among them was his American naturalization certificate. Anticipating a plea by the defence that Riel as an American citizen could not be charged with treason, the Crown had framed its charge of treason on six counts, on three of which he was charged as a British subject, and on three as a resident of Canada, with armed revolt at Duck Lake, Fish Creek, and Batoche.

Driven from its preliminary arguments of unconstitutionality and Riel's American citizenship, the defence devoted most of its attention to proving that Riel was insane. Unfortunately for this contention, Dr. [François] Roy [of the Beauport Asylum], the only medical witness with any real acquaintance with Riel's mental condition, who pronounced him irresponsible and of unsound mind, became entangled in linguistic difficulties under [B. B.] Osler's ruthless cross-examination, while [Dr. Daniel] Clark of Toronto [Superintendent of the Toronto Asylum] and Dr. [James] Wallace of Hamilton refused to pronounce Riel incapable of distinguishing between right and wrong, though they thought him of unsound mind. Dr. [A.] Jukes, the Mounted Police surgeon, flatly pronounced him sane. Riel himself, who in the early stages of the trial tried to cross-examine the government witnesses and was told that he must either repudiate his counsel or keep silent, in his two remarkable addresses to the court at the end of the trial denied the plea of insanity upon which his defence had rested.

He spoke with remarkable if confused eloquence, calling himself the "founder of Manitoba" and "prophet of the New World" and clearly revealing his religious mania as he recapitulated his career and his dream of the West as a haven for the oppressed nationalities of Europe, in which the ancient opposition between Catholics and Protestants would be overcome. He mentioned many things which the government would have wished unsaid, including the details of his dealings with Macdonald and Cartier after the first rising, the provocative role of the Mounted Police in 1885, the failure to give first Manitoba and then the North-West Territories real representation at Ottawa, and the administration's broken promises to the *Métis*. Although he turned against the clergy—even against his lifelong protector Archbishop Taché—and made heretical statements, his deep religiosity was very manifest in a moving plea which is quite as effective despite its imperfect English as Bartolommeo Vanzetti's. He concluded with a request to be tried before a full jury and to be examined by a medical commission, for the Crown's implication that he was shamming insanity pricked his intellectual pride. After the seven days' trial, the jury brought in a verdict of guilty, with a recommendation of mercy. On August 1 Justice [Hugh] Richardson sentenced Riel to be hanged on September 18 at Regina.

William McCartney Davidson, *The Life and Times of Louis Riel*, (Calgary, Albertan Printers, 1952), pp. 104-105. Reprinted by permission of the Albertan Printers.

# Recommendation of Mercy

The jury members had never seen Riel before. But they had a keen sense of their responsibility and felt obliged to listen to the evidence with greater care than the spectators, and they were six men who had a good general knowledge of the conditions of the territory. They were kept together and under guard throughout the trial and permitted no contact with the public, so that they were uninfluenced by the reactions of the spectators. They influenced each other in their private intercourse shut up together.

What they were thinking was not evident to the spectators. Something of what they were thinking they told years later. Mr. W. G. Brooks of Indian Head, the only member of the jury surviving when this biography of Riel was written (1926-28) describes their state of mind in these, his own terms:

"He seemed to us no more insane than any of the lawyers and they were the ablest men in Canada. He was even more interesting than some of them.

"We were in sympathy with the Metis because we knew they had good cause for what they did. We often remarked during the trial that we would like to have the Minister of the Interior in the prisoner's box charged with inciting the Metis to revolt by his gross neglect and careless indifference. We developed a liking for Riel too, although we had never seen him until the trial began.

"One of the other members of the jury said, 'This man is in a bad hole. I wish we knew a way to help him out.' That was the concern of all of us. There was no division or difference of any kind. We just couldn't believe the man was insane."

In their preoccupation with this problem, Fitzpatrick's potent eloquence failed to impress them with the conviction he was trying to establish; but that eloquence distracted their everyday non-legal minds so that to them the issue became not whether or not Riel was guilty of high treason according to the absurd sounding definition of high treason in the formal charge, but whether or not Riel was guilty of insanity—and in 1885 the popular feeling about insanity was not that it was a disease but was rather, somehow, an offence, a repulsive abnormality associated with bad behavior in general.

High treason was not a familiar crime. No person of whom the jury knew or had heard in their own times had been hanged for high treason. The Metis and Riel had done nothing to endanger Queen Victoria—that was just absurb legal terminology of no practical significance; lawyer's fancy talk. Their commonsense did not accept the idea that men struggling to get redress of visible wrongs were in any way comparable with the traitors of history books, and that what Riel had done could lead to any such severe punishment as hanging. . . .

The device of Riel's counsel to plead insanity and the shift of their entire attention to that question had given the trial a shape such that Riel's activities had never been analysed in any detail, nor had they been analysed and examined in any detail in relation to the definition of high treason. But the jury knew that he had been the leader of the half breeds who, in an agitation to obtain rights of wrongs with which every man on the jury sympathized, had gone the length of resisting the Mounted Police in unusual force against them, with arms, and of shedding blood in the encounters, and that they had fought the Canadian Army fiercely until they ran out of ammunition. The jurymen entertained strong private doubts about the wisdom of the government in ordering the police and the troops to behave as they had. But there was no getting round the fact that Riel had led the Metis and that they had made resistance with armed violence, which was a kind of treason. The jury was out half an hour.

They brought in a verdict of "guilty," but attached a rider recommending mercy. They could have given their main decision without leaving the box; they spent the half hour debating what they could do to help Riel effectively, and in that desire they were unanimous.

"We were in a dilemma" Mr. Brooks, the only surviving juryman at the time this biography was written, told the writer. "We could not pass judgment on the Minister of Interior, who was not on trial; and we had to give our finding on Riel according to the evidence. We refused to find him insane. The only thing we could do was to add the clause to our verdict, recommending mercy. We knew it wasn't much, but it was not an empty formal expression, and it expressed the serious desire of every one of the six of us."

Speech of Edward Blake, Liberal Leader, House of Commons, March 19, 1886.

## The Jury Elaborates

. . . It is common talk, and this House has not been wholly free from that common talk, that there should be no interference with the verdict or sentence in capital cases—talk which, if it were acted on, would render it impossible to maintain capital punishment on the Statute-book for twelve months in any civilised country. . . . I maintain that there is no duty on the part of the Executive, to leave the law to take its course, when, in this particular case, it is the maximum punishment which the law obliges the judge to award, and when as I have shown, as often as not that maximum punishment is not inflicted. . . . Now, I ventured to observe, on the only occasion on which I have spoken in public on this case until to-day, that it was a matter of regret that the jury were not asked to state what their reason was for the recommendation [of mercy]—I do not mean by the Executive, of course, but by the judge at the trial, as it was fitting that he should have done. . . . At the time of the trial, the [Toronto] *Mail* correspondent at that trial telegraphed to the *Mail* newspaper as follows:—

Regina, N.W.T., 3rd August.—Three of the jurors in Riel's case tell me that the meaning of that recommendation to mercy is that in their opinion Riel should not be hanged, as they think that, while he is not absolutely insane in the ordinary accepted meaning of the word, he is a very decided 'crank.' The other three jurors I have not been able to see, but this is their view also. Most of the witnesses for the Crown admitted on cross-examination that Riel, in their estimation, was 'not all there'; and this, with the testimony of the experts and that of Rev. Father André, of Prince Albert, who fought with might and main against Riel during the agitation which culminated in the rebellion, produced a profound impression upon the minds of the jury. Lastly, the jury saw and heard the prisoner in the box.

That was the only information which, at the time I spoke, I had as to the meaning of the recommendation. A gentleman residing in the North-West, with whom I had no acquaintance, wrote to me, stating that he had seen the statement made that it was not known what the meaning of the recommendation was, and he enclosed to me a letter addressed to himself from one of the jury, which I think it necessary to give to the House as the only information I have had since on the subject, given to me without any solicitation on my part, and simply coming in the way I have stated. That letter is as follows:—

My Dear Sir,—In answer to your enquiries regarding our verdict, etc., in the Riel trial, I would say that as a friend I have no objections whatever to giving you our reasons for recommending the prisoner to the mercy of the Crown, but I would ask you as a favor not to make public my name or residence.

The judge, in his charge, told us distinctly that we must take into consideration these two points, the prisoner's implication in the rebellion and the state of his mind at the time. He said: 'If you are perfectly satisfied in your own mind that the prisoner was implicated in the rebellion, directly or indirectly, and at the same time able to distinguish between right and wrong, you must bring him in guilty; if, on the other hand, you find him implicated in the rebellion, but of unsound mind, you must bring him in not guilty, and state, on account of his insanity.' This was the purport of the charge, although by no means the whole of it.

After we had retired to consider the verdict, our foreman asked each and every one of us the following questions:— 'Is the prisoner guilty or not guilty? and, is he sane or insane.' We each answered in our turn. Guilty and perfectly sane.

In recommending him to the mercy of the court, we did so because we considered that while the prisoner was guilty and we could not by any means justify him in his acts of rebellion, at the same time we felt that had the Government done their duty and redressed the grievances of the halfbreeds of the Saskatchewan, as they had been requested time and again to do, there never would have been a second Riel rebellion, and consequently no prisoner to try and condemn. We could not but condemn in the strongest terms possible the extraordinary dilatoriness of Sir John Macdonald, Sir David McPherson and Lieutenant-Governor Dewdney, and I firmly believe that had these three been on trial as accessories, very little mercy, if any, would have been shown them by the jury.

Although I say we, in nearly every case in the above, it may possibly be that not everyone held the same views as myself, but I certainly thought at the time that they did so, and am still of the same opinion.

You are at perfect liberty to make use of this letter in any way you see fit, provided anything therein relating to myself is not made public.

Correspondence of John A. Macdonald and Governor General Lansdowne. Printed in Joseph Pope, *Correspondence of Sir John Macdonald,* (Toronto, Oxford University Press 1921), pp. 354-358.

# A Mere Domestic Trouble

John A. Macdonald to Governor General Lansdowne, August 28, 1885.

Riel's case comes before the Queen's Bench on 2nd September.

That Court cannot try him again, but on appeal can decide as to the jurisdiction of the local Court and the legality of its proceedings.

If the application is for a new trial on the usual grounds of misdirection of the judge—or that the verdict was against evidence or the weight of evidence—or for the rejection of admissible or the reception of inadmissible evidence, or the like—then the Court will, if the application is in its opinion well founded, send Riel back to Regina for a second trial. But it is not at all unlikely that the Court will intervene. It has already in Connor's case decided as to the competence of the Stipendiary Magistrate's Court, and there does not appear from the newspaper report of the trial (I have not yet seen the judge's report) to be any ground for a new trial. The judgment will probably—nay certainly—be promptly given. Then if the judge—Richardson—reports as he will do—that he is satisfied with the verdict, it seems to me that the sentence must be carried into effect.

I don't think that we should by a respite anticipate—and as it were court—the interference of the Judicial Committee. If an appeal lay as a matter of course, or as in civil cases, it might be different—but it is not so in criminal matters.

An appeal against a criminal conviction like the present, is merely an exercise of the prerogative which should only be exercised (as interfering with the administration of justice) in a case of supreme necessity. Your Excellency draws a distinction between treason as having a political aspect, and other crimes. Now there are treasons and treasons—any armed resistance to the Queen's authority is technically treason, but may have no political significance. If there were any international complications likely to arise with the United States, the distinction would be obvious. In 1838 the burning of the *Caroline* and the arrest of McLeod, nearly caused a war with the United States. Here Imperial considerations gave the right—I may say imposed the necessity on the Home Government—of Imperial interference. So in the case of the Fenian invasions by citizens of the United States.

But this Northwest outbreak was a mere domestic trouble, and ought not to be elevated to the rank of a rebellion.

The offences of Riel were riot and murder of such an extensive nature as to make them technically amount to treason. The whole insurrection should properly be classed with the Rebecca riots of some years ago in England, where there was armed resistance and a conflict with Her Majesty's troops, and loss of life. These riots and the rising under Thorn (I think that was the name) were held technically to be treason, but really amounted only to riot and murder.

There is a feeling of such intensity among the English-speaking people of Canada on this subject, that any appearance of a desire on the part of the Government to facilitate appeal to England would have, in my opinion. serious and far-reaching consequences of a disastrous character, greatly affecting the friendly relations between English and French.

There is, it is true, some sympathy in the Province of Quebec, with Riel. This is principally worked up by the Rouge party for political purposes. Among the habitants of Quebec, the recollection of their own rising in 1837 and of their "martyrs" still lingers, and Riel's rebellion in 1869 was believed by them then to be under the same circumstances as caused their own Holy War.

The attempt now made to revive that feeling in his favour will not extend far, and will be evanescent.

The murder of the priests—the incitement of the Indians to murder and pillage, and Riel's abandonment of the faith of his fathers, added to his cowardice, will prevent any anticipated sentiment in his favour. I send you a copy of a memo signed by the Catholic priests of the Prince Albert district which was sent to Mr. D'Alton McCarthy in June last. In consequence of his absence in England it did not reach him until his return the other day. This shows the estimates of the Catholic clergy residing in the disturbed district, of Riel's character and conduct.

The execution of Riel stands for 18th September and, if necessary, the Stipen-

diary Magistrate will postpone it of his own motion without any direct intervention on the part of the Government. See 43 Victoria, C. 25, sec. 76.

Governor-General Lansdowne to John A. Macdonald, August 31, 1885.

Thanks for your letter of the 28th which I have read with attention. We are, I think, entirely at one upon the general principle, but I am not sure that I should apply it as you do in Riel's case. I still think that there are features in that case which give it an aspect distinct from that of ordinary criminal cases.

You regard the recent outbreak in the N.W. as a merely "domestic trouble" which should not be "elevated to the rank of a rebellion."

The outbreak was, no doubt, confined to our own territory and may therefore properly be described as a domestic trouble, but I am afraid we have all of us been doing what we could to elevate it to the rank of a rebellion, and with so much success that we cannot now reduce it to the rank of a common riot.

If the movement had been at once stamped out by the N.W.M. police, the case would have been different, but we were within an ace of an Indian war; the progress of the outbreak and its suppression has been described in glowing language by the press all over the world: we brought up troops from all parts of the Dominion: those troops have been thanked by Parliament: they are to receive an Imperial medal. Will not all this be regarded as placing the insurrection in a category quite different from that of the Rebecca riots with which you compare it? No one would have proposed to confer a medal upon the troops or a decoration upon the Commanding Officer engaged in the suppression of these.

I should not like to go a step further than could be helped in facilitating an appeal to England, and there would no doubt be an objection to the postponement of the execution by directions sent from Ottawa at this stage. On the other hand, assuming that the Court of Queen's Bench refuses to order a new trial, and that thereupon Riel at once appeals to the Privy Council, could we hang him before that tribunal had disposed of his application?

It seems to me that if there is any feeling at all on the subject in the Dominion (and I observe what you say as to the extent of this) that feeling would be greatly embittered and prolonged by such a course.

I should much prefer that whatever is done should take place as much as possible in the ordinary modes of procedure and as little as possible by direct intervention on the part of the Government. Under the section of the N.W. Territories Act to which you refer me (S. 76. s. s. 8) the Stipendiary is required to postpone the execution from time to time until his report has been received and *the pleasure of the Governor thereon communicated to the Lieutenant-Governor*.

If in the interval between the termination of the proceedings at Winnipeg and the date fixed for the execution, we become aware that Riel has appeared by counsel before the Judicial Committee, my "communication" to the Lieutenant-Governor might be deferred. Whereupon the Stipendiary, without special instructions, would, I apprehend, postpone the execution.

What do you say to this?

John A. Macdonald to Governor-General Lansdowne, September 3, 1885.

I fear that you *have me* with respect to the character given to the outbreak. We have certainly made it assume large proportions in the public eye. This has been done however for our own purposes, and, I think, wisely done. Still it was a rising within a limited area, and was confined to a small number of persons. It never endangered the safety of the State, nor did it involve international complications. True it involved the danger of an Indian war, and in that would be similar to the arson of a small house, in the vicinity of a powder magazine.

What I ventured to suggest in my letter was that the persons convicted at Regina, should be dealt with as guilty of municipal and not political offences.

I quite agree with Your Excellency that if notice is given of an intention to appeal to the Judicial Committee, it would not do to hurry the execution as it were—in order to prevent such appeal.

The mode suggested by Your Excellency of deferring the significance of your pleasure, without any positive action on the part of the Government, seems the best solution of the matter.

I shall be obliged by Your Excellency not mentioning your views to anyone. These things do get out in an extraordinary way, and if it were suspected that there was a prearranged intention of postponing the execution of the sentence, there would, I fear, be a popular burst of indignation in Ontario and the Northwest, that may as well be avoided.

Louis Riel to John A. Macdonald, July 16, 1885. Printed in Joseph Pope, *Correspondence of Sir John Macdonald,* (Toonto, Oxford University Press, 1921), pp. 348-350.

## Riel's Appeal

I beg for a full trial and by the Supreme Court. I wish to clear myself of the accusations which have weighed on me for fifteen years. If you grant my entreaties, if you accord me all the latitude I need to defend myself, God helping me, not only will I clear myself, but the great responsibility for the troubles in the North-west in 69-70 and in 85 will fall heavily on the Honorable gentlemen Blake and Mackenzie and on the newspapers, their principal organs. Your policy toward the North-west will find itself extricated from the obstacles which these powerful men endeavoured to create for you since 69.

My interest is not only in clearing myself. I desire to rehabilitate myself. If through the support of God and the kindness of men I am permitted to aspire to the advantages of a true rehabilitation and an equitable indemnity, it will be to re-enter Manitoba politics.

It is painful for me to abandon my country, my mother, my brothers, my sisters, my relatives, my friends.

Moreover I have a heart to continue my work, I appreciate the great talent of men who governed and are still governing Manitoba at this time. But it seems to me that they do not understand its founding. This is the reason the province is not at ease and the Confederation is conscious of it. Manitoba thrives; but it makes me think of those people who grow fat without being healthy. It would perhaps not be useless if I were one day to attain to its Ministry. And it would be particularly advantageous for me to attain this position and to continue with your Government, what was begun, fifteen years ago, by the Manitoba Act.

I had the honour to say to you in my communication of the 6th inst., that I think Ireland could become happy and at the same time the English landlords continue to have their revenue as usual.

The principle I would propose to obtain this result appears to me clear and simple. If my native country honoured me one day to the point of placing me at the head of its Ministry, I would submit my views to you. In the case it would be possible for you to approve of them I would submit them to you to put an end to the "Better Terms" which tire Confederation without bringing any definite amelioration to Manitoba. You would procure for me no doubt the advantage of modifying for the better what I have not yet sufficiently matured in my ways of seeing it. After seeing them inaugurated in the young province you would be in a position to examine how my ideas would function. If they succeeded, you would be able to employ them generally throughout the Dominion. Then the Mother Country would judge them herself. And before too long perhaps you would have the glory and I the pleasure of seeing them employed in the situation of Ireland by the

High Authority of the English Parliament itself.

The principle and the views of which I have the honour to say a word to you are in germ in the constitution, the Manitoba Act.

Mr. Prime Minister, the best ideas need to be understood to be put into practice. And then even if the hand of God and that of my friends get me out of prison to place me at the head of the Provincial Ministry of Manitoba, it would seem to me very difficult for me to make my way if there was not there a Governor who understands me.

Since I have been in Regina all my writings have passed through the hands of Captain Dean. This noble officer knows my way of thinking. And in order not to embarrass him by singing his praises to you in a letter which has to go through his office I will say to you quite briefly that it would be, in my opinion, an honour for Manitoba, to have a Lieutenant Governor like him; and for the Honourable Mr. Aikins to have a successor of such great merit and for me a guide whose advice would be so useful to me.

My benevolent lawyers arrived yesterday. I have had the joy of an interview with them. They are going to insist that my trial take place in Lower Canada and before the Supreme Court. Would you grant me that. Would you accede to the good representations of my learned lawyers.

When they take me East, if you consent that I be taken, arrangement could be made that on my arrival three Conservative lawyers, a French Canadian, an Irishman and an English Protestant offer me their good services. My gratitude would be great for such an honour. My cause would be pleaded from the point of view of the interests of your party, as well as from the point of view of the interests of the opposition party.

The Captain would be able to take me. He could follow the complete trial. He would see you often. It would be natural that you could name him Lieutenant Governor of Manitoba. As for me I would have the pleasure of returning to St. Vital, to appreciate the peace which has been waiting for me there for fifteen years.

And you (may my vows never make you suspicious) you would greatly increase your reward. If my good wishes can pass through the bars of my little and gloomy cell, if my strict confinement does not prevent my voice from being heard, you could one day occupy the Vice Regal throne of the Dominion, for the greater benefit of this Confederation of which you are one of the glorious founders.

*Memorandum Respecting the Case of The Queen v. Riel, prepared at the Request of the Committee of the Privy Council, by Alexander Campbell, Minister of Justice, November 25, 1885.* Canada Sessional Papers 1886, Vol. 19, No. 43a.

# The Government States its Case

The case of Louis Riel, convicted and executed for high treason, has excited unusual attention and interest, not merely in the Dominion of Canada but beyond its limits. Here it has been made the subject of party, religious and national feeling and discussion; and elsewhere it has been regarded by some as a case in which, for the first time in this generation, what is assumed to have been a political crime only, has been punished with death.

The opponents of the Government have asserted that the rebellion was provoked, if not justified, by their maladministration of the affairs of the North-West Territories, and inattention to the just claims of the half-breeds.

With this question, which has been made one of party politics, it is not thought becoming to deal here.

Upon such a charge, when made in a constitutional manner, the Government will be responsible to the representatives of the people, and before them they will be prepared to meet and disprove it.

Appeals to the animosities of race

have been made in one of the Provinces, with momentary success. Should these prevail, the future of the country must suffer. Parliament will not meet for some time, and in the interval, unless some action is taken to remove these animosities, they will gain ground, and it will become more difficult to dispel belief in the grounds which are used to provoke them.

It is thought right, therefore, that the true facts of the case, and the considerations which have influenced the Government, should be known, so that those who desire to judge of their conduct impartially may have the information which is essential for that purpose.

It has been asserted that the trial was an unfair one, and before a tribunal not legally constituted; that the crime being one of rebellion and inspired by political motives, the sentence, according to modern custom and sentiment, should not have been carried out; and that the prisoner's state of mind was such as to relieve him from responsibility for his acts.

After the most anxious consideration of each one of these grounds the Government have felt it impossible to give effect to any of them, and have deemed it their duty to let the law take its course.

I am now desired, in a matter of such grave importance and responsibility, to place on record the considerations which have impelled them to this conclusion:

1. As to the jurisdiction of the court and the fairness of the trial.

It should be sufficient to say that the legality of the tribunal by which he was tried has been affirmed by the Privy Council, the highest court in the Empire, and has seemed to them so clear that the eminent counsel who represented the prisoner could not advance arguments against it which were thought even to require an answer. . . .

Of the competency of the court, which had been affirmed by the full court in Manitoba, the Government saw no reason to entertain doubt; but having regard to the exceptional character of the case, the usual course was departed from in the prisoner's favor, and a respite was granted, to enable him to apply to the ultimate tribunal in England, and thus to take advantage to the very utmost of every right which the law could afford to him.

The fairness of the trial has not been disputed by the prisoner's counsel, nor challenged either before the Court of Appeal in Manitoba or the Privy Council. It has, on the contrary, been admitted, not tacitly alone by this omission, but expressly and publicly. . . .

The evidence of the prisoner's guilt, both upon written documents signed by himself and by other testimony, was so conclusive that it was not disputed by his counsel. They contended, however, that he was not responsible for his acts, and rested their defence upon the ground of insanity.

The case was left to the jury in a very full charge, and the law, as regards the defence of insanity, clearly stated in a manner to which no exception was taken, either at the trial or in the Court of Queen's Bench of Manitoba, or before the Privy Council.

2. With regard to the sanity of the prisoner and his responsibility in law for his acts, there has been much public discussion.

Here again it should be sufficient to point out that this defence was expressly raised before the jury, the proper tribunal for its discussion; that the propriety of their unanimous verdict was challenged before the full court in Manitoba, when the evidence was discussed at length and the verdict unanimously affirmed. Before the Privy Council no attempt was made to dispute the correctness of this decision.

The learned Chief Justice of Manitoba says in his judgment: "I have carefully read the evidence and it appears to me that the jury could not reasonably have come to any other conclusion than the verdict of guilty. There is not only evidence to support the verdict, but it vastly preponderates."

And again: "I think the evidence upon the question of insanity shows that the prisoner did know that he was acting illegally, and that he was responsible for his acts."

Mr. Justice Taylor's conclusion is: "After a critical examination of the evidence, I find it impossible to come to any other conclusion than that at which the jury arrived. The appellant is, beyond all doubt, a man of inordinate vanity, excitable, irritable, and impatient of contradiction. He seems to have at times acted in an extraordinary manner; to have said many strange things, and to have entertained, or at least professed to entertain, absurd views on religious and political subjects. But it all stops short of establishing such unsoundness of mind as would render him irresponsible, not accountable for his actions. His course of conduct indeed shows, in many ways, that the whole of his apparently extraordinary conduct, his claims to Divine inspiration and the prophetic character, was only part of a cunningly devised scheme to gain, and hold, influence and power over the simple-minded people around him, and to secure personal immunity in the event of his ever being called to account for his actions. He seems to have had in view, while professing to champion the interests of the Métis, the securing of pecuniary advantage for himself." . . .

Mr. Justice Killam says: "I have read very carefully the report of the charge of the Magistrate, and it appears to have been so clearly put that the jury could have no doubt of their duty in case they thought the prisoner insane when he committed the acts in question. They could not have listened to that charge without understanding fully that to bring in a verdict of guilty was to declare emphatically their disbelief in the insanity of the prisoner."

And again: "In my opinion, the evidence was such that the jury would not have been justified in any other verdict than that which they gave. * * * I hesitate to add anything to the remarks of my brother Taylor upon the evidence on the question of insanity. I have read over very carefully all the evidence that was laid before the jury, and I could say nothing that would more fully express the opinions I have formed from its perusal than what is expressed by him. I agree with him also in saying that the prisoner has been ably and zealously defended, and that nothing that could assist his case appears to have been left untouched."

The organization and direction of such a movement is in itself irreconcilable with this defence; and the admitted facts appear wholly to displace it. The prisoner, eight months before this rebellion broke out, was living in the United States, where he had become naturalized under their laws, and was occupied as a school teacher. He was solicited to come, it is said, by a deputation of prominent men among the French half-breeds who went to him from the North-West Territories, and, after a conference, requested him to return with them, and assist in obtaining certain rights which they claimed from the Dominion Government, and the redress of certain alleged grievances. He arrived in the Territories in July, 1884, and for a period of eight months was actively engaged in discussing, both publicly and privately, the matters for which he had come, addressing many public meetings upon them in a settlement composed of about six hundred French and a larger number of English half-breeds, together with others. The English half-breeds and other settlers observed his course, and saw reason to fear the outbreak which followed; but the suggestion of insanity never occurred, either to those who dreaded his influence in public matters over his race, and would have been glad to counteract it, or to the many hundreds who unhappily listened to him and were guided by his evil counsels to their ruin.

If, up to the eve of the resort to arms, his sanity was open to question, it is unaccountable that no one, either among his followers or his opponents, should have called public attention to it. If the Government had then attempted to place him under restraint as a lunatic, it is believed that no one would have been found to justify their action, and that those who now assert him to have been irresponsible would have been loud and well warranted in their protest. It may be well also to call attention to the obvious inconsistency of those persons—not a few—who have urged the alleged maladministration of the affairs of the North-West Territory by the Government as a ground for interfering with the sentence, without ceasing to insist upon the plea of insanity. The prisoner cannot have been entitled to consideration both as the patriotic representative of his race and an irresponsible lunatic. It may be asked, too, if the leader was insane, upon what fair ground those who were persuaded by and followed him could be held responsible; and, if not, who could have been punished for crimes which so unquestionably called for it?

It has been urged, however, that his nature was excitable, and his mental balance uncertain; that as the agitation increased his natural disposition overcame him, and that the resort to violence was the result of over-wrought feelings, ending in insanity for which he cannot fairly be held accountable—that, in short, he was overcome by events not foreseen or intended by him. . . .

A simple statement of the facts will show that this view is wholly without foundation; that throughout he controlled and created the events, and was the leader, not the follower; and that the resort to armed violence was designed and carried out by him deliberately, and with a premeditation which leaves no room whatever for this plea. . . .

It may be asserted with confidence that there never has been a rebellion more completely dependent upon one man; that had he at any moment so desired, it would have come to an end; and that had he been removed a day before the outbreak, it would, in all probability, never have occurred. A dispassionate perusal of the whole evidence will leave no room for doubt upon this point, and that this was his own opinion appears by his statement to Father André, to be presently referred to.

Finally, under this head, as regards the mental state of the prisoner, after his trial and before execution, careful enquiry was made into this question by medical experts employed confidentially by the Government for that purpose, and nothing was elicited showing any change in his

mental powers or casting any doubt upon his perfect knowledge of his crime, or justifying the idea that he had not such mental capacity as to know the nature and quality of the act for which he was convicted, as to know that the act was wrong, and as to be able to control his own conduct.

3. It has been urged that the prisoner's crime was a political one, inspired by political motives alone; that a rebellion prompted only for the redress of alleged political grievances, differs widely from an ordinary crime, and that however erroneous may be the judgment of its leader, in endeavoring to redress the supposed wrongs of others, he is entitled, at least, to be regarded as unselfish, and as in his own view, patriotic.

This ground has been most earnestly considered, but the Government has been unable to recognize in the prisoner a political offender only, or to see that upon the evidence there can be any doubt that his motives were mainly selfish. On the contrary, it seems plain that he was willing at any moment, for the sake of gain, to desert his deluded followers, and to abandon his efforts for the redress of their alleged grievances, if, under cover of them, he could have obtained satisfaction for his own personal money demands.

It is believed that many who have espoused his crime and desired to avert from him the sentence which the law pronounced must have been ignorant of this fact, or cannot duly have considered its proper effect, for it seems incredible that anyone knowing it could regard the prisoner as entitled to the character of a patriot, or adopt him as the representative of an honorable race.

It is to be remembered that the prisoner had left this country and gone to the United States, where he had become an American citizen. He was brought here, therefore, avowedly to represent the claims of others, although in his letter of acceptance to the delegates he mentioned his own grievances as enabling him to make common cause with them. It is clear, however, from the evidence of Dr. Willoughby and Mr. Astley, that from the beginning his own demand, which he himself claimed against the Government, was uppermost in his thoughts, and as early as December he attempted to make a direct bargain with the Government for its satisfaction. . . .

The counsel for the other half-breeds who pleaded guilty also stated in court that Riel had himself procured the request to him to come to this country; and on two occasions in court these learned gentlemen most earnestly and indignantly denounced the prisoner as one who had misled and deceived their clients, and to whom all the misery and ruin which this unhappy rebellion had brought upon them was to be attributed.

But if an unselfish desire could be credited to the prisoner to redress political wrongs even by armed rebellion, it would at least have been necessary to disprove the charge which lies against him, that in his own mind the claims of humanity had no place, but that he was prepared to carry out his designs by bringing upon an unoffending people all the horrors of an Indian rising with the outrages and atrocities which, as he knew full well, must inevitably accompany it. That this cannot be disproved, but that it is beyond all dispute true, the evidence makes plain.

From the beginning, even before Duck Lake, he was found in company with Indians armed, and to the end he availed himself of their assistance. . . .

It could not be overlooked either,

upon an application for executive clemency, that upon the trials of One Arrow, Poundmaker, White Cap and other Indians, it was apparent that they were excited to the acts of rebellion by the prisoner and his emissaries. Many of these Indians so incited and acting with him from the commencement were refugee Sioux from the United States, said to have been concerned in the Minnesota massacre and the Custer affair, and therefore of a most dangerous class.

It is to the credit of the Indian chiefs that their influence was used to prevent barbarity, but by individuals among them several cold-blooded, deliberate murders were committed, for which the perpetrators now lie under sentence of death. These crimes took place during the rebellion, and can be attributed only to the excitement arising out of it.

4. Whether rebellion alone should be punished with death is a question upon which opinions may differ. Treason will probably ever remain what it always has been among civilized nations, the highest of all crimes; but each conviction for that offence must be treated and disposed of by the Executive Government upon its own merits, and with a full consideration of all the attendant circumstances. In this particular instance, it was a second offence and, as on the first occasion, accompanied by bloodshed under the direct and immediate order of the prisoner, and by the atrocity of attempting to incite an Indian warfare, the possible results of which the prisoner could and did thoroughly appreciate. In deciding upon the application for the commutation of the sentence passed upon the prisoner the Government was obliged to keep in view the need of exemplary and deterrent punishment for crimes committed in a country situated in regard to settlement and population as are

the North-West Territories; the isolation and defenceless position of the settlers already there; the horrors to which they would be exposed in the event of an Indian outbreak; the effect upon intending settlers of any weakness in the administration of the law; and the consequences which must follow in such a country if it came to be believed that such crimes as Riel's could be committed, without incurring the extreme penalty of the law, by anyone who was either subject to delusions, or could lead people to believe that he was so subject. The crime of the prisoner was no constructive treason; it was accompanied by much bloodshed, inflicted by his own direct orders; and the Government have felt, upon a full and most earnest consideration of the case, that they would be unworthy of the power with which they are entrusted by the whole people, and would have neglected their plain duty to all classes, had they interfered with the due execution of a sentence pronounced as the result of a just verdict, and sanctioned by a righteous law.

Statement made by Riel at his trial, Regina, 1885. The full proceedings at the trial are in *Canada Sessional Papers* 1886, Vol. 19, No. 43c.

# A Statement to the Court

Prisoner.—Can I speak now?

Mr. Justice Richardson.—Oh, yes.

Prisoner.—Your Honors, gentlemen of the jury——

Mr. Justice Richardson.—There is no jury now, they are discharged.

Prisoner.—Well, they have passed away before me.

Mr. Justice Richardson.—Yes, they have passed away.

Prisoner.—But at the same time I consider them yet still there, still in their seat. The court has done the work for me, and although at first appearance it seems to be against me, I am so confident in the ideas which I have had the honor to express yesterday, that I think it is for good, and not for my loss. Up to this moment I have been considered by a certain party as insane, by another party as a criminal, by another party as a man with whom it was doubtful whether to have any intercourse. So there was hostility, and there was contempt, and there was avoidance. Today, by the verdict of the court, one of those three situations has disappeared.

I suppose that after having been condemned, I will cease to be called a fool, and for me, it is a great advantage. I consider it as a great advantage. If I have a mission—I say "if," for the sake of those who doubt, but for my part it means "since," since I have a mission, I cannot fulfil my mission as long as I am looked upon as an insane being—human being, as the moment I begin to ascend that scale I begin to succeed.

You have asked me, your Honors, if I have anything to say why my sentence should not be passed. Yes, it is on that point particularly my attention is directed.

Before saying anything about it, I wish to take notice that if there has ever been any contradiction in my life, it is at this moment, and do I appear excited? Am I very irritable? Can I control myself? And it is just on religion and on politics, and I am contradicted at this moment on politics, and the smile that comes to my face is not an act of my will so much as it comes naturally from the satisfaction that I proved that I experienced seeing one of my difficulties disappearing. Should I be executed—at least if I were going to be executed—I would not be executed as an insane man. It would be a great consolation for my mother, for my wife, for my children, for my brothers, for my relatives, even for my protectors, for my countrymen. I thank the gentlemen who were composing the jury for having recommended me to the clemency of the court. When I expressed the great hopes that I have just expressed to you, I don't express it without grounds. My hopes are reasonable, and since they are recommended, since the recommendation of the jury to the Crown is for clemency, it would be easy for me, your Honor, to make an incendiary protest and take the three reasons which have been reasonably put forward by my good lawyers and learned lawyers about the jury, about their selection, about the one who selected them, and about the complacency of the court; but why should I do it since the court has undertaken to prove that I am a reasonable man? Must not I take advantage of the situation to show that they are right, and that I am reasonable? And yesterday, when I said, by repeating the evidence which had been given against me, when I said in conclusion that you had a decent prophet, I have just today the great opportunity of proving it is so. Besides clearing me of the stain of insanity, clearing my career of the stain of insanity, I think the verdict that has been given against me is a proof that I am more than ordinary myself, but that the circumstances and the help which is given to me is more than ordinary, are more than ordinary, and although I consider myself only as others, yet by the will of God, by His Providence, by the circumstances which have surrounded me for fifteen years, I think I have been called on to do something which, at least in the North-West, nobody has done yet. And in some way I think, that, to a certain number of people, the verdict against me today is a proof that maybe I am a prophet, maybe Riel is a prophet, he suffered enough for it. Now, I have been hunted as an elk for fifteen years. David has been seventeen, I think I will have to be about two years still. If the misfortunes that I have had to go through were to be as long as those of old David, I would have two years still, but I hope it will come sooner. I have two reasons why I would ask that sentence should not be passed upon me, against me. You will excuse me, you know my difficulty in speaking English, and have had no time to prepare, your Honor, and even had I prepared anything, it

would have been imperfect enough, and I have not prepared, and I wish you would excuse what I have to say, the way which I will be able to perhaps express it.

The troubles of the Saskatchewan are not to be taken as an isolated fact. They are the result of fifteen years' war. The head of that difficulty lies in the difficulty of Red River. The troubles of Red River were called the troubles of the North-West, and I would like to know if the troubles of the Saskatchewan have not the name today of being the troubles of the North West. So the troubles of 1869 being the troubles of the North-West, and the troubles of 1885 being still the troubles of the North-West, the suggestion comes naturally to the mind of the observer if it is a continuation. The troubles of the North-West in 1885 are the continuation of the troubles in 1869, or if they are two troubles entirely different—I say they are not. Canada—no, I ought not to say Canada, because it was a certain number of individuals, perhaps 700 or 800, that can have passed for Canada, but they came to the Red River, and they wanted to take possession of the country without consulting the people. True, it was the half-breed people. There were a certain number of white pioneers among the population, but the great majority were half-breeds. We took up arms against the invaders of the east without knowing them. They were so far apart of us, on the other side of the lakes, that it cannot be said we had any hatred against them. We did not know them. They came without notification, they came boldly. We said, who are they, they said, we are the possessors of the country. Well, knowing that it was not true, we done against those parties coming from the east, what we used to do against the Indians from the south and the west, when they would invade us. . . . We took up arms, as I stated, and we made hundreds of prisoners, and we negotiated. A treaty was made. That treaty was made by a delegation of both parties. Whether you consider that organization of the Red River people at that time a provisional government, or not, the fact is that they were recognized as a body tribal, if you like to call it, as a social body with whom the Canadian Government treated. . . . What was the treaty? Was it an Indian affair? If it had been an Indian affair Manitoba would not have been as it is, would not be as it is. We have the Manitoba Act. There was an agreement between the two delegates how the whole North-West interest would be considered and how the Canadian Government would treat with the North-West. And then, having settled on the matters of principle, those very principles, the agreement was made that those very principles would be inaugurated in Manitoba first. There was a province erected with responsible government; the lands, they were kept by the Dominion. As the half-breed people were the majority of Manitoba, as at their stage of civilization they were not supposed to be able to administer their lands, we thought that at that time is was a reasonable concession to let them go, not because we were willing to let them go, but because it seemed impracticable to have the administration of the lands. Still, one of the conditions was that the lands were that the people of the North-West wanted the administration of their lands. The half-breeds had a million, and the land grant of 1,400,000 acres owned about 9,500,000, if I mistake not, which is about one-seventh of the lands of Manitoba. You will see the origin of my insanity and of my foreign policy. One-seventh of the land was granted to the people, to the half-breeds of Manitoba—English and French, Protestant and Catholic; there was no distinction whatever. But in the sub-division, in the allotment of those lands between the half-breeds of Manitoba, it came that they had 240 acres of land. Now, the Canadian Government say that we will give to the half-breeds of the North-West 240 acres. If I was insane I would say yes, but as I have had, thank God, all the time the consciousness that I had a certain degree of reason, I have made up my mind to make use of it, and to say that one-seventh of the lands in Manitoba, as to the inauguration of a principle in the North West, had to bring to the half-breeds of the North-West at least as soon as possible the guarantee for the future that a seventh of the lands will also be given to them; and seeing and yourself understanding how it is difficult for a small population, as the half-breed population, to have their voices heard, I said what belongs to us ought to be ours. Our right to the North-West is acknowledged, our co-proprietorship with the Indians is acknowledged, since one-seventh of the land is given us, but we have not the means to be heard. What will we do? I said to some of my friends if there is no other way we will make the people who have no country understand that we have a country here which we have ceded on condition. We want a seventh of the lands, and if the bargain is not kept, it is null and void, and we have no right to retreat again. And if we cannot have our seventh of the lands from Canada, we will ask the people of the States, the Italians, to come and help us as emigrants. The Irish, I will count them. Now, it is my turn; I thank you. I count them, and I will show you if I made an insane enumeration of the parties. I said we will invite the Italians of the States, the Irish of the States, the Bavarians of the States, the Poles of the States, the Belgians of the States, and if they come and help us here to have the seventh, we will give them each a seventh; and to show that we are not fanatics, that we are not partizans, that we do not wish only for the Catholic, but that we have a consideration for those who are not Catholics. I said we will invite the Danes, we will invite the Swedes who are numerous in the States, and the Norwegians, to come around, and as there are Indians and half-breeds in British Columbia, and as British Columbia is a part of the immense North-West, we said not only for ourselves, but speaking of our children, we will make the proposition, that if they help us to have our seventh on the two sides of the Rocky Mountains, they will each have a seventh, and if the Jews will help us, on condition that they acknowledge Jesus Christ as the son of God and the only Saviour of human kind, and if they will help us with their money, we will give them a seventh; and I said also, if the principle of giving a seventh of the lands in the North-West—if the principle of giving a seventh of the lands in the North-West to the half-breeds is good, it ought to be good in the east also, and I said if it is not possible that our views should be heard, we will meet as American citizens. I will invite the Germans of the States, and I will say if you ever have an opportunity of crossing the line in the east, do it, and help the Indians and the half-breeds of the east to have a revenue equivalent to about one-seventh. And what would be the reward of the Germans? The reward of the Germans would be, if they were successful, to take a part of the country and make a new German-Indian world somewhere in British North America; but that is the last resort, and if

I had not had a verdict of guilty against me, I would have never said it. Yesterday it is just those things that I have just avoided to say; when I said I have a reason to not mention them, and when I said, as one of the witnesses said, that my proclamation was in Pembina, I think I am right, because of this trial you see that my pretension is, that I can speak a little of the future events. My trial has brought out the question of the seventh, and although no one has explained the things as I do now, still there is enough said about the seventh of the land and that the division of the lands into seven, seven nationalities, while it ought to have been said between ten nationalities, that by telegraph today my proclamation is in Pembina, truly, and the States have my idea; they have my idea. The Fenian element, without any tangible object, have crossed the lines several times for the only sake of what they called revenge, but now that Riel, whose name is somewhat prominent for fifteen years, is known to be in his trouble for life and death, for himself and his nationality, now that my trial gives me a certain increase of the celebrity, now that those questions are appearing now before the public, that there is a land league in the States, that that very same element which possesses Fenianism is still there, and quiet, because they have no plan, because they have no idea around which gather their numbers, and when they catch at it do they think that they will smile? And Gabriel Dumont on the other side of the line, is that Gabriel Dumont inactive? I believe not. He is trying to save me from this box. . . . If Canada is just with me, if Canada respects my life, my life my liberty and by [sic] reputation, they will give men all that they have taken from me, and as I said yesterday, that immense influence which my acts are gathering for the last fifteen years, and which, as the power of steam contained in an engine will have its sway, then what will it do? It will do that Riel will go perhaps to the Dominion ministry, and there instead of calling the parties in the States, he will by means, constitutional means of the country, invite the same parties from Europe as emigration, but let it be well understood that as my right has been acknowledged as a co-proprietor of the soil with the Indian, I want to assert that right. It is constitutionally acknowledged in the Manitoba Act by the 31st clause of that Act, and it does not say to extinguish the Indian title. It says two words, extinguishing, and 1,400,000 acres of land, two words and as each child of the half-breeds got one-seventh, naturally I am at least entitled to the same. It is why I spoke of the seventh for the Indians, not of the lands but of the revenue as it increases. But somebody will say, on what grounds do you ask one-seventh of the lands? Do you own the lands? In England, in France, the French and the English have lands, the first was in England, they were the owners of the soil and they transmitted to generations. Now, by the soil they have had their start as a nation. Who starts the nations? The very one who creates them, God. God is the master of the universe, our planet is his land, and the nation and the tribes are members of His family, and as a good father, he gives a portion of his lands to that nation, to that tribe, to everyone, that is his heritage, that is his share of the inheritance, of the people, or nation or tribe. Now, here is a nation strong as it may be, it has its inheritance from God. When they have crowded their country because they had no room to stay any more at home, it does not give them the right to come and take the share of all

tribes besides them. When they come they ought to say, well, my little sister, the Cree tribe, you have a great territory, but that territory has been given to you as our own land, it has been given to our fathers in England or in France and of course you cannot exist without having that spot of land. This is the principle God cannot create a tribe without locating it. . . . They made the treaty with us. As they have made the treaty, I say they have to observe it, and did they observe the treaty? No. There was a question of amnesty then, and when the treaty was made one of the questions was that before the Canadian Government would send a governor into Manitoba an Imperial amnesty should be proclaimed so as to blot out all the difficulties of the past. Instead of proclaiming a general amnesty before the arrival of the governor which took place on the 2nd of September, 1870, the amnesty was proclaimed the 25th April, 1875, so I suffered for five years unprotected, besides I was expelled from the House twice. I was they say outlawed, but, as I was busy as a member of the east, and had a trial in the west, I could not be in two places, and they say that I was outlawed, but no notification was sent to my house of any proceedings of the court. They say that I was outlawed and when the amnesty came five years after the time that it should have come, I was banished for five years and Lepine deprived of his political rights for ever. Why? Because he had given political rights to Manitoba? Is that all? No. Did the amnesty come from the Imperial Government? Not at all. It came from our sister colony in the east, and mind you, to make a miracle of it I said the one being great, and Riel being small, I will go on the other side and I am banished. It is a wonder I did not take and go to Mexico. Naturally I went to the States, amnesty was given by the Secretary of State at Ottawa, the party who treated with us. That is no amnesty. It is an insult to me. It has always been an insult to me. I said in Manitoba two years ago that it was an insult and I considered it as such, but are there proofs that amnesty has been promised? Yes, many. Archbishop Taché the delegate who has been called, the prelate who has been called from Rome to come and pacify the North-West received a commission to make, to accomplish that pacification, and in general terms was written his commission, and when he came into the North-West before I sent delegates, he said I will give you my word of honor as a delegate, that there will be an Imperial amnesty, not because I can promise it on my own responsibility, but because it has been guaranteed to me by the representative of the Crown and the Ministers themselves, the Minister of the Crown, and instead of the Imperial amnesty came the amnesty of which I spoke and besides, an amnesty came five years too late, and which took the trouble of banishing me five years more.

Mr. Justice Richardson.—Is that all?

Prisoner.—No, excuse me, I feel weak and if I stop at times, I wish you would be kind enough to——

But the last clause of the Manitoba Act speaks also a little of the North-West, speaks that a temporary government will be put into the North-West until a certain time, not more than five years, and, gentlemen, the temporary government, how long has it lasted now? How long has it existed now? For fifteen years, and it will be temporary yet. It is against the Manitoba, it is against the treaty of the North-West that this North-West Council should continue to be in existence, and

against the spirit of the understanding. Have I anything to say against the gentlemen who compose the North-West Council? Not at all, not more than I had yesterday to say against the jury and to say against the officials of this court, whom I respect all, but I speak of the institution. No; I speak of the institutions in the North-West. The Manitoba treaty has not been fulfilled, neither in regard to me, neither in regard to Lepine. Besides the population of the half-breeds who have found in the troubles of the North-West in Manitoba in 1870, and who have been found in the troubles of the North-West, what right have they to be there? Have they not received their 240 acres? I suppose that the half-breeds in Manitoba in 1870 did not fight for 240 acres of land, but it is to be understood that there were two societies who treated together; one was small, but in its smallness it had its rights. The other was great, but by its greatness it had no greater rights than the rights of the small, because the rights is the same for every one, and when they began by treating the leaders of the small community as bandits, as outlaws, leaving them without protection, they disorganized that community. The right of nations wanted that the treaty of Manitoba should be fulfilled towards the little community of Red River in the same condition that they were when they treated. That is the right of nations, and when the treaty would have been fulfilled towards that small community in the same state as when it was when she treated, then the obligations would have been fulfilled and the half-breeds might have gone to the North-West, the Saskatchewan, and have no right to call for any other things for themselves, although they had a right to help their neighbors if they thought that they were in a bad fix, because charity is always charity. Now I say that the people of Manitoba have not been satisfied, nor the leaders nor the people, because during those five years, which elapsed between 1870 and 1875, there were laws made and those laws they embraced the people, the half-breed people, and because they hadn't their rights, because their leaders were always threatened in their existence, the people themselves did not feel any security and they sold their lands, because they thought they would never get first that seventh of the lands. . . . The amnesty has not been given by the right parties. Amnesty has not been given to Lepine, one of the leaders, who was then, as Dumont is today and myself. I was allowed to come back into the country after ten years; after I would be completely deprived of the chances which I had in 1870 to do something for my people and myself and for emigration, so as to cut down my influence for ever. It is why I did not come at that time, and I thought I would never come to the country. Did I take my American paper, put my papers of American naturalization during my five years' banishment? No, I did not want to give to the States a citizen of banishment, but when my banishment had expired, when an officer at Battleford—somewhere on this side of the line, in Benton—invited me to come to the North-West I said: No, I will go to an American court, I will declare my intent, now that I am free to go back, and choose another land. It sored my heart. It sored my heart to say that kind of adieu to my mother, to my brothers, to my sisters, to my friends, to my countrymen, my native land, but I felt that in coming back to this country I could not re-enter it without protesting against all the injustice which I had been suffering, and in doing it I was renewing a struggle which I had not been able to continue as a sound man, as I thought I was, I thought it better to begin a career on the other side of the line. In Manitoba is that all about the amnesty? No, my share of the 1,400,000 acres of land, have I received it? No, I have not received it. My friends, my mother have applied to have it. No, I could not. Everyone else could apply for theirs. Father, mother, would apply for their sons and that was all right, but for my honor, to apply for me it was not, I did not get it. Last year there was a proof. Here, in the box, not long ago when I asked an indemnity, I was refused. Was that indemnity based on a fancy? I wanted my lands in Manitoba to be paid. Besides, when they treatied, the treaty was completed on the 31st May, 1870, it was agreed to the 24th June, and Sir Geo. Cartier had said, let Riel govern the country until the troops get there, and from the 24th June till the 23rd August I governed the country in fact, and what was the reward for it? . . . When I speak of an indemnity of $35,000, to call for something to complete the $100,000, I don't believe that I am exaggerating, your Honor. In 1871 the Fenians came in Pembina. Major Irvine, one of the witnesses, I was introduced to him, and when I brought to the governor 250 men, Governor Archibald was then anxious to have my help because he knew that we were the door of Manitoba, and he said as the question of amnesty came he said if Riel comes forward we will protect him. "Pour la circonstance actuelle," we will protect him. As long as we need him, we will protect him, but as soon as we don't want him, as soon as we don't need him, we want him to fall back in the same position he is today, and that answer had been brought because it had been represented that while I would be helping the Government the parties would be trying to shoot me in the back. "Pour la circonstance actuelle," they said, I will protect him. What reward have I had by that? The first reward that I had was that that took place in the first days of October, 1871, before the year was ended.

Of course they gave the chance to Riel to come out. A rebel had a chance to be loyal then. My friends, my glorious friend in Upper Canada, now the leader of the opposition, Mr. Blake, said, we must prevent Mr. Riel from arriving. When he was Minister in Upper Canada he issued a proclamation of $5,000 for those who would arrest Riel. That was my reward, my dowry, but the Canadian Government, what reward would they give me? In the next year there was going to be an election—1872. If Riel remains in the country for the elections, it will be trouble, and he has a right to speak. We have made a treaty with him, we do not fulfil it; we promise him amnesty; he is outlawed; we take his country and he has no room even to sleep. He comes to our help. He governs the country during two months and the reward is that he is a bandit. He comes to the help of the Government with 250 men and the reward is $5,000 for his head. It was at that time that I took the name of David and didn't I take it myself? The hon. judge of the court at Manitoba, Mr. [Joseph] Dubuc, today is the one who gave me the name of David. When I had to hide myself in the woods and when he wanted to write me that he should write me under the name which would not be known, so that my letter could come to me, and I may say that in that way it is a legal name. From that point of view even, and I put in a parenthesis, why I have a right, I think as a souvenir of my friend in Upper Canada who caused the

circumstances, who brought me that name, to make nothing special about it, and besides, when the King of Judea was speaking of the public services of David didn't he refer us to refer to him in that way? Yes, he did, and as something similar I thought it was only proper that I should take the name of David, but it was suggested to me in a mighty manner, and I could not avoid it. The Canadian Government said well, Riel will be in the elections here, and he will have the right with all those grievances to speak, and he will embarrass the Government, so they called on my great protector, Archbishop Taché, I don't know what; but in the month of February, 1872 Archbishop Tache [sic] came to me and said the authorities in Lower Canada want you to go on the other side of the line until the crisis is passed. Well, I said, if the crisis is concerning me only, it would be my interest to go there, but I am in a crisis which is the crisis of the people of the country, and as it concerns the public besides me I will speak to the public as the public are speaking to me, but the Archbishop gave me so good reason that although I could not yield to those reasons, I came to a conclusion with him, and I said, my Lord, you have titles to my acknowledgment which shall never be blotted out of my heart, and although my judgment in this matter altogether differs from yours, I don't consider my judgment above yours and what seems to me reasonable might be more reasonable, although I think my course of action reasonable, perhaps yours is more reasonable. I said if you command me, as my Archbishop, to go, and take on your shoulders the responsibility of leaving my people in the crisis I will go, but let it be known that it is not my word, that I do it to please you, and yet after you command me to do it—to show that in politics when I am contradicted I can give way, and they offered me £10 a month to stay on the other side of the line. I said to be in gaol I have a chance here in Manitoba, and I want something. They asked me how much I wanted, and I said how long do you want me to stay away? Well, he said, perhaps a year. I tell you beforehand that I want to be here during the elections; that is what I asserted. I want to be here during the elections and it was agreed that they would give £800; £400 to Lepine, £400 to me, £300 to me personally, £300 for Lepine, £100 for my family, £100 for Lepine's family. That makes £800. How was it agreed that I should receive that money? I said to his lordship that the Canadian Government owe me money, they libel me, and even on the question of libel, they do it so clearly that it does not need any trial to come to judgment. They have a judgment and will they make use of it? They owe me something for my reputation that they abuse every day. Besides I have done work and they never paid me for it. I will take that money as an account of what they will have to pay me one day. It was agreed in that manner and the money was given me in the chapel of St. Vital in the presence of Mr. Dubuc, judge now, and when I did not know at that time where the money came, surely came from, and when the little sack of £300 of gold was handed me there on the table, I said to his lordship, my Lord, if the one who wants me to go away was here, and if I had to treat him as he is trying to treat me, this little sack of gold ought to go through his head. That was my last protest. At that time, but before the election, public opinion was so excited against the one who had taken the responsibility of advising my leaving, that he called me back, and

during the elections I was present, it was three years to-day. I am rewarded for what I have done through those three years. Sir George Cartier in 1872, just in that summer was beaten in Montreal. I speak of him not as a man of party, I speak of him as a Canadian, as public man. He was beaten by Mr. Jetté, of Montreal, by 1,200 majority, and they came to me. My election was sure in Provencher. I had fifteen or twenty men against me, and they came to me. Riel, do you want to resign your seat? I have not it yet. Oh, well you are to get it. Allow George Cartier to be elected here, and I said yes, to show that if I had at the time any inclination to become insane when I was contradicted in politics. But Lower Canada has more than paid me for the little consideration, great as my consideration, but that little mark I considered it a little mark of consideration, a little mark of a great consideration for them. . . . I struggled not only for myself but I struggled for the rights, for the inauguration of the principles of responsible and constitutional government in Manitoba. That was conceded about the time I was banished. While I was in the States was I happy? Yes, I was very happy to find a refuge, but I have met men who have come to me several times and say, here, look out, here is a man on the other side of the line, and he is trying to take a revenge at you, when you water your horses, because they have left stains as much as possible on my name. I could not even water my horses on the Missouri without being guarded against those who wanted my life. And it is an irony for me that I should be called David. . . .

. . . I did not hide my thoughts, I went through the channel of natural emigration, of peaceful emigration, through the channel of constitutional means, to start the idea, and if possible to inaugurate it, but if I can't do it during my life I leave the ideas to be fulfilled in the future, and if it is not possible, you are reasonable men and you know that the interests that I propose are of an immense interest, and if it is not, if the peaceful channel of emigration is not open to those races into the North-West, they are in such numbers in the States that when you expect it least, they will perhaps try to come on your borders and to look at the land, whether it is worth paying it a visit or not. That is the seventh of the lands, that is about the seventh of the lands. So you see that by the very nature of the evidence that has been given here when the witnesses speak of a seventh of the land, that very same question originates from 1870, from the troubles of Red River which brought a treaty where the seventh of the lands took its existence, and I say if this court tries me for what has taken place in the North-West they are trying me for something which was in existence before then. This court was not in existence when the difficulties of which we speak now in the Saskatchewan, began; it is the difficulties of 1869, and what I say is, I wish that I have a trial. My wish is this, your Honor, that a commission be appointed by the proper authorities, but amongst the proper authorities of course I count on English authorities, that is the first proper authorities; that a commission be appointed; that that commission examines into this question, or if they are appointed to try me, if a special tribunal is appointed to try me, that I am tried first on this question: Has Riel rebelled in 1869? Second question. Was Riel a murderer of Thomas Scott, when Thomas Scott was executed? Third question. When Riel received the money from Archbishop Taché, reported to be the

money of Sir John, was it corruption money? Fourth. When Riel seized, with the council of Red River, on the property of the Hudson Bay Company, did he commit pillage? Fifth. When Riel was expelled from the House as a fugitive of justice in 1874, was he a fugitive of justice? . . . In the month of April I was expelled from the House. Lepine was arrested in 1873, and I was not; not because they did not want to take me. And while I was in the woods waiting for my election Sir John sent parties to me offering $35,000 if I would leave the country for three years, and if that was not enough to say what I wanted, and that I might take a trip over the water, besides over the world. At the time I refused it. This is not the first time that the $35,000 comes up, and if at that time I refused it was it not reasonable for me that I should think it a sound souvenir to Sir John? Am I insulting? No, I do not insult. You don't mean to insult me when you declare me guilty; you act according to your convictions, I do also according to mine. I speak true. I say they should try me on this question, whether I rebelled on the Saskatchewan in 1885. There is another question. I want to have one trial; I wish to have a trial that will cover the space of fifteen years, on which public opinion is not satisfied. I have, without meaning any offence, I have heard, without meaning any offence, when I spoke of one of the articles I mentioned, some gentlemen behind me saying, "yes, he was a murderer." You see what remarks. It shows there is something not told. If I told by law it would not be said. I wish to have my trial, as I am tried for nothing; and as I am tried for my career, I wish my career should be tried; not the last part of it. On the other side I am declared to be guilty of high treason, and I give myself as a prophet to the new world. If I am guilty of high treason I say that I am a prophet of the new world. I wish that while a commission sits on one side a commission of doctors should also sit and examine fully whether I am sane, whether I am a prophet or not; not insanity, because it is disposed of, but whether I am a deceiver and impostor. I have said to my good lawyers, I have written things which were said to me last night and which have taken place to-day; I said that before the court opened. Last night the spirit that guides and assists me told me the court will make an effort—your Honor, allow me to speak of your charge, which appeared to me to go on one side —the court made an effort, and I think that word is justified. At the same time there was another thing said to me; a commission will sit; there will be a commission. I did not hear yet that a commission is to take place. I ask for it. You will see if I am an impostor thereby. The doctors will say when I speak of these things whether I am deceiving. If they say I am deceiving, I am not an impostor by will. I may be declared insane because I seek an idea which drives me to something right. I tell you in all what I say in most things I do, I do according to what is told to me. In Batoche any things which I said have already happened. It was said to me not far from here and that is why I never wanted to send the half-breeds far, I wanted to keep them, and it was said to me I will not begin to work before 12 o'clock, and when the first battle opened I was taking my dinner at Duck Lake. When the battle began it was a little after 12 o'clock. I will not begin to work before 12 o'clock, and what has happened? And it was said to me if you do not meet the troops on such a road, you will have to meet them at the foot of a hill, and the half-breeds facing it. It is said my papers have been published. If they have been published, examine what took place, and you will see we had to meet General Middleton at the foot of the hill. It was also told me that men would stay in the "belle prairie," and the spirit spoke of those who would remain on the "belle prairie," and there were men who remained on the "belle prairie." And he admits it was looked upon as something very correct in the line of military art, it was not come from me or Dumont, it was the spirit that guides me.

I have two reasons why I wish the sentence of the court should not be passed upon me. The first, I wish my trial should take place as I said, whether that wish is practical or not, I bow respectfully to the court. I ask that a commission of doctors examine me. As I am declared guilty I would like to leave my name, as far as conscience is concerned, all right. If a commission of doctors sits and if they examine me, they can see if I was sincere or not. I will give them the whole history, and I think while I am declared guilty of high treason it is only right I should be granted the advantages of giving my proofs whether I am sincere, that I am sincere. Now, I am judged a sane man, the cause of my guilt is that I am an impostor, that would be the consequence. I wish a commission to sit and examine me. There have been witnesses around me for ten years, about the time they have declared me insane, and they will show if there is in me the character of an impostor. If they declare me insane, if I have been astray. I have been astray not as an impostor, but according to my conscience. Your Honor that is all what I have to say.

Evidence of Dr. James Wallace, trial of Louis Riel 1885. The full proceedings of the trial are in *Canada Sessional Papers* 1886, Vol. 19, No. 43c.

# Medical Opinion

DR. JAMES M. WALLACE sworn:—

*Examined by Mr. Osler:*

Q. Doctor, what is your position? A. I am medical superintendent of the Asylum for the Insane at Hamilton, Ontario.

Q. An institution having about how many patients, on the average? A. Somewhere over 600.

Q. How long have you been making a branch a specialty of the study of the insane? A. I have been in charge of that asylum nearly nine years, but I have been studying insanity for a few years more than that.

Q. For more than nine years? A. Yes.

Q. And you see every variety of it I suppose? A. All shades and variety.

Q. Now, do you devote yourself to the medical branch of it? A. Entirely.

Q. You have nothing to do with keeping the hotel or boarding house. A. Well, I have the general superintendence of the house; but I devote nearly all my time to the medical department of the asylum.

Q. Have you been listening to the evidence in this case? A. Yes.

Q. Have you examined or had an opportunity of seeing the prisoner. A. I saw him for about half an hour, that is, alone, not in court.

Q. And you have been here during the——? A. During the sitting of the court.

Q. Have you formed an opinion of his mental responsibility, of his sanity or insanity? A. I have so far as my time and opportunities enabled me to do so.

Q. What is that opinion? A. I have not discovered any insanity about him, no indication of insanity.

Q. What would you say then in view of the evidence and your examination? Is he of sound mind or is he not? A. I think he is of sound mind.

Q. And capable of distinguishing right from wrong? A. I think so.

Q. And know the nature and quality of any act he would commit? A. Very acutely.

*Cross-examined by Mr. Fitzpatrick:*

Q. You have no doubt whatever in your mind from the examination you have made of this man during half an hour, and from the evidence which you have heard here, that he is of perfectly sound mind? A. Well, I should qualify, I should qualify my answer to that question. I have only had a limited examination of him, and in any case of obscure mental disease, it sometimes takes a very long time before one can make up their mind; but from what I have seen of him, I say that I have discovered no symptoms of insanty.

Q. So what you say now, doctor, is purely and simply this, not that he is not insane, but that you have not been able to discover any symptoms of insanity? A. That is what I say. I say I have not discovered it. It would be presumption for me to say he is not insane, from the opportunities that I have had; but at the same time my opinion is pretty fairly fixed in my mind that he is not insane.

Q. You are aware that a great many cases exist in which men are found to be perfectly insane without its being possible to discover any trace of insanity, are you not? A. O, sir, I have had patients in my asylum for weeks sometimes before I found any symptoms of insanity.

Q. You are aware also, are you not, that there have been cases in England in which men were examined for a whole day, and cross-examined by such men as Erskine for instance, perfectly insane, and during the whole day it was impossible for Erskine to discover that the man was insane? A. Yes, I daresay such cases may exist. I am quite certain such cases have existed.

Q. You are quite certain such cases are in existence? A. Yes.

Q. Therefore you are obliged to say that all that you have discovered in this case, or all you are in a position now to say is that you have not discovered any traces of insanity? A. That is all that my conscience will allow me to say.

Q. You have heard of that particular form of mental disease known as magalomania probably? A. Yes.

Q. Would you tell us what are the symptoms which are the characteristics of this disease? A. That is a simple complication. That is a term which is scarcely ever used, and I think it is only used by one writer. I don't remember any other who uses it in the English language, and he simply introduces it and says——

Q. But one writer uses that name? A. Only one that I can think of at the present time in the English language, and he says that it is a condition in which the patient has delusions, grandiose delusions, delusions of greatness, and most commonly complicated with that form of insanity called paralytic insanity or gentle paralysis.

Q. You are aware that this particular form of insanity is characterized, among other things, by extreme irritability on the part of the patient? A. Not magalomania. Magalomania simply applies to grandiose ideas. It can have no other definition than that. And these definitions allow me to explain are delusions; they are delusions such as a person holding or believing himself to be a king or possessed of immense wealth, and that the world is at his feet. These are the kind of delusions that are meant by magalomania, as I understand them, and it has not any other meaning that I know of.

Q. The delusions are that he is rich? A. Yes.

Q. And powerful? A. Yes.

Q. A great general? A. Yes.

Q. A great minister? A. He may be a great anything and everything.

Q. A great prophet? A. Yes.

Q. Or divinely inspired, or that he is a poet or a musician, in fact that he is an egotist, and a selfish man? A. Yes.

Q. But you are quite sure that the character of irritability is not one of the characters of this malady? A. It is not a malady, it is merely a symptom.

Q. That is a form of mental disease? A. It is not a mental disease, it is only a symptom of mental disease. . . .

Q. But in magalomania irritability is laid down by the book as one of the characteristics, at all events? A. Yes.

Q. So that now, doctor, you are of the opinion that the idea of grandeur and of power is not to be found anywhere except in cases of paralytic insanity? A. Oh, yes; we find it in simple mania. We find it in simple mania, but these are fixed delusions; these are fixed delusions, and persons who hold them say they are, believe themselves to be kings and queens or great leaders or wealthy people. They may be great in anything and great in everything, and they actually believe this and act upon their belief, constantly act upon their belief.

Q. Did I understand you to say, doctor, that the idea of grandeur is exclusively a symptom of paralytic insanity, that that is not to be met in other cases? A. No; I have just stated now that you will find delusions of grandeur in other forms of insanity.

Q. Now is it not a fact that in cases of magalomania one of the characteristics, one of the very essential characteristics, is that the individual who suffers from that particular form of mental disease is able in a very large measure to hide the disease from any person who endeavors to find it out? A. Well, insane persons are able, as I said before, to conceal their delusions sometimes for a length of time, but a person suffering from magalomania does not attempt to do it; he is too proud to expose his delusion.

Q. So that one of the characteristics of it is pride? A. Yes.

Q. Is there a case in which a man, for instance, would be under the insane delusion that he was destined to fill a great mission, that he was in a position to take possession of a country such as this one is—would not that man be in a position to take such means as would be necessary to arrive at his ends, and to take those means with a great amount of shrewdness and precaution? A. That is quite inconsistent with my idea of magalomania. As I said before, my idea of magalomania is, as defined by Clouston, for instance, that a man is already in possession of all these things, and he does not want any more.

Q. So that your idea is, doctor, that a man who is suffering from this particular disease is not in a position, and it is utterly impossible for him to take any steps to arrive at the conclusion which he pretends he ought to arrive at? A. Oh, he does not require any plans at all; everything flows into him; he is the greatest man in the world, and everything is subservient to him; wealth comes into him; he does not want, and he can command everybody and they will obey him.

Q. So that he does not make any calculations at all, and does not adopt any means at all to arrive at his end? A. Not at all.

Q. It is one of the characteristics of the malady that he is unable to do that? A. Not unable; because he does not ask to do it; he is self-possessed and so self-contented.

Q. Now, doctor, we will just read this little book again on that subject: "it is so much the more dangerous that he still retains the necessary faculty to be able to make calculations which are necessary to arrive at his ends"? A. But is that speaking of magalomania?

Q. Under the chapter entitled "Magalomania"? A. Well, would you allow me to quote from Clouston? He is speaking of mental depression, and he says, there are a few cases of depressed feeling with exalted intellectual condition. Many persons exaggerate their former notions of wealth and position by way of contrast with their present misery. I had a woman, in excited melancholia, groaning all the time, and then considered herself a queen; and another a king, and of immense wealth. Some cases are of the nature of what the French call magalomania, that is, expansive grandiose, exalted state of the mind, which, as a mental symptom, is best seen in gentle paralysis, coupled with ideas of persecution, and with depressed feeling, especially at times.

Q. Do you think there is anything in what you have read there that is inconsistent with what I have read to you, that contradicts that? A. Well, there is nothing contradicts it; but I say magalomania is——

Q. That is simply an interpretation of what this book has said here? A. Well, we are not very far apart; we are only apart this far, that you wish to contend for magalomania as a disease, while I contend that it is only a symptom.

Q. We are not talking about symptoms of diseases at all, I ask you was that one of the symptoms of magalomania and you said that it did not exist in a case, and the book says that it does? A. You are not giving me justice.

Q. I don't mean to do you an injustice. I don't mean to adopt any bullying process, it is not my habit and I don't do it, I don't pretend to set my knowledge against yours in a matter of this kind, you are free to explain it. This magalomania was called formerly intellectual monomania, was it not? A. Yes, it is a monomania.

Q. It came under that general class of cases formerly? A. Yes.

Q. Now, one of the symptoms of that malady—you have heard of a book written by Ducelle? A. No, I never heard of that.

Q. You don't know Legrand Ducelle, a French author? A. No, I don't know the book.

Q. You never heard of a book of that kind, at all events I cannot put the authority in evidence as you say you don't know it, but I might ask you, for instance, whether or not that particular

form of disease which I have spoken to you about, that is intellectual monomania, that insane persons believe they are in constant intercourse with God, and they believe themselves to be inspired, and believe themselves to be prophets, and their hallucinations are such they suppose they are in constant intercourse with the Supreme Being? A. Yes, I have known patients of that kind.

Q. Have you ever heard of: (giving the name of another French author)? A. I don't want to hear of any French authors. I never read them.

Q. You never get that far? A. No.

Q. Persons suffering from delusions of grandeur are perfectly harmless as a rule are they not? A. No; as a rule they are not. Not always. They sometimes are and sometimes they are not.

Q. In cases in which they would be harmless, would you put two of these persons together in the same ward? A. I never put two lunatics together anywhere. They are always kept, either one, or more than two.

Q. Would you put more than two together? A. Yes.

Q. Without any impropriety whatever? A. Yes. Our buildings are put up with a view to that.

Q. I don't know if you understand my question—I supposed several persons suffering from the same, two kings and a queen or two queens, you would put all those persons together in the same ward? A. They might be or they might not.

Q. You would not see any objection in that? A. There would be no impropriety in putting them together, I think not.

*By Mr. Osler:*

Q. Where the disease exists, is the idea, the result of disease, fixed and constant? A. It is the result of the disease.

Q. But is it fixed or intermittent?

A. In those cases they are fixed.

Q. So that when a person has taken herself a queen, she remains a queen? A. She usually dies a queen.

Q. In her own idea? A. Yes.

Q. And she is a queen to everybody to whom she talks? A. Yes.

Q. Not sometimes a queen and sometimes otherwise? A. No.

Evidence of Dr. A. Jukes, trial of Louis Riel 1885. The full proceedings of the trial are in *Canada Sessional Papers* 1886, Vol. 19, No. 43c.


# Another Doctor's Testimony


DR. JUKES, sworn:—

*Examined by Mr. Robinson:*

Q. You are at present the medical officer attached to the Mounted Police force? A. I am the senior surgeon of the Mounted Police.

Q. And how long have you been in medical practice? A. Thirty-five years.

Q. Have you devoted your attention to insanity at all specially or not? A. Never specially. There are cases, of course, occasionally will come under the notice of every general practitioner, but as a special study I have never done so.

Q. Every medical practitioner, I suppose, has his attention more or less directed to it? A. Occasionally I have been called upon to certify in cases of insanity.

Q. You are also surgeon to the gaol here I am told? A. At present until a gaol has been erected in the North-West Territories, the guard room at Regina constitutes the gaol, the guard room headquarters constitutes the gaol.

Q. In that capacity insane persons would pass under your hands—any person supposed to be insane? A. Yes. I remember during the last three years a number of persons of unsound mind have been sent there as a place of confinement.

Q. And in that way they have come under your observation? A. They have come under my observation for the time.

Q. Now, you know the prisoner I believe? A. Yes.

Q. How long have you known him? A. I don't remember the exact day that he was brought to Regina, but I think it must have been between the 20th and 24th of May.

Q. But whatever it was—between the 20th and 24th? A. About that time I am not sure.

Q. Since that time how often have you seen him? A. I have seen him almost every day. There have been one or two or perhaps three days that I have missed seeing him, owing to pressure of other business, other work at that time, but I have seen him uniformly every day.

Q. As a rule you have seen him every day, although you have missed two or three or four days during that time? A. Yes.

Q. Then you have had an opportunity I suppose of observing his mental condition? A. I would speak to him on every occasion in passing him, and he has generally acquainted me with what he conceived to be his wants and his necessities, and I would examine into the condition of his physical—the general health and ascertain how his diet was agreeing with him, and things of that kind, such as came under my special duty, and occasionally he would speak to me on other matters, occasionally he would delay me and speak on other subjects.

Q. Then you have formed an opinion as to his mental state? I am speaking now of his insanity—sanity or insanity? A. I have never seen anything during my intercourse with Mr. Riel to leave any impression upon my mind that he was insane.

Q. Then as I understand you believe him to be sane? A. I believe him to be sane so far as my knowledge of such matter goes. I have seen nothing to induce me to believe otherwise.

Q. I suppose you have had your attention directed to that part of his character more or less, I mean his mental condition more or less? A. No, I have never seen anything to make me question his mental condition, and therefore have never led the conversation under any circumstances to draw out any possible insane notion. I have never made any effort to do so, because my duty was otherwise.

Q. What I meant is, doctor, you have heard, I suppose, from time to time, rumors that there was an assertion of the unsoundness of his mind? A. I have heard it rumored that he had been formerly insane and that he had been confined, I think, in the Beauport Asylum, and I have heard it also rumored that it was the intention to bring forward a plea of insanity in his defence on the present occasion, that is a general rumor.

Q. Therefore, I suppose you have had this thing in your mind, that is all, that part of his condition in your own mind in speaking to him? That is all that I mean? A. Yes; Oh, I have always watched him very carefully so as to notice if possible any appearance of unsoundness of mind, and if I had noticed it, I would have placed him under special treatment as far as my knowledge enabled me to do, or have advised further treatment for him as I have done in other cases.

*Cross-examined by Mr. Fitzpatrick:*

Q. You said, doctor, that you had not made any endeavor to ascertain during the intercourse which you had with Mr. Riel, whether or not he suffered from any particular mental disease, did you? or any form of insanity or any mental disease, unsoundness of mind? A. I never specially examined him as a lunatic. I never made a special examination of him as a lunatic.

Q. You never made any special endeavor to discover whether or not he was suffering from any particular form of mental disease? A. Never any special endeavor, anything beyond ordinary conversation of the day.

Q. Is it not a fact that there are, doctor, forms of insanity which are not discoverable except after considerable endeavors have been made to discover them? A. Yes; it is so, unquestionably, that you may converse with a man continually and not be aware of his insanity until you touch accidentally, or some other person touches accidentally upon that point upon which he is insane.

Q. Had you been informed at any time of the particular mental disease from which Mr. Riel was supposed to have been suffering? A. I don't think I ever knew as much of it as I have learned here.

Q. So that you never made any endeavor to? A. I never did, that is, I never spoke to him specially with regard to what he believes to be his mission, knowing that many very sane men might be so, and yet the man might be perfectly sane.

Q. So that you have no doubt at all, doctor, from the evidence that you have heard here given by the different witnesses who were examined, the conduct of Mr. Riel is perfectly compatible with a perfectly sound mind? A. Well, I regret to say that my hearing is rather imperfect in the courtroom, and that I have not been able to hear as well as I could wish the translations that were made to the examinations in French, but so far as my understanding has gone of the evidence which has been given, I have heard nothing which would satisfy me that he was of unsound mind. I have heard nothing which might not be accounted for by other causes, that for instance, of fraud or deception. A man might really believe that he had a mission, as many great men have believed, or he might only pretend for a purpose that he had that belief.

Q. A man might also labor under the insane delusion that he had a mission? A. He might also labor under the insane delusion, but the fact of his laboring under that insane delusion would not necessarily imply that he was otherwise insane or incompetent either to perform business in a successful manner or to be responsible for his actions. That would be my own judgment.

Q. But *quoad* the particular delusion, in so far as the particular delusion under which he is suffering is concerned, he would be still responsible in your opinion, doctor. Supposing for instance that a man labored under the delusion that his neighbor was a savage dog and was endeavoring to destroy him and bite him, and that he killed his neighbor, he might be perfectly sane in other respects? A. You misunderstand me if you think I entertain that opinion.

Q. That is not the opinion you entertain? A. Certainly not.

Q. So that if a man is laboring under an insane delusion the acts which he does while he is under that insane delusion *quoad* the particular delusion he is not responsible for? A. If a man is clearly— if it can be proved that a man is acting— if it is proved that the man is acting under an insane delusion, then any act I should consider which he performed under that delusion, any act having special relation to his delusion I should consider that he was not personally responsible for, if it could be shown clearly that that delusion

was an insane one, and that it was not rather a feigned one for a purpose.

Q. So that if it can be proved that a man is laboring under an insane delusion that he was in direct communication with the Holy Ghost and was acting under the direct inspiration of God and he was bound to do a certain act, and he did it, would he be responsible for that act? A. Views on subjects of that kind are so different even among those who are confessedly sane, that it is hardly one on which I could base an opinion. There are men who have held very remarkable views with respect to religion and who have been always declared to be insane until they gathered together great numbers of followers and became leaders of a new sect, then they became great prophets and great men. It is extremely difficult to tell how far a delusion of that kind may begin as a direct attempt at fraud and may at last so take possession of a man's mind that he may believe himself divinely inspired. I think that cases of that kind could be produced,—and it would depend very much upon the mental condition of a man whether he were responsible. If it could be shown that he was clearly insane, he is clearly irresponsible on that point. That would be my own view.

Q. So that if it can be clearly shown that he was laboring under a delusion that he was divinely inspired directly from God, you think he would not be responsible for his actions? A. Responsible for what?

Q. Responsible for his actions in connection with delusion of course? A. What actions would they be, such actions as what?

Q. Such actions as he might do for the purpose of carrying out his insane delusion? A. Well, take Mahomet for instance, that was exactly Mahomet's belief.

He believed and few believed with him, even of his own people, that he was divinely inspired, but he acted upon his belief and he carried his whole belief with him. He believed it and he carried it out at the point of the sword and with the whole world, and he convinced the people of what, if he had failed, would have been simply regarded as a delusion of his own mind.

Q. So that you think the conduct of Mr. Riel perfectly compatible with the conduct for instance of a man like Mahomet or a man like Smith or a man like Young? A. No, I don't regard him so far as I understand them—Mr. Riel's views in that light. My opinion is rather, in regard to Mr. Riel, if you will allow me to say it, as far as I have been able to judge from my own personal knowledge, that he is a man of great shrewdness and very great depth, and that he might choose, knowing the great influence which he exercised over these people who had a much inferior education to his own, that they regard him in the light almost of a Saviour, I have thought that he might have assumed for the purpose of maintaining his influence with them, more than he really believed.

Q. That is your impression, doctor? A. I have thought it might be so. I don't think it is, for I have never heard him speak on the subject. I have never heard him speak on that subject, and I gather that knowledge only from a general knowledge of what has taken place and from personal knowledge which I acquired in speaking with Mr. Riel, but never on that subject.

Q. And of course that knowledge is also based upon a very imperfect hearing of the evidence? A. Of this evidence today—on this evidence today it is not based. I had a very imperfect hearing of the evidence today. I am speaking only of the general judgment I formed in my own mind entirely apart from the evidence as given in this room. That is what I speak of.

Q. That is entirely outside of what you have heard here? A. Yes, not—let me observe—contrary to what I have heard, though it may be contrary to what I have not heard.

Q. So that now, doctor, you are perfectly aware, are you not, that insane men have exhibited very great shrewdness in some respects? A. Yes.

Q. Now, are you in a position to say, doctor, on your oath, that this man here is not insane? A. I am in a position to say that after a very considerable amount of conversation with him and daily communication with him, I have never spoken to him on a single subject on which he has spoken irrationally.

Q. And you have never spoken to him on the particular subjects with reference to which he is supposed to have his delusions? A. Name the subject?

Q. On religion, and on his mission with reference to the North-West Territories? A. I have never spoken to him on either.

Daniel Clark, M.D. (Medical Superintendent of the Asylum for the Insane, Toronto), "A Psycho-Medical History of
Louis Riel", *American Journal of Insanity,* Vol. 44, No. 1, July 1887.

# A Psycho-Medical History

# of Riel, 1887

. . . On July 28, 1885, the writer
made a first visit to Riel in the prison at
Regina, Northwest Territory. . . . He was
very talkative, and his egotism made itself
manifest, not only in his movements, but
also in his expressed pleasure in being
the central figure of a State trial, which
was likely to become historic. . . . During
a long conversation with him, I found him
quite rational on subjects outside of those
connected with his "mission" and personal greatness. He walked about a good
deal as he talked, at the same time putting on his hat and taking it off in a nervous way. His fidgety way, his swagger,
his egotistic attitudes, his evident delight
at such a trying hour—in being so conspicuous a personage—impressed me very
strongly as being so like the insane with
delusions of greatness, whether paretics or
not. A hundred and one little things in
appearance, movement and conversation,
which cannot be described in writing, are
matters of every day observation by
asylum medical officers. I may say they

are almost intuitions in this respect. Such
knowledge as this, which we acquire by
every day acquaintance with the insane,
would be laughed out of court by the legal
profession, who can not discern any valid
evidence that does not tally with a meta-
physical and obsolete definition. . . .

I wish again to repeat the statement
which is a truism to alienists. He had a
look and movement so characteristic of
insane people, which it is impossible to
put in words, but known so well to us.
He had that peculiar appearance, which
is hard to be described, of a man who is
honest and sincere in his insane convictions and statements. There could be no
doubt he was stating what he himself believed to be true. In acting as he did he
was **not a pretender,** and he did not
assume **those feelings** to his own hurt
for the occasion. The most cunning deceiver could not simulate the appearance
and actions which he presented. A ma-
lingerer would never utter so much wisdom, mixed with so much that showed
insanity. Riel's great aim, even at the
trial, was to falsify the charge of insanity,
and to show by his words his mental
capacity to be a leader of men. Anyone
who has read his letters and addresses
to the jury will see that a great deal of
shrewdness, and irony, and sarcasm of
rather an intelligent kind, were mingled
with his delusions of greatness. This is
perfectly consistent with his form of insanity. Every asylum could produce men
and women just as clever, cunning, and
able to write as good letters as Riel did,
and even hide their delusions when it suits
their purpose so to do. His frowns, facial
disgust and deprecatory shakes of the
head when evidence was given to prove
his insanity, and his egotistic walking up
and down the dock, with swinging arms
and erect head when his sanity was wit-

nessed to, were no actor's part. His actions and speeches carried conviction of their genuineness even to the minds of many who were bitterly hostile to him. Much evidence was given by the Crown after mine was rendered. His two speeches made to the jury and much of his excited conduct in the dock towards the end of his trial impressed me very strongly as to the prisoner's mental unsoundness. His whole aim was to show that he was responsible in all his conduct, and not demented. He was a saviour and leader of his people, and this glorious position was to be taken from him by his friends trying to prove his insanity. He repudiated the plea with scorn. . . .

Since his execution up to a few months ago his death was made to do duty as a political war-cry. It was felt that the recommendation to mercy by a Protestant and English speaking jury; that the strong evidence of the prisoner's insanity, which was adduced at the trial and after it; that the repeated postponements of the day of execution; that the fact of his having been only the nominal head of the rebellion should have had due weight with the executive. A living lunatic in an asylum would soon have been forgotten, but a dead Riel has roused into unwonted activity, influences which will not easily be allayed. . . .

Dr. R. E. Turner, "The Life and Death of Louis Riel, a Study in Forensic Psychiatry. Part III—Medico-Legal Issues," *Canadian Psychiatric Association Journal,* Vol. 10, No. 4, August, 1965. Reprinted by permission of *The Canadian Psychiatric Journal.*

# Medico-Legal Issues, 1965

The life and death of Louis Riel poses many problems and issues, none more interesting than his state of mind at the time of the rebellion, trial, and prior to his execution. The medico-legal issues arise at distinct points during that turbulent year of 1885—his fitness to stand trial, his mental condition at the time of the rebellion, i.e. offence, and while awaiting execution.

It is a matter of law and procedure at the outset of a trial to consider whether the accused is fit to stand trial. This is a question of possible insanity at the time of trial, not at the time of the alleged offence or with regard to criminal responsibility. An insane person must not be tried. A court may at any time before verdict decide whether the accused is capable of conducting his defence. This means that the accused person must be mentally as well as physically present in the court to appreciate the proceedings and to make full answer and defence to the charge against him. This is an issue of enough importance that the 1956

Royal Commission on the Law of Insanity as a Defence in Criminal Cases commended the practice in some provinces whereby those charged with capital offences are examined by at least one psychiatrist, on arrest, later, and immediately before trial; suggesting that this practice be made uniform throughout Canada. The report did make it clear that all accused persons have a right to remain silent, none the less, and therefore such examination should not be compulsory by law. One of the difficulties in Riel's trial was that he refused to co-operate with a defence of insanity.

The issue of fitness to stand trial was not introduced at Riel's trial, yet there were ample provisions for such procedure at that time. The Act relating to Procedure in Criminal Cases in Canada of 1869, Chapter 29, s. 102, read:—

"If any person indicted for any offence be insane, and upon arraignment be so found by a jury empannelled for that purpose, so that such person cannot be tried upon such indictment, or if, upon the trial of any person so indicted, such person appears to the jury charged with the indictment to be insane, the Court, before whom such person is brought to be arraigned, or is tried as aforesaid, may direct such finding to be recorded, and thereupon may order such person to be kept in strict custody until the pleasure of the Lieutenant-Governor be known."

This followed closely the Criminal Lunatic Act, 1800, of England, concerning insanity at the time of trial. This is curious because just four days previously, William Henry Jackson, secretary to Riel, was tried for treason-felony, (Riel was charged with high treason). His defence counsel, Mr. McArthur, Q.C., answered "not guilty on the ground of insanity" to the charge. The evidence introduced came from the medical men who examined Jackson on the part of the

Crown. The prosecutor, Mr. Osler, Q.C. stated that, "evidence that has come to the knowledge of counsel for the Crown during the course of preparation for other trials is conclusive that at the time he committed the acts he was not responsible for them". Dr. Jukes was called by the defence and gave his opinion that Jackson was . . . "unquestionably of unsound mind". He gave evidence that Jackson became much worse as arrangements for the trial proceeded. "He is labouring under a mild form of insanity". On cross-examination by Mr. Osler, Dr. Jukes stated that, "I don't think that to bring him at a moment's notice that he would be capable of conducting his trial or doing justice to himself in any manner". "He holds peculiar ideas on religious matters in connection with this trouble, and in connection with the new religion of which he thinks Riel is the founder". Dr. Jukes believed that if Jackson committed any acts in the condition he was in at the time of the trial, he could not be held responsible. Mr. Osler was satisfied that the jury should return a verdict of 'not guilty on the ground of insanity' upon this evidence. It was recommended that he be kept in strict custody until the pleasure of the Lieutenant-Governor be known. The jury returned such a verdict. . . .

Since July 1893 when our Criminal Law was first codified, the M'Naghten Rules have not been the test of criminal responsibility in Canada. Since that time, the test has been "disease of the mind to an extent that renders him incapable of appreciating the nature and quality of the act or omission, and of knowing that an act or omission was wrong". The M'Naghten Rules used the word 'know' rather than 'appreciate'—'know' being much more limiting.

In trials today both Crown and Defence take great care in establishing the credentials, qualifications and experience of expert witnesses. What were the qualifications of the witnesses for the Defence and Crown with regard to the matter of Riel's insanity? Dr. Roy, of undoubted experience who, you will remember, was Superintendent of the Beauport Asylum for fifteen or sixteen years, was Superintendent of that asylum at the time Louis Riel was a patient there. He was present for part of the examination of other witnesses that took place that day and the day before. He did compare the symptoms disclosed by the witnesses with those disclosed while the patient was at Beauport. Yet how well was Riel served by the defence witnesses? Dr. Roy did not have the papers under which Riel was held, with him in court nor did he have any paper showing what disease he had and under whose certificates he was confined. Apparently, these papers were kept by the provincial secretary. The witness spoke from a note taken from the register and from his memory which, after eight years, was not entirely reliable. He took no book or copy of a medical book with him to court and Mr. Osler, for the prosecution, cross-examined Dr. Roy on this point. The length of time of his examination of the day before was not indicated.

The second defence expert, Dr. Clark, was an experienced mental hospital superintendent. He had given expert evidence in capital cases. He indicated in his evidence that he examined the prisoner three times, twice the day before and on the morning that he gave evidence. He heard the evidence given by other witnesses. When pressed he refused to give an unqualified answer whether Riel was insane.

What witnesses did the Crown call in rebuttal? Dr. Wallace in cross-examination admitted that his examination was limited, and said, "It would be presumptuous of me to say that he is not insane from the opportunities I have had. But at the same time my opinion is pretty fairly fixed in my mind that he is not insane"— that Riel was of sound mind and capable of distinguishing right from wrong.

The other Crown witnesses had no medical qualifications whatsoever, yet they were asked to give opinions about possible insanity. This would be considered a curious manoeuvre in present-day trial practices, particularly calling such witnesses, not only as experts, but after the evidence of the experts. It is usual in trial practices of our experience that the psychiatrist is called at the conclusion of evidence, so that the opinion he forms is based on previous evidence, in addition to his own examination. . . .

Dr. E. R. Markson, "The Life and Death of Louis Riel, a Study in Forensic Psychiatry. Part I—A Psychoanalytic Commentary", *Canadian Psychiatric Association Journal,* Vol. 10, No. 4, August 1965. Reprinted by permission of *The Canadian Psychiatric Association Journal.*

# A Psychoanalytic Commentary

. . . The intention of this brief communication is to provide a longitudinal study of Riel's psychological disorder, and to elaborate upon some of the theoretical and dynamic factors involved in his illness. Perhaps we may then gain a clearer understanding of his psychosis and of the ways in which it influenced and was influenced by the historical events of his day.

Riel was a Metis, born in the Red River Settlement in 1844. He was the oldest of nine children and throughout his lifetime enjoyed the special favour of his revered and suffering mother. A religious and abstemious atmosphere pervaded the home, both parents having prepared to enter religious orders prior to their marriage. Throughout his life Louis idolized his parents unwaveringly. When he was five, his father became a local hero as a result of his success in obtaining greater freedom of trade for the Metis from the Hudson Bay Company, which until then had monopolized the fur trade. As far as we know, Riel was a quiet, re-

served and inhibited boy during his early childhood. At the age of fourteen he travelled to Montreal where he entered a seminary to prepare himself for the priesthood. He remained in this school for seven years, was a good student, but was hot-headed, intolerant of criticism and opposition, extreme in his views and not averse to arguing with his teachers.

His illness first manifested itself overtly in February 1864 when he learned of his father's death. He abruptly left the seminary and entered a prolonged period of pathological mourning. Strange ideas began to make their appearance. For a time he believed that Louis Riel was dead and that he himself was in fact David Mordecai, a Jew from Marseilles, and as such he was not entitled to the immense inheritance of Louis Riel, which was bequeathed by his father. It is important to note that in fact the actual estate of Louis' father was of little value. He was seized with religious fervour and declared that he was going to astonish the world by becoming the head of a new religious movement. He felt it was his duty to redeem both Jew and Gentile from temporal, political and spiritual bondage. He developed the notion of founding a Metis Republic to protect the rights of his persecuted brethren. He wrote his mother that he would follow the footsteps of his father who was a great benefactor of the Metis. He asked her to share her sorrows with him ". . . . for now I have the right to suffer with you". . . .

In November 1874 Riel had a divine revelation while he sat atop Mount Vernon near Washington. He was appointed by God to be a prophet, to serve as the chosen instrument for the regeneration of the Metis, and to protect all French speaking Canadians from their enemies. This sense of mission remained with him to the day he died. His illness progressed rapidly. His religious fervour and submissiveness increased. While in church he was suddenly seized with uncontrollable sobbing. He now felt called upon "to regenerate the whole world". He began to believe that he was one of a trilogy of bulls, and was to be found bellowing and roaring in the streets and in church. He believed he could create miracles, and he expressed great guilt over his pride and youthful vanity which had diverted him from his career within the church. Episodes of uncontrollable violence alternated with periods of profound and abject submissiveness, in which he felt that he was the willing and helpless instrument of the Holy Spirit.

In March 1876, he was admitted to the Hospital of St. Jean de Dieu at Longue Pointe. He was now in the throes of a psychotic disintegration, suffering from hallucinations and from grandiose and persecutory delusions. He imagined that he was in telegraphic communication with important political figures in Europe. He scribbled bizarre notes, verses and messages. He stood against the wall in the posture of the crucifixion to show the nuns that he was Christ crucified. He declared that the Holy Spirit had told him that he must sacrifice everything, even his clothing.

In May 1876 he was transferred to Beauport Asylum in Quebec City. He was violent, required physical restraint, ran through the corridors naked, and destroyed the articles on the chapel altar in obedience to God's command. His messianic visions and prophecies flourished and he signed himself grandiosely as "Louis David Riel, Prophet, Infallible Pontiff and Priest King". He prophesied the decay of the old world and the removal of the Papacy to Montreal and St.

Vital. It was his destiny to be the leader in these fateful events. He identified himself with Moses who was the redeemer of his people. He believed that he was superior to the priests and ordered them to do as he commanded. Gradually the acute symptoms subsided, his penitence and submissiveness increased and he began to regard his illness as a punishment and a humiliation imposed upon him by God for his wilfulness, his thirst for power and his vanity. He was released from hospital in January 1878 and, in my view, although there were apparent remissions subsequently, he was never really well from that time on. . . .

In June 1883 he left Montana to lead the Metis of the Saskatchewan Valley in their struggles with the Canadian Government. He was also preoccupied with his own personal grievance with the government which had failed to compensate him for his property in Manitoba. From this time on he was a victim of his own prophetic and megalomanic zeal, and a progressive deterioration of his mental state ensued. His grandiosity and religious fervour increased. His heterodoxy became extreme and he reviled and abused the local clergy, claiming his own supremacy and his appointment by God to re-organize the spiritual and temporal affairs of the territory. He was worshipped by the Metis who regarded him as a prophet, a saviour and a saint.

By this time he was referring to himself as "The Prophet of the New World", whose every thought and action was determined by the spirit of God through the Holy Ghost. He declared the Papacy overthrown and the removal of the church seat to Canada. He renounced the Divine Trinity, declaring that Christ was not God but was merely the Son of God. Similarly, Mary was not the Mother of God but the mother of the Son of God. He elaborated a fantastic scheme for the resettlement of the West by various American and European ethnic and national groups. As the Metis began to arm and prepare for rebellion his violent outbursts became uncontrollable. He shouted that he was after blood and the extermination of the enemies of the Metis. He now included stewed bullocks blood in his diet. He formed a committee known as the Exovedate which, under his influence, issued bizarre declarations even during the heat of battle. It declared that Riel was a prophet, resolved that Hell would not last for ever; it discussed trans-substantiation, changed the names of the days of the week; altered the signs of the Zodiac and changed the Sabbath to Saturday. These resolutions were the product of Riel's nocturnal visions and his conviction that he was the representative of the Holy Ghost, come to reform Christ's church. . . .

His mother wrote to him while he was imprisoned in Regina reminding him once more of all her suffering. He answered, justifying his behaviour and placing all blame upon his enemies. His psychosis flourished while he was in jail. There was an endless stream of visions and prophecies. He declared Bishop Tache as the vicar of Christ's church on earth and St. Boniface the religious capital of Christendom. The Metis were Christ's chosen people. He further elaborated his bizarre scheme of land distribution which was of great importance to him. For example, Vancouver Island was to be given to the Belgians and Jews, Quebec to the Prussians, etc. He petitioned Grover Cleveland, President of the United States, requesting the abolishment of the boundary line between Canada and the United States, proposed that the American Consul at Winnipeg be made Governor Gen-

eral of the new territory and that Riel be appointed First Minister and Secretary.

I would like to refer briefly to some of his remarks to the court. He stated . . . "the day of my birth I was helpless and my mother took care of me . . . the North West is also my mother . . . I am sure that my mother country will not kill me more than my mother did forty years ago when I came into the world, because a mother is always a mother and, even if I have my faults, if she can see I am true, she will be full of love for me". He later stated . . . "God is the master of the Universe and as a good father he gives a portion of his lands . . . to everyone . . . that is his share of the inheritance".

Riel possessed many of the characteristics of the leaders of millennian movements. He was a great orator, a fascinating personality, and possessed those charismatic qualities essential to reformers. They were expressed in "the megalomaniac view of himself as the Elect, wholly good, abominably persecuted, yet assured of ultimate triumph; the attribution of gigantic and demonic powers to the adversary; the refusal to adopt the ineluctable limitations and imperfections of human existence, such as transcience, dissension, conflict, fallibility whether intellectual or moral . . . and an obsession with inerrable prophecies . . ."

The most striking feature of his disorder was the unmitigated idealization of both his mother and father. He worshipped them uncritically and unswervingly throughout his life. The normal resolution of infantile ambivalence conflicts was never achieved. Profoundly regressive mechanisms were necessary to maintain the idealized object, and with it his own sense of power and worthiness. Since the idealized objects with whom he identified were devoid of badness, either of a sexual or aggressive nature, grave difficulties developed in respect to his instinctual life.

An additional feature of his illness was the masochistic identification with his suffering, martyred mother. This is amply supported by the clinical history. He was guilt-ridden because of his mother's suffering and even because of his own birth and existence which had created hardship for her. . . .

. . . The unconscious rage and guilt which he felt toward the parents, and his own sense of inner corruption and badness, were expressed in his desires to reform and redeem the world. His prophetic zeal and his sense of mission helped him to maintain his love objects. His own badness and all bad attributes of the parents were projected on to his enemies in the external world. His enemies were many and even included the clergy who were the direct temporal representatives of God. By cleansing the world and himself he could continue to feel both loved and powerful and so to avoid despair. Through his appointment by God to a prophetic destiny, he obtained divine licence for the expression of his primitive hatred and murderous impulses upon his enemies. Since his enemies represented aspects of his parents it was inevitable that Riel should feel guilt and anxiety for his attacks upon the persecutors. He dealt with this danger by fortifying his submissiveness to God through an incessant struggle to remain pious, humble and in God's good grace. His behaviour was therefore characterized by sharp vaccilations between violence and passivity, humility and grandiosity, love and hate. He could be omnipotently destructive or completely subservient to the will of God, or both simultaneously. . . .

One can see how the historical events of his day lent themselves to the expression of his psychopathology. In addition, the awe and reverence afforded him by the Metis served to strengthen his feelings of omnipotence and his mission of divine service to mankind.

The death of his father triggered the overt expression of his illness. Because of his narcissistic identification with the father, Louis lost his identity for a brief period. This phenomenon was also fostered by his inability to cope effectively with his guilt about the death of the ambivalently loved father. He recovered his identification with the omnipotent father at this time by formulating a great purpose for his life, which was to redeem the Metis. The Metis were the persecuted children with whom he identified. The persecutors represented the bad father as well as other projected bad introjects. He could simultaneously preserve his illusory omnipotence, retain the love of the father-God, and preserve the threatened motherland from the alien robbers. Although Louis spoke of assuming his father's responsibilities and burdens, he never actually did so except by way of his delusional creations. In fact, he neglected his mother and siblings and was prevented by his conflicts from properly attending to their welfare. His preoccupation with a fair division of the territories is related to the guilt and anxiety which he experienced in connection with his own inheritance. Just as he wished to claim all of his father's possessions for himself, he wished to claim all the territory, but was unable to do so. He was never able to claim the ultimate position of authority but had to relinquish it to one other person, in relation to whom Riel maintained a subsidiary position.

In the end the effectiveness of his paranoid constructions collapsed and he surrendered himself to pay the ultimate penalty for his violent rebellious struggle against authority. By forgiving everyone, including his enemies and by restoring his feeling of unity with God he was able to die, having created in his last days an inner world which seemed full of love and free of hate.

# Part VI

# Public and Political Reaction

Magistrate Hugh Richardson sentenced Louis Riel to be hanged on September 18, 1885. Appeals to the Court of Queen's Bench of Manitoba and to the Judicial Committee of the Privy Council in London failed when these bodies upheld the judgment of the Territorial Court. To permit these appeals to be heard Riel was granted a reprieve to October 16th, then again to November 12th. The final reprieve was to permit a medical commission to inquire into the state of Riel's mind. The appointment of this commission was a concession forced on John A. Macdonald in response to the increasing agitation in the country over Riel's fate. Macdonald was hoping desperately that the French Canadian members of his cabinet would not be forced into resigning by Quebec's demand for a pardon. The three doctors of the commission reported early in November that while Riel suffered from delusions on religious and political matters he was otherwise an accountable being and responsible for his actions. Macdonald could not delay any longer. The sentence of the court was to be carried out and on November 16, 1885 Riel went to the gallows.

The passions aroused by Louis Riel in 1870 and inflamed in succeeding years by the issue of the amnesty and his expulsion from Parliament never fully abated. Extremists in both English and French Canada remained unreconciled and in 1885 their tempers flared anew. Press, public, and politicians drew battle lines once more, raging and storming in their respective racial and religious camps. Demands for vengeance on the "murderer" and the "traitor" were echoed by cries of justice and mercy for the "saint" and "hero."

In Parliament the argument centred on the issues of the legality of the trial, the mental state of the prisoner and the government's responsibility in the rebellion. Hector Langevin and Adolphe Caron who had been called traitors to their race by Honoré Mercier, the Quebec Liberal leader, defended their decision to remain in the Conservative cabinet. Wilfrid Laurier coupled a spirited attack on the government of John A. Macdonald with a warning to Quebec of the danger in organizing, as Mercier was doing, a political party based on race.

Macdonald's decision in 1885 to let Riel hang is directly associated by many writers with the rise of Laurier as a national figure, the defeat of the Conservative party in the election of 1896 and the long-lasting support enjoyed by the Liberal party thereafter in Quebec. The clearest statement of this sequence of events is that of John W. Dafoe's study of Laurier published in 1922.

Only slight or vague modification of this thesis has been indicated to date in Canadian historical writing. The thesis is perhaps too attractive a generalization and requires qualification. Research presently underway into the complex nature of Quebec provincial politics will undoubtedly provide further insight into the relationships of the Riel phenomena to Quebec and Canadian party politics. The article by H. Blair Neatby and John Saywell, an excerpt from which is included in this section, suggests one qualification of the traditional thesis. It is not possible to reprint the full article in this compilation and the student is advised to follow the argument in its totality in the *Canadian Historical Review*.

Mason Wade, *The French Canadians,
1760-1945,* (Toronto, The Macmillan
Co., 1955), pp. 414-423, 440. Reprinted
by permission of The Macmillan Co. of
Canada Ltd.

## Political Necessity

Meanwhile an agitation arose in Ontario for immediate execution of a double
traitor and Quebec was swept by a great
popular movement which demanded that
Riel be reprieved as the irresponsible victim of the government's maladministration of the North-West. The Quebec press
cited [William Henry] Jackson's easy fate
and compared it with that allotted to Riel,
with the observation: "If madness is an
excuse for an Englishman, it ought to be
one for Riel, even if he is a *Métis.*" Riel
defence committees had been organized
as early as June in Montreal and Quebec.
Their sponsor was L.-O. David, who considered Riel the spiritual heir of the
*Patriotes* of 1837. Thanks to his efforts,
protest meetings began to be held throughout the province, with the watchword
"Riel must be saved."

During July, before the trial began,
the Liberal leaders [Edward] Blake and
[Wilfrid] Laurier had attacked the government. Blake tabled seventy-six *Métis*
petitions of grievances, while Laurier accused the government of treating the

*Métis* as the Russians did the Poles. Although Archbishop Taché and most of
the Western clergy warned against mistaken sympathy with Riel, Quebec was
won to his cause by Father André's account of the distress of the *Métis* after
they had been ruthlessly pillaged by
Middleton's English-Canadian troops.
Gradually the question became not one
of Riel's guilt or innocence, but the execution or pardon of a compatriot. This
development of ethnic feeling determined
[J. A.] Chapleau's decision not to resign
from the federal cabinet and to form a
French-Canadian party. He and his French
colleagues were denounced by Quebec,
while petitions rained upon Ottawa from
all quarters of French Canada, from Manitoba, the North-West, the United States,
and even from England and France. The
great majority of them urged mercy, although the Ontario Orangemen and the
English settlers of Regina recommended
that the sentence be executed. While the
government allowed three successive stays
of execution until every avenue of appeal
had been exhausted, and appointed a
medical commission composed of Dr.
[A.] Jukes, Dr. F.-X. Valade of Ottawa,
and Dr. [Michael] Lavell of Hamilton,
who decided early in November that Riel
was not legally insane, the decision had
already been made, in the words attributed to Sir John Macdonald, that
"Riel must swing."

In the last analysis the decision not
to show the same mercy to Riel as to the
other convicted rebellion prisoners was
based upon political necessities. English-
Canadian feeling had risen to the explo-
sive point as French pressure for Riel's
pardon grew stronger. . . . Macdonald
decided that he could better afford to lose
a few seats in Quebec than to have English Canada turn solidly against him.

Riel was not allowed to rest in peace. The agitation in Quebec against the execution of a French Canadian summarily condemned by an English judge and jury became a political revolution. The minority group of the assembly, which had in March 1885 censured the federal government for settling by force a disturbance which had been occasioned by its own culpable neglect, became an overpowering majority as Quebec opinion rose against Sir John Macdonald and the French-Canadian ministers, Sir Hector Langevin, Sir Adolphe Caron, and Adolphe Chapleau, who had refused to break with their leader, though privately they opposed his course in the matter. The Ministers were burnt in effigy as Quebec mourned Riel.

On November 22 [1885] the greatest mass meeting ever held in the province took place on the Champ de Mars at Montreal, where Conservatives and Liberals alike voiced violent protests and adopted resolutions severely condemning the government. *La Presse* had sounded the war-cry on the day after Riel's execution: "Henceforward they are no more Conservatives nor Liberals nor Castors. There are only PATRIOTS AND TRAITORS." For once the Quebec press ceased its habitual political axe-grinding and united in a unanimity to which was flatly opposed the equally rare unanimity of the English press, summed up by a Toronto dispatch of November 17 thus: "A general sentiment of satisfaction prevails." Three platforms had been raised on the Champ de Mars, around which gathered a crowd of forty or fifty thousand, and from them orator after orator held forth. The three great speeches of this day in which a people voiced its indignation were made by the Liberal Laurier, who with a rare vehemence proclaimed: "If I had

been born on the banks of the Saskatchewan, I, too, would have shouldered my musket"; by the ultramontane [Senator F. X. A.] Trudel, who compared Riel to Christ and Joan of Arc; and by Honoré Mercier who won the leadership of French Canada at this moment of crisis. . . Mercier called for the formation of a national party, uniting all those who were outraged by Riel's death, to drive Macdonald's government from office and to preserve the French-Canadian solidarity created by this crisis. The crowd enthusiastically adopted the "Resolutions of the Champ de Mars" which had been previously drafted to embody Mercier's ideas.

The agitation in Quebec, which Macdonald had dismissed as "a blaze of straw," spread like a forest fire, with assemblies in each parish adopting resolutions based upon those of the great meeting at Montreal, and with anti-ministerial demonstrations taking place throughout the province. Trudel and others wanted a national movement in which the old party lines would be preserved, except for the Riel matter and national questions; but Mercier succeeded in imposing his doctrine of a racial party founded on the newly made grave of Riel. Quebec rallied like one man to the defence of the outlying minority groups. Riel was enshrined as a national hero and a saint despite his treason and his heresies, and despite the resolute opposition of the Quebec hierarchy, whose attitude had been prompted by Archbishop Taché and who became increasingly alarmed by a movement which began to take on revolutionary tendencies, with public disorders, the burning in effigy of the federal ministers, and the singing of the *Marseillaise*. . . .

Under the goad of Mercier's burning eloquence, heard in all regions of the province as he tirelessly sought to break down old party lines and to unite the people under his leadership, the movement was only checked, not halted, by the opposition of the hierarchy, the English Liberals, Chapleau and his friends, and Laurier, who was alarmed at the growing isolation of Quebec from the rest of Canada. At the Champ de Mars meeting the latter had been swept by the wave of public indignation from his lifelong conviction that the formation of a Catholic or French-Canadian party would be suicidal for his people, since it would unite the English Protestants against them and pave the way for a war of religion or race. Once that party began to take form, Laurier withdrew his support from Mercier.

The beginnings of this English reaction which Laurier had anticipated had already been produced by the Quebec agitation. On November 23 the *Toronto Mail* published an editorial in which it warned the French Canadians, "now seeking to compel us to recognize their right to suspend the operation of the law when a representative of their race is in the toils," that "rather than to submit to such a yoke, Ontario would smash Confederation into its original fragments, preferring that the dream of a united Canada should be shattered forever, than that unity should be purchased at the price of inequality." Two days later the *Mail* told Mercier and his friends that "if the cabinet should fall as a result of the intrigues of French influence, if such is the fruit of Mr. Mercier's programme, in that case, as Britons, we believe that the Conquest will have to be fought over again. Lower Canada may depend upon it, there will be no new treaty of 1763. The victors will not capitulate next time." To these

utterances of the *Mail,* which was considered the chief mouthpiece of the government, but at this moment was running quite as free of political harness as the ministerial organs in Quebec were on the other side of the question, were added the observations of the *Orange Sentinel:* "Must it be said that the rights and liberties of the English people in this English colony depend upon a foreign race? . . . The day is near when an appeal to arms will be heard in all parts of Canada. Then, certainly, our soldiers, benefiting by the lessons of the past, will have to complete the work they began in the North-West." Such statements only furthered Mercier's game by increasing the ethnic tension. . . .

When parliament met at the end of February 1886, the first clash on the Riel question occurred in the Senate, where censure by government supporters of the raising in the press of racial and religious prejudices was opposed by followers of Mercier. In the House early in March the Conservative Philippe Landry offered a motion expressing profound regret at Riel's execution, which had the effect of embarrassing the Liberals, who were divided on this question, although agreed on the government's responsibility for the execution. Archbishop Taché appeared in the visitors' gallery during the debate which followed, and counselled the French-Canadian Conservatives who consulted him not to vote against the government. This well-meant effort to quell the storm was taken in Orange quarters as new proof that Rome was running Canada.

Relief from the ever-growing tension was provided by Laurier's speech in the House on March 16. He denied the *Mail's* charges and foreswore Mercier's suicidal policy of forming a French-Canadian party, but he indicted the government for its long neglect of the *Métis* grievances. . . .

[Edward] Blake . . . made one of his greatest efforts in this debate, speaking for five hours as he indicted the government for negligence and he piled up proof of Riel's insanity and precedents against holding madmen responsible for their acts. But in spite of these notable speeches by the leading Liberals and the general weakness of Conservative replies, the government was sustained by a large majority, as Macdonald had foreseen, with losses among the Quebec Conservatives offset by support from Liberals from the English-speaking provinces. The vote gave evidence that the Riel question had become an ethnic rather than a party or a sectional one. It was to ease the ethnic tension that Laurier discussed the question at Toronto the following December, in the same terms that he had used at Ottawa. Quebec, however, turned against its Conservative government, since it placed party loyalty before ethnic considerations. The provincial administration crumbled before Mercier's assault in the October elections, and in January 1887 the *Parti National* took power.

A whole generation in Quebec was filled with emotional hatred for all things English by the Riel affair, while the gallophobia and "no-popery" agitation aroused by it in Ontario were fed by the course of Mercier's administration and sustained by conflicts over the rights of the French language and of separate schools in the West. Mercier, who had won power by invoking the gibbet of Regina at ninety political meetings and had built his government on Riel's grave, did much to further the division between French and English in 1885 and to make it permanent. Faced with the political necessity of maintaining the coalition which the Riel crisis had forged between French-Canadian Liberals and Conservatives, Mercier disregarded the solemn warning which Laurier had given him in the Ottawa debate on Riel's execution. . . . But Mercier had discovered how easy it was to organize a party in Quebec on the basis of nationality, and he attempted to govern by using the emotions conjured up by the words "national," "French," and "Catholic," rather than by the reasoned arguments demanded by questions of policy and administration.

. . . it was not difficult for Mercier's enemies to use his nationalism to turn the English Canadians against him; and Mercier himself, lacking Laurier's understanding of the English mentality or caring less for its reactions, soon lost caution as power made him domineering. The incorporation in 1887 of the Jesuits, who had educated Mercier at their Collège Sainte-Marie in Montreal, did not cause much comment in the English-speaking world, although some English Quebeckers were disgruntled by the spectacle of the legislature receiving delegates of the Jesuits and Cardinal Taschereau, who opposed the measure in the interests of Laval, and that of politicians discussing the fine points of theology and canon law. But when Mercier went to New York in search of a loan, and there received the honors appropriate to the head of a state; when Mercier summoned an inter-provincial conference—the first held since Confederation—in October 1887 at Quebec and induced the delegates of five provinces (Prince Edward Island and British Columbia abstained from attendance) to reaffirm vigorously the principle of provincial autonomy; and finally when Mercier, unsuccessful in New York, went to Paris to obtain a loan from the Crédit Lyonnais and to Rome to consult the Holy See on the Jesuit Estates question, the English Canadians began to take alarm at this provincial premier whose watchword was "national" and who acted like the ruler of an independent state. Dark rumors of Mercier's plan to set up a French-Canadian state began to go the rounds. Mercier's actions did nothing to dispel these suspicions. In New York, on the eve of sailing for France, he had closeted himself in the rectory of the French-Canadian church with Bishop Grandin of Saint-Albert and Gabriel Dumont, the *Métis* "general" in 1885. In Paris Mercier was given a royal reception and the Legion of Honor, and in his speeches stressed Quebec's ties with France; in Rome he was received in private audience by the Pope. His success abroad in winning popularity and in achieving his commercial and diplomatic ends greatly strengthened his position in Quebec, which felt itself honored through the honor paid to its premier but Mercier's doings were entirely too French and Catholic for English-Canadian taste. . . .

Cartier's dream of another Quebec in the West was doomed forever by the flood of multi-national immigration into that region under the Laurier regime. But Riel's dream came true, as the West became the new home of the poor and oppressed of Europe. The growing domin-ance of English Canadians in the West, the reaction to the Riel troubles, and the desire to force assimilation, deprived the western French Canadians of the constitutional guarantees for the language and their schools which Cartier had carefully written into the Manitoba Act. The Laurier-Greenway Agreement was the first of a series of compromises in the matter of educational rights in the West which embittered French-Canadian feeling and furthered the development of a provincial nationalism in Quebec.

The French Canadians became convinced that they stood on a basis of equality with their English compatriots only in Quebec, despite their constitutional guarantees, and that their brethren in the West were oppressed by the English majority. The question of the rights of minority groups in the West has remained a thorn in the flesh of French Canada down to the present day, and the only hope of healing this old wound lies in English-Canadian acceptance of the doctrine that Canada is a bilingual and bicultural nation, and that the rights of the French language are not confined to Quebec. Some evidence that this hope may be realized lies in the growing tendency of English Canadians in the West to regard Riel as a regional hero rather than a French traitor.

Robert Rumilly, *Histoire du Canada,* (Paris, La Clé d'Or, 1951), pp. 411-414. Reprinted by permission of the Author.


# A National Party


Ontario was in exultation. The Prime Minister [Oliver] Mowat, former follower of George Brown, had gradually evolved to the point of becoming the champion of tolerance towards the Catholics. But he had not transformed his people. The newspapers relished in advance the spectacle of a French Canadian dancing at the end of a rope. In the province of Quebec . . . emotion mounted like a groundswell. A wave of protest and entreaty arose. Meetings were organized in all the parishes. Committees formed to obtain mercy for Riel. The emotion overflowed into the French-American centres of New England. . . .

All of French Canada lived in anguish. The Privy Council rejected the appeal. The Orangemen still wanted to avenge the death of Thomas Scott. The French Canadians again besieged Chapleau, his colleagues and the federal members. . . .

The government remained silent. Letters, addresses, telegrams flowed into Ottawa. Ultramontanes, Conservatives,

Liberals, Radicals forgot their differences. In every home of the province of Quebec they prayed for Riel. Conservative members warned the government to be on guard against a political mistake. The execution was postponed until November 16.

The Orangemen, furious, demanded death. The French Canadians demanded mercy. The federal cabinet weighed the number of votes to be gained or lost in each province. Ontario won out in the reckoning. Riel would hang. Some French Canadian members threatened to break away. For an entire night Chapleau argued with his advisers, and submitted. Louis Riel died courageously on the scaffold November 16, 1885.

The English provinces were gratified. The French province was convulsed. Pictures of Riel set in veils of crepe appeared in shop windows. In every town people gathered in the streets. Laurent-Olivier David at first had been the soul of the committees formed to demand mercy for Riel but he lacked the support of the leaders. Honoré Mercier, leader of the provincial opposition and traditional rival of Chapleau, remained in the background, to avoid compromising the cause he wished passionately to serve. Riel dead, there was no longer any reason to be cautious. Mercier assumed the leadership of the movement which brought together Conservatives and Liberals of all shades of opinion. A gathering held at the Champ de Mars in Montreal November 22 was the greatest and most moving which had till then ever been held in Canada. Thirty thousand, forty thousand, fifty thousand human molecules were turned into a enormous, united whole. Francois-Xavier Trudel, chief ultramontane, and Rodolphe Laflamme, chief radical defended the same cause with one heart. Wilfrid

Laurier revealed his indignation. . . . But Honoré Mercier especially gripped the crowd in demanding that the martyr Riel, a victim of fanaticism, cement a union of all French Canadians.

Mercier had cherished this idea for a long time. Under his guidance a "National Party" was organized reuniting indignant Conservatives and Liberals. The agitation did not abate in spite of the reticence of some members of the clergy. Mercier and his friends kept it up. At full speed, all winter, they travelled throughout the province arousing and uplifting it. The ministers, "rogues," were hooted, burned in effigy. Chapleau attempted, without great success to organize the resistance. His great popularity foundered.

All the province wished to avenge Riel. Vengeance could only be exercised by means of electoral sanctions. First came the provincial election in October 1886.

[J. A.] Mousseau, overshadowed by Chapleau, had been prime minister for only eighteen months. He sought refuge in the judiciary in January 1884. His successor, John J. Ross, was a man of goodwill, a diocesan of Monseigneur Laflèche, and inclined toward the ultramontanes. Stressing the concept of the separation of powers he refused to place any official blame on the federal government in the Riel affair. Mercier and his friends linked John J. Ross with John A. Macdonald, and the provincial Conservatives jointly with the federal "rogues." A small number of Conservatives, their anger subdued, abandoned the "National Party." But the "National Conservatives," embracing the greater part of the ultramontanes, remained in the new party with the majority of the Liberals. Young men, breaking with family tradition, and abhoring the "assassins of Riel" adhered to the national party with the Liberals. In this fashion the provincial campaign was a continuation of the Riel campaign.

Ardent youth, haunted by a vision of a French Canadian on the gallows, accompanied Mercier as he threw himself into the conquest of his province. On October 14, 1886 the opposition, doubled in number, became just barely stronger than the ministerial party. John J. Ross resigned. An energetic minister, Louis-Olivier Taillon, formed a Conservative cabinet which lasted only four days. Mercier, prime minister, formed a "national" cabinet (January 27, 1887).

The province of Quebec was relieved. The federal elections were held in turn in February 1887. Once again the "rogues" were reviled, but with attenuated force Chapleau organized the defence and limited the damage. The Conservative party did not suffer losses as great as in the provincial elections. They gained a little in the other provinces, and preserved a reduced majority, but sufficient to continue in office.

The Riel affair was nearly over. But the hold of the Conservative party in Quebec was shaken for a long time.

George F. G. Stanley, *Louis Riel: Patriot or Rebel?*, (Ottawa, Canadian Historical Association, 1954), Historical Booklet No. 2, pp. 22-24. Reprinted by permission of the Author.

## Quebec Turns to the Liberals

On July 6th, 1885, a formal charge of treason was laid against Louis Riel, then in gaol at Regina. This was the beginning of that trial which was to have such drastic consequences, not only for Riel himself, but for the whole of Canada. The jury was entirely Anglo-Saxon and Protestant, the defendant French and, by training at least, Catholic. Here were the old familiar elements of discord. And into the little courtroom stalked the ghost of Tom Scott, whose memory his Orange brethren had never permitted to rest. As the howl for vengeance grew louder in Orange Ontario so too did the cry for clemency in Catholic Quebec. A madman, a heretic, a métis he might be, to the people of Quebec Louis Riel was nevertheless a French Canadian, a victim of Anglo-Saxon persecution. Even while shots were still being fired at Canadian soldiers on the plains, Quebeckers had expressed admiration for Riel's heroic battle for the rights of his people, and when he surrendered they sprang to his defence and provided him with eminent counsel.

The argument adopted by the defence lawyers was that Riel was insane. It was pointed out that he had twice been in asylums, that he had committed the folly of attacking the church, that he had planned the establishment of a Canadian Pope and spent valuable time during the actual rising changing the names of the days of the week. But Riel would not accept this defence. He repudiated the plea of insanity. "I cannot abandon my dignity!" he cried. "Here I have to defend myself against the accusation of high treason, or I have to consent to the animal life of an asylum. I don't care much about animal life if I am not allowed to carry with it the moral existence of an intellectual being . . ." Twice he addressed the court in long rambling speeches; but the jury was only bored, and after one hour and twenty minutes deliberation they declared him guilty. Henry Jackson, despite similar denials of insanity and an expressed desire to share the fate of his leader, was acquitted within a few minutes. To an English-speaking jury the English-speaking Jackson must obviously have been insane to have taken part in the rebellion. There was much truth in the statement made by one of the jurors fifty years later: "We tried Riel for treason, and he was hanged for the murder of Scott."

As the date set for Riel's execution approached feelings throughout Canada became more and more intense. Efforts to save the métis leader were redoubled in Quebec; efforts to ensure his death never slackened in Ontario. The Prime Minister temporized. He was uncertain what course to follow. The execution was postponed, and then put off again while a medical commission examined the question of Riel's sanity. But the terms of reference of the commission limited it to a determination of Riel's capacity to distinguish right from wrong and did not allow an investigation of his delusions; and when the report of the commission was published it was published in a truncated form. Throughout the autumn months petitions and letters from all parts of the world poured into Ottawa. Sir John had not a jot of sympathy for Riel, but he had to balance the political consequences of death or reprieve. There was danger of political disaster if Riel were hanged, but perhaps Sir John could trust to the loyalty of his French Canadian colleagues, Hector Langevin, Adolphe Caron and Adolphe Chapleau, and to the support of a Catholic hierarchy offended at Riel's apostasy. There might be still greater danger of political disaster if Riel were not hanged with every Orangeman in Ontario baying for his death. So Riel was hanged. On November 16th, once more a son of the church, the métis, Louis Riel, mounted the gibbet of Regina. The madman became a martyr.

It is hard to escape the conclusion that Riel's execution, to some extent at least, was determined by political expediency, that, in the final analysis, it represented the careful assessment by the Canadian government of the relative voting strengths and political loyalties of the two racial groups in Canada. If this were so then, for the moment, Macdonald's choice was not unsound. Admittedly the "nation-

alists" in Quebec, led by Honoré Mercier, succeeded in 1886 in overthrowing the provincial Conservative government in an election fought largely on the Riel issue; but in the federal election of 1887 Macdonald, with the support of his French Canadian ministers, still retained a sufficient number of Quebec seats to keep in power.

Yet he had lost ground. And even if he did not recognize it, the election results were an ominous warning of the fate which awaited the Conservative party in Quebec. In the long run the trial and execution of Louis Riel and the racial bitterness which it engendered led to a profound revolution in Canadian politics. As a result of the crisis of 1885 the most conservative province in Canada swung over to the Liberal party, a change in political allegiance which was cemented by the selection of a French Canadian, Wilfrid Laurier, as leader of that party. This shift in the political weight in Quebec, not as the result of any fundamental change in political outlook, but under the stress of a racial emotion, brought about a new orientation in Liberal policy. The old radical tradition of Clear Grittism and Rougeism was swamped by a basic rural conservatism; and for over seventy years the paradox endured of the backbone of the Liberal party being provided by rural Quebec.

John W. Dafoe, *Laurier: A Study in Canadian Politics*, (Toronto, Thomas Allen, 1922), pp. 15, 17-23. Reprinted by permission of Thomas Allen.

## Laurier's Star

In almost one rush he [Laurier] passed from the comparative obscurity of a new member in 1874 to the leadership of the French Liberals in 1877; and then he suffered a decline which seemed to mark him as one of those political shooting stars which blaze in the firmament for a season and then go back; . . . A political accident, fortunate for him, opened the gates again to a career; and he set his foot upon a road which took him very far. . . .

The "accident" which restored Laurier to public life and opened up for him an extraordinary career was the Riel rebellion of 1885. In the session of 1885, the rebellion being then in progress, he was heard from to some purpose on the subject of the ill-treatment of the Saskatchewan half-breeds by the Dominion government. The execution of Riel in the following November changed the whole course of Canadian politics. It pulled the foundations from under the Conservative party by destroying the position of supremacy which it had held for a generation in the most Conservative of provinces and condemned it to a slow decline to the ruin of today; and it profoundly affected the Liberal party, giving it a new orientation and producing the leader who was to make it the dominating force in Canadian politics. These things were not realized at the time, but they are clear enough in retrospect. Party policy, party discipline, party philosophy are all determined by the way the constituent elements of the party combine; and the shifting from the Conservative to the Liberal party of the political weight of Quebec, not as the result of any profound change of conviction but under the influence of a powerful racial emotion, was bound to register itself in time in the party outlook and morale. The current of the older tradition ran strong for some time, but within the space of about twenty years the party was pretty thoroughly transformed. The Liberal party of to-day with its complete dependence upon the solid support it gets in Quebec is the ultimate result of the forces which came into play as the result of the hanging of Riel.

After the lapse of so many years there is no need for lack of candor in discussing the events of 1885. To put it plainly Riel's fate turned almost entirely upon political considerations. Which was the less dangerous course—to reprieve him or let him hang? The issue was canvassed back and forth by the distracted ministry up to the day before that fixed for the execution when a decision was reached to let the law take its course. The feeling in Quebec in support of the commutation was so intense and overwhelming that it was accepted as a matter of course that Riel would be reprieved; and the news of the contrary decision was to them, as Professor Skelton says, "unbelievable." The actual announcement of the hanging was a match to a powder magazine. That night there were mobs on the streets of Montreal and Sir John Macdonald was burned in effigy in Dominion square. On the following Sunday forty thousand people swarmed around the hustings on Champ de Mars and heard the government denounced in every conceivable term of verbal violence by speakers of every tinge of political belief. This outpouring of a common indignation with its obliteration of all the usual lines of demarcation was the result of the "wounding of the national self-esteem" by the flouting of the demand for leniency, as it was put by La Minerve [sic]. Mercier put it still more strongly when he declared that "the murder of Riel was a declaration of war upon French-Canadian influence in Confederation." A binding cement for this union of elements ordinarily at war was sought for in the creation of the "parti national" which a year later captured the provincial Conservative citadel at Quebec and turned it over to Honoré Mercier.

This violent racial movement raged unchecked in the provincial arena, but in the federal field it was held in leash by Laurier. That he saw the possibilities of the situation is not to be doubted. He took part in the demonstration on Champ de Mars and in his speech made a declaration—"Had I been born on the banks of Saskatchewan I myself would have shouldered a musket"—which riveted nation-wide attention upon him. Laurier followed this by his impassioned apology for the half-breeds and their leader in the House of Commons, of which deliverance Thomas White, of the assailed ministry, justly said: "It was the finest parliamentary speech ever pronounced in the parliament of Canada since Confederation." In

the debate on the execution of Riel all the orators of parliament took part. It was the occasion for one of Blake's greatest efforts. Sir John Thompson, in his reply to Blake, revealed himself to parliament and the country as one worthy of crossing swords with the great Liberal tribune. But they and all the other "big guns" of the Commons were thrown into complete eclipse by Laurier's performance. It is easy to recall after the lapse of thirty-six years the extraordinary impression which that speech made upon the great audience which heard it—a crowded House of Commons and the public galleries packed to the roof.

In the early winter of 1886-7 Laurier went boldly into Ontario where, addressing great audiences in Toronto, London and other points, he defended his position and preferred his indictment against the government. This was Laurier's first introduction to Ontario, under circumstances which, while actually threatening, were in reality auspicious. It was at once an exhibition of moral and physical courage and a manifestation of Laurier's remarkable qualities as a public speaker. Within a few months Laurier passed from the comparative obscurity to which he had condemned himself by his apparent indifference to politics to a position in public life where he divided public attention and interest with Edward Blake and Sir John Macdonald. When a few months later Blake, in a rare fit of the sulks, retired to his tent, refusing to play any longer with people who did not appreciate his abilities, Laurier succeeded to the leadership—apparently upon the nomination of Blake, actually at the imperious call of those inescapable forces and interests which men call Destiny.

Lionel Groulx, *Histoire du Canada Francais Depuis la Découverte*, (Montreal, L'Action Nationale, 1952), pp. 139-142. Reprinted by permission of Editions Fides.

## Quebec Nationalism

Could one not say that Quebec's reactions were almost inevitable? And should one even be surprised that they were frequent if not continual? These were the consequences of the isolation of a French and Catholic province in the setting and surroundings we know. This was the attitude of a people condemned to be on the alert or on guard perpetually. In fact, in the some forty years following Confederation several nationalist outbreaks took place and from the beginnings of the new regime much anxiety was aroused in Quebec. First, there was at the end of 1871, the formation of the "national party," a union of moderate Liberals and Conservatives, some anxious to free themselves from the anticlerical wing of their party, others tired of Georges-Etienne Cartier's dictatorship, but a party particularly of young patriots sympathetic with Louis Riel and disgusted with Canadian policy in the west and in the New Brunswick schools affair. In 1874, after the death of Cartier and the retirement of the Liberal leader Antoine-Aimé Dorion, J.-A. Mousseau, supported by several newspapers, proposed, in turn, a political organization of the same type, soon called derisively "the party of angels." The essential thing to remember is that these plans and groups arose from the same concern; to resist the encroachment of Ottawa in the affairs of Quebec through a French Canadian front, to constitute a political force to safeguard national interests. They drew inspiration from the theory that in Parliament at Ottawa the members "were invested with full powers in matters relating to the provinces." Two of these nationalist outbursts, better organized, more durable have a place in history as a result of the notable role they played. Both, moreover, crystallized around two strong personalities, both first-rate leaders: Honoré Mercier, Henri Bourassa. Of the first, could we say that he personified the reaction to centralization, and the second, the reaction to colonialism? It is an acceptable generalization but from which both greatly deviated.

It is a tradition among historians to attribute the advent of Mercier to the movement in support of Riel. But does this take into account all the uneasiness of the period, and in particular, of two misfortunes or dangers which particularly alarmed opinion between 1880 and 1890? We would mention: the constant diminution of French influence at Ottawa and the already formidable inclination of the national spirit in Quebec. "French Canadian influence amounts to nothing in the cabinet, nothing in the direction of policy," confessed a federal cabinet minister in 1888, and not one of the least, Adolphe Chapleau, was in favour of "provincial politics which would at last be concerned with the interests of Lower Canada without reference to the convenience or needs of Ottawa." The new orientation of provincial and French sentiment went so far that future political leaders such as Thomas-Chase Casgrain and Edmund James Flynn made it a point to recommend to the Quebec parliament in 1888, an outline of today's centralization and the fusion of the races in a single Canadian nationality. Having said this, let us grant that the powerful agitation in the outburst of 1886 grew out of the Riel movement. Let each recall the facts: the genuine grievances and misery of the Métis, driven back, thrown into disorder by immigration into the North-West, seriously affected in their way of life by the disappearance of the buffalo; faced with this distress, persistent and inexplicable neglect in Ottawa; then the approach of the Métis to the exiled Louis Riel who left the United States and became their leader; a campaign of petitions and claims which turned into rebellion; armed intervention by the Canadian government; surrender of Riel, his trial at Regina, before an English-speaking judge and half-jury; after exhausting all judicial recourse including the appeal to the Privy Council in England and to the mercy of the Governor-General, death by hanging of the Métis leader in Regina prison, November 16, 1885; hanging of a man for a political crime, and a man affected, at least in the past, by mental troubles, duly stated, declared, moreover during his trial by the alienists of the defence, irresponsible in regard to matters of religion and politics. The Riel affair, I have already written, was for Canada, what one day would be the "Dreyfus Affair" in France. Had they hanged an innocent man? Had they committed a judicial murder? If it is difficult to decide on the guilt or innocence of Riel, all just minds, we believe, can agree on the inopportunity, if not the in-

justice of capital punishment. *La Minerve*, the obsequious newspaper of the Conservative government, admitted that the Métis had rightly complained of serious grievances. The bishops, the western missionaries had wasted warning after warning on Canadian authorities. In fact, the government at Ottawa was so guilty that it did not want to appear severe. Crimes of the people against authority are assuredly serious, crimes of authority against the people are no less so. This realization of injustices committed by the federal government and especially the judicial murder at Regina, aroused an almost unanimous French-Canadian opinion. To the same extent English-Canadian opinion almost solidly, without valid cause, associated the events of 1885 with those of 1869-70 in Manitoba, and petitioned demanding the execution of the Métis leader. *L'Electeur* newspaper had observed: "Requests have been heard until now for the pardon or the commutation of the death penalty, but demands for his death, never." The *News* of Winnipeg, on its part, wrote: "If Riel's sentence is commuted, the government should not be surprised that a loyal though exasperated people, would feel justice done to them." On both sides of the barricade, moreover, people did their best to give the controversy the character of a racial conflict. One reads, for example, in the *Toronto Mail:* "If the collapse of the cabinet should result from the withdrawal of its French partisans . . . in this case, we, British subjects, are convinced that it would be necessary to undertake the Conquest again; and Lower Canada may be assured there will be no 1763 treaty. This time the conqueror will not capitulate." The French newspapers quickly reached the same pitch. One reads, for example, in *La Presse* of Montreal, lines such as this: "Riel expiated not only the crime of having demanded the rights of his compatriots; he expiated especially and above all the crime of belonging to our race." The newspaper continued: "The execution of Riel destroys all the party lines which were formed in the past. Henceforth there will be neither Conservatives, nor Liberals, nor Castors. There will be only Patriots or Traitors. The national party and the party of the rope."

H. Blair Neatby and John T. Saywell, "Chapleau and the Conservative Party in Quebec", *Canadian Historical Review,* Vol. 37, No. 1, March 1956, pp. 1-2, 22. Reprinted by permission of the University of Toronto Press and the Authors.

# Quebec and the Conservatives

Until the 1890's Quebec was considered a Conservative province; since the 1890's it has been a Liberal stronghold. This transfer of political allegiance has long been recognized as one of the most significant developments in Canadian political history. And yet historians have never satisfactorily explained why the change occurred. Possibly Canadians have been too concerned with national parties and national leaders, and so have concentrated on Laurier's assumption of national leadership and his policy as a national figure. It is apparently assumed that French Canadian voters deserted the Conservatives in 1896 because Laurier was a French Canadian, although he had become leader of the national party in 1887; or because Louis Riel was hanged, although the execution took place in 1885. In concentrating on Laurier's victory, the role of regional and provincial leaders and the interaction of provincial and national politics has been overlooked or drastically simplified.

In 1896 the Conservatives lost Quebec. They lost Quebec because the party was divided and leaderless as it had seldom been before, at a time when both unity and leadership were essential. [J. A. Chapleau] might have provided that leadership and saved Quebec for the party in 1896 as he had done in the past, but he made no effort to do so. A study of Chapleau's career gives some insight into the complexities of Canadian politics, and also provides a partial explanation for the transition from the Macdonald era to the Laurier era in Canada.

The *débâcle* of the Conservative party in 1896 might be said to have its origins in 1871 with the publication of the *Programme catholique.* This political manifesto signified the formation of an ultra-Catholic lay party corresponding to the ultramontane faction within the church. Weak in numbers but influential because of its leadership and its rigid principles, this group maintained that politics must have a firm religious and moral basis and that "la séparation de l'Eglise et de l'Etat est une doctrine absurde et impie." The group—soon to be labelled the Castors—became the right wing of the Conservative party, but as the *Programme* stated, it was not concerned with party loyalty in the political sense. . . .

In spite of his talent and ambition he [Chapleau] had failed to dominate Quebec as Cartier had done. Yet his career is significant in the history of his province and his country. He had consistently fought against the ultra-clerical faction and had probably saved the Quebec Conservative party from becoming a narrow Roman Catholic party. His failure to unite his party might be attributed to his temperament, to his instinctive preference for destroying the Castor faction rather than compromise, but he was not entirely to blame. The Castors were no less determined to destroy him. Nor would it be just to describe him as no more than an ambitious or self-seeking politician. He was an ambitious man, it is true, but in two national crises, the execution of Riel and the Manitoba School question, he refused to seek personal power at the expense of the interests of his compatriots and the nation. His career illustrates the dilemma of a national politician represent- ing a minority group. It helps to explain why Quebec became a Liberal province. And it should be a warning to historians that to speak exclusively of national parties and national leaders is to superimpose on a pattern of great variety and intricate design another of the utmost simplicity which, while simplifying Canadian political history, may at times tend to distort it.

*The Mail,* Toronto, November 23, 1885.

# A Grave Crisis

After due deliberation, the active leaders of the English-speaking Reformers have determined to join the Bleu-Rouge coalition that has been formed for the purpose of avenging the execution of RIEL. The *Globe* makes the announcement in an article, reproduced elsewhere, which bears all the ear marks of careful preparation. The rebellion is justified and RIEL's course defended; in a word, our contemporary accepts the whole French platform, and urges the Reformers of Ontario to unite with Lower Canada in destroying the Ministry at Ottawa, which in upholding the law of the land sent RIEL to the scaffold. The *Globe* plea is, that unless Sir JOHN MACDONALD be punished, permanent antagonism between the two races will be established.

The issue thus created is perhaps the most momentous ever presented to the Canadian people. The overthrow of the present Administration purely on political grounds would be a matter of very little consequence. Twenty Tory Cabinets might rise and fall in the ordinary way,

and the country would still live. But it is proposed by this combination of Bleus and Rouges to assert the doctrine that Quebec's demands in RIEL's behalf should have been sufficient to ensure the setting aside of the sentence of the court; and the Reform leaders have agreed to support them in defeating the Ministry which dared to challenge their right thus to overawe and supersede the Executive. So that if Sir JOHN MACDONALD should be beaten, the result would involve not merely a change of parties at Ottawa, such as under ordinary circumstances would ensue, but the establishment once for all of the principle that the French-Canadian race is above, beyond and superior to the Canadian constitution. Such, stripped of verbiage and other adornments, is the issue now forced upon the country by this new and unnatural alliance. It is in no sense a party question, but one vitally concerning the whole English-speaking race, which has always contended for, and is bound at any cost to insist upon perfect equality under the law. We tell the *Globe* deliberately that it would be better a thousand times to create permanent antagonism between the two peoples, and precipitate the disruption of Confederation, than to set up the permanent supremacy of the minority.

The blindness of the Bleus and Rouges in combining to defeat the Government, which for the time being represents constituted authority in the Dominion, upon such an issue as the execution of RIEL is astounding. Do they suppose that if with the aid of their Reform allies they should succeed, the English people in Ontario, the Maritime Provinces and the North-West would long submit to the monstrous injustice which would triumph with them? Does it not strike them that the English majority might be provoked to retaliate and say, "If the equality of the races is to be disturbed, we are entitled by virtue of numbers to be supreme?" and that, instead of gaining by the movement, they might lose? Hitherto the French race in Canada has been fairly treated. We are free to confess that, in the early days, under the regime of Lord DORCHESTER and others, injustice was oftentimes done to them. But the fault lay not so much with the English Canadians as with the colonial system of the period and the obliquity of the military governors sent out to administer it. Since 1841, however, when the people began to rule, to the present hour, a spirit of the broadest justice and generosity has characterized the dealings of Upper Canada with the sister province. We challenge the press of Quebec and Montreal to point to a wrong wittingly done, or to name any country in the wide world where the rights of a minority have been more conscientiously respected. As this is a time for the plainest speaking, let us add that the sincere desire of the English provinces to do right by Lower Canada has undoubtedly hampered their material progress. The English-speaking majority in the United States would never have tolerated the demands which the British portion of Canada has cheerfully complied with, much less submitted to the maintenance of those peculiar institutions which British Canada has fostered as though they had been her own. Yet, after all our efforts to establish amicable relations with them, even at the sacrifice of prosperity, the French-Canadians are now seeking to compel us to recognize their right to suspend the operation of the law whenever a representative of their race is in the toils. But let us solemnly assure them again that, rather than submit to such a yoke, Ontario would smash Con-

federation into its original fragments, preferring that the dream of a united Canada should be shattered forever, than that unity should be purchased at the expense of equality.

If the French desire to destroy Sir JOHN MACDONALD, in God's name let them do it on grounds other than the execution of RIEL. The Dominion is not bound up in the fate of any one political leader or party. But if he should be overthrown simply because he upheld the majesty of the law and resisted the bold demand that this felon should be saved because he had become the hero of French mass meetings, then Canadian institutions cannot survive him. The English people are willing, now as in the past, to recognize equal rights for the French, but they will never whilst they breathe consent to the establishment of a French *imperium in imperio;* and we beg and entreat the Bleu and Rouge leaders, as they value the welfare of the Dominion, to withdraw from so dangerous an experiment before it is too late.

That Ontario Reformers, whose policy for forty years has been one long cry against French domination in the ordinary affairs of the country, should now consent to recognize French domination in so sacred a domain as that of the administration of the law, is a phenomenon only to be accounted for by the depth and profundity of their desire for office. We do not believe, however, that the wirepullers who have thus conspired to sacrifice the basis of stable government in order that they may enjoy the sweets of power, will be supported by the rank and file of the party. There are tens of thousands of Liberals in Ontario who must agree with us that in the face of the sinister movement now in progress in Lower Canada the ups and downs of the English factions is but a paltry consideration. To these men, and to all who believe that the life of the country can be preserved only by conserving the elementary principle of one law for all, we appeal, no matter by what name they may have been known in the politics of the past. Quebec cannot succeed at this audacious attempt to plant a dictatorship, even with the aid of the renegades who may follow the *Globe,* provided we stand together and conduct ourselves as men sincerely desirous of peace, and willing to go a full half-way towards perpetuating it, but determined nevertheless to submit to no trick for imposing the tyranny of a French minority upon a country consecrated by British blood to British freedom.

*Le Monde,* Montreal, November 20, 1885.

## The Orangemen

Let us be calm, let us reflect, let us ponder the situation; it is solemn, it is serious and dangerous.

There is at this moment a hastily conceived movement which could throw the country into abysmal depths.

Let us quieten the indignant voices of national and humanitarian sentiment. Let us hold back the tears that show in our eyes and attempt to view dispassionately and with all possible dignity the present political situation in Canada.

The cause of this situation is known. We will not go over the offensive and humiliating details again. One word will suffice.

The death of Riel on the scaffold at Regina is perhaps a legal execution, but in these circumstances a political crime. It is contrary to the custom of civilized countries in this last half of the 19th century.

But fanaticism needs a victim. Riel has been offered as a sacrifice, and Orangeism has hanged him through hatred and to gratify a vengeance already outdated.

At first Sir John thought he had the power, as formerly, to control this dangerous element in our population. He has been powerless.

No further French domination, said Upper Canada, Riel's head or yours.

*No further French domination, said the Orangemen: Riel's head or yours.*

In the end the old chief gave in, and the gallows, the hideous gallows was built deep in the far off wilderness of the West. The rest is known.

Should Sir John be surprised today if Lower Canada withdraws the unbounded confidence that it has given him for forty years.

His career, so glorious to him, and which has been so valuable to the country, he owes to the Conservative party of Lower Canada which never failed him.

As recompense for forty years of service he refuses its prayer for mercy and gives it instead a gallows.

They have found it necessary to burn the Orange rope which hanged Riel. This is a useless precaution. The wind will disperse the ashes to the four corners of the country. The ingrates and the executioners will be poisoned.

The Conservative party in our province can not be held responsible for the blood of this man. He degraded himself in the eyes of humanity. All of Canada recoils from this act of cruelty the consequences of which could be terrible.

We had fashioned beautiful dreams, great hopes for the future of our country.

Especially since the establishment of Confederation, the work of Cartier, the different races who lived under the Canadian flag seemed to draw together to work in harmony and peace for the expansion, the success and the wealth of the common homeland.

Former hatreds disappeared and

gave way to esteem and mutual confidence between citizens of a single country.

The memory of former unhappy days disappeared, buried in the joy of the present and hopes for a future filled with glory and good fortune.

Why had these tender dreams to be shattered so soon?

Why had these hopes to vanish so quickly?

Why was it necessary, in a single day, in a single hour, abhorred forever, to revive all the former hatreds of the past and compromise perhaps forever the peace and the future of this Confederation?

We demand no sacrifice of the rights of other national groups—not even the Orangemen;—Why not permit us to enjoy ours in peace.

Are French Canadians disloyal? Are 150 years of struggle and work to maintain the flag and influence of England on this continent not sufficient to prove our attachment, our fidelity, our love for the British crown? The Orangeman was born in the blood of Ireland. He is the disturbing element.

The crown of England has no greater enemy under the sun than the organization of Orange Lodges. It is to this faction that England owes all the shame and dishonour which tarnishes its Coat of Arms.

Let us not permit this branch of tyranny to grow stronger in this free soil of Canada.

The Canadian sun shines for every man who wishes to work and to develop for himself a happy and tranquil homeland;—Fomenters of injustice and disorder have no right to citizenship here. It is clear Orangeism has no part to play in the well-being and good fortunes of states.

It has become the tormentor of Ireland and the shame of England. Its conduct in Canada will lead us to the destruction and utter ruin of Confederation. May all the friends of good order, justice and national well-being unite to rescue from peril the country which now finds itself slipping into an abyss.

Let us meditate calmly.

Let us reflect seriously on the grave and perilous situation of our country, which our unfortunate political divisions have contributed so greatly to create. Let us be careful of exaggerated agitation. Anger like meanness is a poor guide.

Mr. Laflamme spoke yesterday of the danger of sectional agitation. He was correct.

Let us be firm in the demand for our racial rights; but let this demand be made within the undeniable constitutional means at our disposal. Vexation and violence will accomplish nothing at all for us.

Let us control the movement so that it does not become a cause for provocation to the other provinces and the other races.

Let us not lose courage. National life has seen days much worse,—has passed through more terrible crises, engaged in battles more perilous,—and has won victories more difficult.

Winds more furious have beat against the ship which carries our destiny; let us act as skilful and experienced captains; in the middle of the tempest let us retain the cool courage necessary to execute the manoeuvres which will bring us victory over the fury of the winds and the waves and which will bring us safely into port.

Speech of Honoré Mercier, Champ de Mars, Montreal, November 22, 1885. Printed in J. O. Pelland (ed.), *Biographie, Discours, Conferences, etc. de l'Hon. Honoré Mercier,* (Montreal, 1890), pp. 328-333.

# The Guilty Must Be Punished

Riel, our brother, is dead, a victim of his devotion to the cause of the Métis whose chief he was, a victim of fanaticism and of betrayal; of the fanaticism of Sir John and of his friends; of the betrayal of three of our own people who, to maintain their cabinet posts, have sold their brother.

Riel died on the scaffold, as the patriots of 1837 died, as brave and Christian men! In surrendering his head to the executioner as did [Francois] Lorimier, he has given his heart to his country; as Christ he forgave his murderers.

He went up to the scaffold with a firm and sure step; not a muscle of his face trembled; his soul, strengthened by martyrdom, knew not the weakness of agony.

In killing Riel, Sir John has not only struck at the heart of our race but especially at the cause of justice and humanity which, represented in all languages and sanctified by all religious beliefs, demanded mercy for the prisoner of Regina, our poor friend of the North-West.

Riel's last gasp has echoed sorrowfully throughout the entire world; it has reverberated as a piercing cry from the soul of all civilized peoples; and this cry has had the same effect on the Minister and the executioner; both, their hands stained with blood, tried to hide their shame: the one in an Orange Lodge hearing the howls of gratified fanaticism; the other, [Macdonald], on the ocean in order not to hear the curses of a whole people in sorrow.

There are about fifty thousand free citizens here [on the Champ de Mars] gathered together under the protecting shield of the constitution, in the name of humanity which cries for vengeance, in the name of all friends of justice which has been trampled under foot, in the name of two million French who are in tears, in order to cast on the Minister in flight a final curse which, reverberating from echo to echo along the banks of our great river, will overtake him as he loses sight of the soil of Canada, which he has soiled through a judicial murder.

As to those who remain; as to the three who represent the province of Quebec in the federal government and who signify nothing but betrayal, let us bow our heads in the face of their shortcoming and let us cry about their sad fate; for the stain of blood they carry on their brow is as indelible as the memory of their cowardice. They will share the fate of their brother Cain; the memory of them will be as detestable as of him; and as the sons of Abel who sought refuge in the desert to avoid meeting again the first brother-killer in the world, our children will turn their heads to avoid seeing the three brother-killers of Canada.

In the face of this crime, in the presence of these failings, what is our duty? We have three things to do: unite to punish the guilty, break the alliance which our deputies made with Orangeism and seek in an alliance more natural and less dangerous, protection of our national interests.

We, united! Oh! how comfortable I feel in speaking these words! Twenty years ago I asked for a union of all the passionate forces of the nation. Twenty years ago I said to my brothers to sacrifice, on the altar of the fatherland in danger, the hatred that was blinding us and the divisions that were destroying us. You replied to this call for unity which came from a patriotic heart, with insults, recriminations, calumnies. It required the national misfortune we deplore, it required the death of one of our own for this cry of unity to be understood.

Today, distracted by grief, we recognize our fault, and faced with the body of Riel we hold out a fraternal hand to one another. Kneeling at the blessed grave, we ask God for pardon and mercy, pardon for our past strife, mercy for our race so grievously attacked. Will this entreaty be heard; will our prayers made in sobs and coming from our souls in despair be granted?

Are there among all the hands clasped in sublime enthusiasm the hands of some traitors? The God who probes the depths of our being, this God alone knows. While waiting till He reveals His secrets to us, till He lifts a corner of the future all of whose mysteries He knows, let us hope and have confidence.

All those who are united in spirit in this day of atonement, are of the same race, speak the same language, kneel at the same altar, the same blood rekindles their heart; these are all brothers! May heaven assure this time that they hear the voice of blood.

Then let us not forget, we who are Liberals, that if the nation is in mourning

as a result of the assassination of Riel, our Conservative brothers are in the depths of grief greater than our own. They are shedding tears over Riel as we are, but they are crying also over the downfall and the betrayal of their leaders. Those who were, with reason, so proud of Chapleau and Langevin, those who saw in the eloquence of one and the competence of the other, the preservation of the country, are forced to bow their heads and curse today those they blest yesterday. Gentlemen, respect this great and legitimate grief; and do not belittle it.

This union, gentlemen, which we have organized and which we beg you to bless, in the name of the fatherland you represent, is not a union of race against other races, of religion against other religions.

We do not wish to atone for a crime with another. Grief renders us neither foolish or unjust, and does not destroy the respect we have for our brothers of other nationalities. We know that the Irish, sons of a race persecuted as ours, are with us in the solemn protest we are making; we know that the English, friends of justice, and the Scotch, friends of liberty, sympathize with us in the misfortune which has struck us; we know too that it is betrayal rather than fanaticism that killed Riel.

Yesterday someone said to me, "If Cartier had been there, Riel would not have been hanged," and I was forced to admit I believed him! Cartier would have defended our brother with the great energy which characterized him; and instead of consenting to his execution he would have thrown his portfolio in Sir John's face!

It must be avowed that the leaders of the Conservative party are degenerating; but I have confidence that the soldiers of this great party remain stout-hearted, and that there will be among them enough patriotism to induce them to join with us, as one man, in the great national movement which is being organized at this moment.

Let us hope also, gentlemen, that our Canadian clergy whose lofty and noble traditions are written in letters of gold in our historic annals, will not fail us at this conjuncture; and that its powerful co-operation, given with prudence and reserve, will assure the realization of our hopes.

We are not unaware that in the neighbouring province and in all other parts of Canada there are generous hearts ready to devote themselves to the common cause, to the cause of justice and humanity.

Just yesterday, an influential newspaper, the Globe, speaking of "the duty of the hour" justifies the demonstrations that the death of Riel has provoked in the province of Quebec, recalls the causes which led to the rebellion in the North West and the readiness of the Ministers, directly after the revolt, to grant the demands of the Métis. . . . "The people of Ontario should not forget that the French Canadians ask nothing but justice. . . . The only way to save Canada is in a cordial union, made between the two provinces, to punish the despicable people who are in power."

That is what they say in Ontario; it is not, therefore, a racial war we want; it is not only an exclusive French Canadian party we ask, but a union of all the friends of justice and humanity whose sacred cause has been outraged by the death of Riel.

This death, the crime of our enemies, will become for us a rallying sign and an instrument of salvation.

Our duty, therefore, is to unite and punish the guilty; may this union be consecrated by our people and let us make an oath before God and man, to fight with all our strength and all our soul and with all the resources provided us by the Constitution, the perfidious government of Sir John, the three traitors who have dishonoured our race and all those who will be wicked enough to seek to imitate or to excuse their crime!

Naively I believed in the patriotism of one of these three men up to the last moment; for four days before the execution, seeing danger imminent, I begged Mr. Bergeron, member for Beauharnois, to go to Mr. Chapleau and say to him for me: "If Riel is hanged and you do not resign, you are finished; if you resign, you save Riel. In the first case, the Liberal party has one powerful adversary less; and the country one shame more. In the second case, the country gains glory and the minister who resigns will become the idol of his compatriots. I have everything to gain as chief of the party if you stay in: you have everything to gain if you resign. Resign, Chapleau and place yourself at the head of the province. I will be at your side to assist you with my feeble efforts, and bless your name beside that of our brother Riel, saved from the scaffold."

Mr. Bergeron said to the committee the other night that he had fulfilled the mission to Chapleau which I, in patriotic despair, had given him.

Mr. Chapleau refused the hand of a brother in order to protect that of Sir John; he preferred the howling of some fanatics to the blessing of all the French-

Canadian nation; he preferred death to life; death for him, death for Riel; his career is destroyed like Riel's! except that the latter fell as a man, the former as a traitor.

A final word, gentlemen, and I am finished.

During the evil times of former days, when the memory of the scaffolds of 1837 crushed the strongest souls, when fanaticism, like today, cried for the blood of those who sought liberty, two men appeared to give this liberty and refuse this blood. It was Baldwin and Lafontaine; Ontario and Quebec! People look! the ship which carries to the other side of the ocean the Tory who burned the Parliament Buildings in 1849, will pass the ship which is bringing here the son of a man who defended our compatriots in that Parliament which was burning.

The son is worthy of the father: it is Blake, a noble Irishman who sympathizes with us.

As formerly, Ontario offers a Baldwin; look in the two parties and find yourself a Lafontaine; the Liberals believe they have him in their ranks; but take him if you wish and if you find him, in the Conservative party; we will acclaim him happily and serve him faithfully.

Hector Langevin, Minister of Public Works, *House of Commons Debates,* March 11, 1886.

# A French Canadian "Traitor"

# Defends The Government

. . . The reason why we allowed the law to take its course has been given already, but there is this to be added, that in this matter we had to deal with a case which affected a large portion of the country, which affected a wild portion of the country; and, if the same action had taken place, if the same crime had been committed in the other parts of the country, we would have acted as we did; and therefore we put to ourselves this question: Is it a reason, because this is in a wild part of the country, far from the strong arm of the law, that this prisoner should escape the punishment which is fixed by law? We thought not; we had to direct us in that fact—and there I know that some of my friends may not agree with me, but, if they allow me to continue my remarks, they will see the reason why I allude to it—we had this before us, we had the fact that Louis Riel had, 15 years before this, committed an act which was considered at the time one that should have been punished in the most severe way. The prisoner, Louis Riel, at that time was not condemned to a severe punishment; he was allowed to remain out of the country for five years, and he was not brought before a tribunal to be tried, and punished or absolved, for the death of Thomas Scott. I know I shall be told that at that time Louis Riel was at the head of a *de facto* Government, that it was the Government for the time being, and that, therefore, the Dominion Government had no right to put him to death for the execution of Scott. I leave that question for the hon. gentlemen to discuss; but if we are not to say a word about the death of Thomas Scott, and if we are met by the reasoning that Louis Riel had a right to put him to death, under circumstances no matter how cruel, then, I ask why should the established Government of this country, the Government that exists here by the Queen's will and by the Constitution of the country—why should we be called to account for having done—what? Not for having condemned Riel to death, but simply for having allowed the tribunals of this country to execute the law of this country. I do not know how hon. gentlemen can get out of this dilemma. Even though Riel may have been justified in putting Scott to death when he was at the head of that *de facto* Government, even with all the cruelty that attended the execution, even though he may have been justified in doing that, we cannot be condemned here for allowing the law to take its course in November last. We are the Government of the country; we had no revenge against this man; he had done us nothing personally; but he had attacked the authority of the Queen; he had revolutionised that country; he had called the half-breeds to his aid and had deceived them in a most shameful way, as the missionaries of that country have all testified;

he had destroyed their faith; he had destroyed their religion to establish one of his own, and my friends from the Province of Quebec call that man a compatriot, a man of their race! No, Mr. Speaker; the sober, second thought of the people will not be so. They will say that whether that man had French blood in his veins, or whether he had English or Irish or Scotch blood, the Government had only to consider whether he was guilty or not. For my part, I am not only a representative of the French Canadians, in the Government, but I, along with my colleagues, am a representative of the whole people of Canada, of all origins; and, therefore, when a case of this kind comes before us, though it may be especially painful for me to see one suffer death who speaks my own language, and who also may have French blood in his veins, nevertheless, I have only one duty to perform, and that is to give even justice to all. Mr. Speaker, I might go further and continue to answer some other remarks made by the hon. gentleman, and other attacks, against the Government made during the last four months;

but I think that I have shown you and this House that the prisoner had a fair trial; I have shown that the courts of the country so declared; I have shown that the Privy Council in England had confirmed that decision; and I have shown that we, as a Government, have taken all the pains and trouble necessary to find out whether the Government of Canada could interfere and should interfere in this case. We found, to our regret, I must say—because it is always a regret for us to see one of our fellow creatures going to his last account—we found, to our great regret, that we could not interfere. We have been blamed for that, and the hon. member for Montmagny (Mr. Landry) has thought proper, under the circumstances, to put in your hands a motion censuring the Government, declaring the regret of this House that the sentence of death against Louis Riel was carried into effect. I hope, Mr. Speaker, that the large majority of this House will not agree with that motion. I hope this House will remember that we did only our duty in the matter, and, though we did it reluctantly, we did it. . . .

Adolphe Caron, Minister of Militia, *House of Commons Debates,* March 17, 18, 1886.

## Duty to the Country

. . . Of all the charges that can be levelled against a public man, of all the grave accusations which can be brought against a public man in the discharge of his official duties, I think the most infamous is that of being a traitor to his country, a traitor to his people. For weeks, nay, for months, my hon. colleagues and myself have been traduced before public opinion in our Province. We have been accused of being traitors to our blood and traitors to our Province. Sir, I wish to ask to day how came it that we could have laid ourselves open to such a grave charge. I want to know how it is possible that men, who for years and years have enjoyed the confidence of their countrymen, of the friends who support us in Parliament, should have rendered themselves guilty of the charge which has been brought against us. Sir, under circumstances of extreme difficulty, knowing as we did know, and as it was our duty to know, what public opinion was in the Province of Quebec in regard to this question, we have been charged with being traitors to our people and our Province, because we allowed the law to take its course. We did so because we considered it our duty not to interfere with the carrying out of the sentence against Louis Riel. . . . I felt, and I feel today, more than I can express, how painful was the duty which we were called upon to perform. I felt that it was not a light thing to sever those ties, political and social, which had bound me to those friends and countrymen who had entrusted me with their confidence and who withdrew it on that occasion. But I felt that it was my imperative duty to my own Province of Quebec, which I love so much, to take the course I did; and I say again, notwithstanding what hon. gentlemen opposite may say, that if the same circumstances should arise again, I would do exactly as I did before. . . .

. . . I have said that I considered it was my bounden duty to my country, to my Province, to act as I have acted as an adviser of the Crown. Mr. Speaker, as Ministers of the Crown, occupying, as we do, the Treasury benches, we are here representing, not one individual Province but the whole Dominion of Canada. I deemed it was an obligation for us, occupying those positions, to maintain the peace and order in the Dominion. I considered it our duty to maintain the credit of this country at home and abroad. I considered that was our duty as Ministers of the Crown, responsible for the peace of the citizens inhabiting this country. I say more. We know, from the public documents of this Parliament, how much treasure Canada has been investing for the purpose of bringing to our vast and fertile prairies of the west, the population of the overcrowded centres of Europe. It is necessary, if we are to hold out inducements to immigrants to come to Canada and to settle in happy homes in our country, to show that Canada can protect those who entrust their future to her care. It is necessary for us to show that, whether in the extreme North-West or in the older Provincess, the Government of Canada is sufficiently strong to protect her people and to maintain law and order. . . . We have, moreover,—and this is a most important feature, as I understand it, in the present debate—thousands of an Indian population in the North-West. I believe every man who desires to see Canada advancing and prosperous must feel that, having acquired those territories which formerly were the uncontested homes of the Indians, we should be true and loyal to those whom we have taken under our protection. We have a large number of Indians in that territory who have a right to expect that they shall be loyally and kindly treated, that the treaties into which they have entered with the Government shall be scrupulously carried out; but it is of greatest importance that they should also learn that peace and order must be maintained in those territories. It is of the greatest importance that they should understand that whatever grounds there may be for agitation, there is a constitutional way of agitating. . . . When all the circumstances of this outbreak are fully gone into, when we come to consider the manner in which it was prepared and organised, when we come to consider the number of lives which it has cost the Dominion, the treasure that has been expended during the revolt, I say it was time for us to consider whether the most energetic possible means should not be taken to prevent the recurrence in the future of any such troubles as we had in the North-West. But, Sir, I hope that within the precincts of this Parliament we shall not find any hon. gentleman who will say that,

in allowing the law to take its course, in not interfering with the execution of the sentence legally passed on Louis Riel the Government has sacrificed a martyr and a hero. I do not see how this is possible, although I have been reading, for the last several months, articles in newspapers which would really indicate that some of those who edited or wrote them must have considered that this man was a great hero and great martyr. I ask myself, reading the evidence which has been taken in his case, knowing the circumstances which attended the rising, knowing everything he did for the purpose of getting up the troubles in the North-West; I ask myself how it is possible that any person having at heart the interests of his country, should consider that the example of Louis Riel is one which should be held out to the admiration of the people of any country, or that he should be considered a hero and a martyr. Is he not the man who stirred up an Indian war with all its horrors? Is he not the man who wrote to Major Crozier that he wanted to commence without delay a war of extermination? . . .

. . . It is almost impossible, the more one goes into the history of this rebellion, the more one reads the documents and papers relating to it, to understand how even an attempt could be made to convert Riel into a hero. . . . We have undoubted proof that he tried to kindle an Indian war in 1879-80; we have also the evidence of Father André, which establishes beyond the possibility of discussion, that the motives of Riel in the agitation were interested, personal motives, and that he stated he was perfectly prepared to give up the Metis cause provided his claims against the Government were satisfied. . . . We have, further, the very important piece of evidence, to my mind, that on the 2nd February, two months before the outbreak, Sir John sent a despatch to Nolin, which was communicated to Father André and to Riel, about the settlement of Metis matters. In this despatch there was no mention of indemnity to Riel, who, in consequence of this, decided to take up arms. We have all this evidence, which cannot be controverted, to show how far this man was deserving of the pedestal on which he is placed today as a hero before the people of Canada. . . . As I stated yesterday, the responsibility which we had to take was a very considerable one, and I think that every hon. member here and every man outside of this House who really takes to heart the interest of Canada will consider that, in a matter of that importance, it became the bounden duty of the Government to consider what would be in the future the result of the course which we were following. Looking to the future of Canada and in the interests of that future, it seems to me that the head, the one who had got up two rebellions within such a comparatively short period, two rebellions which had cost so much treasure to Canada and so many valuable lives, should suffer the penalty of the crime which he had committed. It was important to teach, with a view to the future, those who had some supposed grievance, or who, believing that they had a grievance, imaginary or real, could simply follow the example given them by Riel in trying to do justice to themselves by taking up arms against the Government and the constitution. Such an example as has been given by this unfortunate man, who has paid the penalty of his high crime, certainly will teach others in the future that if they follow such an example they will become liable to the same fate, and that at any cost the constitution and the institutions of this country must be maintained and protected at all

hazards. . . . Twice, Mr. Speaker, had Riel raised the standard of revolt—in 1870 and 1885. Now, I ask any reasonable man, inside or outside of the House, whether we would not have been recreant to our duty if we had allowed him to go on unpunished after a repetition of the rebellion which he had organised in 1869-70? Would we not almost have been inviting him to organise a third rebellion? Would we not have set an example likely to prove disastrous to this country in future? And if we had interfered with the sentence which was passed by the proper tribunal, would we not in effect have said to the world that the Government of Canada winked at such crimes as that rebellion, with all its frightful murders and other sad consequences? I think we would have failed in our duty, we would have lacked that courage which, as public men and as responsible Ministers of the Crown, we ought to possess, if we had not, having regard solely to our duty, allowed the law to take its course and the sentence to be executed. . . . I stated that we simply did our duty towards Canada and towards the Province of Quebec. We claim for our people, for those who are the descendants of the very men who opened up to Christianity and civilisation this vast North American continent, equal rights with the people of other nationalities who inhabit the country. Upon that point we will never give in; I know, for one, I would not consent to give in upon any question of equality of rights with any other Province in the Dominion. In any case it is our interest to have a criminal law in this country which applies equally to French and English, to Scotch and Irish. There must be no law different for one man from that which is applicable to another; there must be no criminal law which applies to one nationality and does not apply to another nationality. We wish to be one Canadian people, united, happy and law abiding, and it is only on that condition we can carry out, or attempt to carry out, what I believe is reserved for us to do upon this continent. I, for one at least, can never agree to pressing upon the people of the Province of Quebec a feeling of jingoism which would be fatal to us. This feeling, if carried out, would mean isolation and the separation of the Province of Quebec from the other Provinces, and it would arouse against the Province of Quebec a hostile feeling from the other component parts of the Dominion. . . . I cannot but ask myself the question, how it can be possible that our people in the Province of Quebec should have any admiration for Riel. As is well known, our people are sincere Catholics; they are led to a very great extent by their clergy, owing to the great attachment existing between the people and the clergy, and how could it be possible that the people of the Province of Quebec would have such an admiration for that man. For his own purposes he gave up his religion; for his own purposes he was ready to give up his own people; and I ask again, how is it possible that this man could be a hero? The letter which I read of Monseigneur Grandin shows what frightful destruction, what misery he had caused to the people in that district. Anyone reading the letters which my hon. friend, the member from Montreal Centre (Mr. Curran), quoted the other day, from the papers published in the *Propagation of the Faith*—I say, for one who has read such papers, and knows anything of the position of those parishes on the Saskatchewan previous to the rebellion, how is it possible to recognise in the man who has laid waste almost every hamlet on the Saskatchewan; how is it possible to have any admiration for such a man, but rather a feeling of hatred than anything else. I never did consider, and I cannot consider now, that his cause has ever been our cause. I cannot for one consent to recognise in him the representative of our race. He is not the representative of our race, and has never been so. . . .

Wilfrid Laurier, *House of Commons Debates,* March 16, 1886.

## To Build a Nation

. . . In every instance in which a Government has carried out the extreme penalty of the law, when mercy was suggested instead, the verdict of history has been the same. Sir, in the Province to which I belong, and especially amongst the race to which I belong, the execution of Louis Riel has been universally condemned as being the sacrifice of a life, not to inexorable justice, but to bitter passion and revenge. And now, Sir, before going any further, it is fitting that, perhaps, I should address myself at once to the state of things which has sprung up in Quebec from the universal condemnation of the Government, not only by their foes, but by their friends as well. The movement which has followed the execution of Riel has been strangely misconceived, or I should say, has been wilfully misrepresented. The Tory press of Ontario at once turned bitterly and savagely upon their French allies of twenty-five years and more. They assailed them, not only in their action but in their motives. They charged them with being animated, not with any honest conviction of opinion, but with being animated with nothing less than race prejudices; they not only charged their former friends, but the whole French race as well, that the only motive which led them to take the course they did in the matter of Riel was simply because Riel was of French origin. They charged against the whole race that they would step between a criminal and justice, the moment the criminal was one of their own race. They charged against the whole French race that they would prevent the execution of the law the moment the law threatened one of their own. Mr. Speaker, on this matter I am not desirous of following the example which has been set before us by hon. gentlemen opposite of citing copious newspaper extracts, although I could cite extracts of the most bitter nature that ever was penned, of the [Toronto] *Mail* newspaper and other Tory organs against French Canadians. . . . It is true that upon the present occasion the French Canadians have shown an unbounded sympathy for the unfortunate man who lost his life upon the scaffold on the 16th November last. But if they came to that conclusion, it was not because they were influenced by race preferences or race prejudice, if you choose to call it so. They were no more influenced in their opinion by race prejudice, than were the foreign papers which deprecated the execution of Riel. It is a fact that the foreign press, the American press, the English press, the French press, almost without exception, have taken the ground that the execution of Riel was unjustified, unwarranted and against the spirit of the age. Certainly, it cannot be charged against that press that they were influenced by race feelings or prejudices, if you choose to call them such. And in the same manner, I say, the French Canadians, in the attitude which they took, were not impelled by race prejudices, but by reasons fairly deducible and deduced from the facts of the case. But if it had been stated that race prejudices, that blood relations had added keenness and feeling to a conviction formed by the mind, that would have been perfectly true. I will not admit that blood relations can so far cloud my judgment as to make me mistake wrong or right, but I cheerfully admit and I will plead guilty to that weakness, if weakness it be, that if an injustice be committed against a fellow-being, the blow will fall deeper into my heart if it should fall upon one of my kith and kin. But I will not admit anything more than that. That race prejudices can so far cloud my judgment as to make me mistake wrong from right, I do not believe to be true. . . . It has been stated, time and again, by the *Mail* newspaper and by other Tory organs, that it was the present intention of the French Canadian leaders to organise a purely French Canadian party, to lay aside all party ties and to have no other bonds of party in this House but that tie of race. I protest against any such assertion. Such assertion is unfounded, it is calculated to do harm, it is not founded on truth. It would be simply suicidal to French Canadians to form a party by themselves. Why, so soon as French Canadians, who are in the minority in this House and in the country, were to organise as a political party, they would compel the majority to organise as a political party, and the result must be disastrous to themselves. We have only one way of organising parties. This country must be governed and can be governed simply on questions of policy and administration, and French Canadians who have had any part in this movement have never had any other intention but to

organise upon those party distinctions and upon no other. . . . It has been stated by sober-minded people that the execution, even if unjust, of the man who was executed and who is believed to have been insane by those who sympathise with him, does not make this a case for the outburst of feeling which has been made in Quebec on the occasion of Riel's execution. I differ from that view. In our age, in our civilisation, every single human life is valuable, and is entitled to protection in the councils of the nation. Not many years ago England sent an expedition and spent millions of her treasure and some of her best blood simply to rescue prisoners whose lives were in the hands of the King of Abyssinia. In the same manner I say that the life of a single subject of Her Majesty here is valuable, and is not to be treated with levity. If there are members in this House who believe that the execution of Riel was not warranted, that under the circumstances of the case it was not judicious, that it was unjust, I say they have a right to arraign the Government for it before this country, and if they arraign the Government for it and the Government have to take their trial upon it, it must be admitted as a consequence that certain parties will feel upon the question more than others. It is not to be supposed that the same causes which influenced public opinion in Lower Canada acted in the same manner with all classes of the community, that the causes which actuated the community at large were identical in all classes of the community. Some there were who believed that the Government had not meted out the same measure of justice to all those that were accused and who took part in the rebellion. Others believed that the state of mind of Riel was such that it was a judicial murder to execute him; but the great mass of the people believed that mercy should have been extended to all the prisoners, Riel included, because the rebellion was the result of the policy followed by the Government against the half-breeds. That was the chief reason which actuated them, and it seems to me it is too late in the day now to seriously attempt to deny that the rebellion was directly the result of the conduct of the Government towards the half-breeds. It is too late in the day to dispute that fact. . . . The half-breeds . . . they sent their friends upon delegations to Ottawa; they sent the hon. member for Provencher; yet the Government never took any action in the matter until the 28th of January, 1885, when the Minister felt his seat shaken by the tempest that was threatening to sweep over the country. But it was then unfortunately too late. When the seeds of discontent have long been germinating, when hearts have long been swelling with long accumulating bitternesses, and when humiliations and disappointments have made men discontented and sullen, a small incident will create a conflagration, just as a spark on the prairie, under certain circumstances, will kindle a widespread and unquenchable fire. Then the Government moved, but it was too late. . . . I have charged the Government with not only having been negligent in the duty they owed to the half-breeds, but with denying to the half-breeds the rights to which they were entitled. I charge them with, not ignoring only, but actually refusing, of design aforethought, the rights to which the half-breeds were entitled. . . . In 1879 the First Minister took power to extend the same privileges to the half-breeds of the North-West. It will be seen that the half-breeds of Manitoba were treated as a special class. They were not treated as Indians; they were not treated as whites, but as participating in the rights of both the whites and the Indians. If they had been treated as Indians they would have been sent to their reserves; if they had been treated as whites they would have been granted homesteads; but as I have said they were treated as a special class, participating in both rights of whites and Indians; as whites they were given a homestead of 160 acres on the plot of land of which they happened to be in possession; as Indians, they were given scrip for lands to the extent of 160 acres for each head of their family, and 240 acres for minors. In 1879, as I have said, the Government passed a statute similar to the statute of Manitoba. Did they act upon it? When did they act upon it? When was the first thing done by the Government of Canada to put in force the Act of 1879? The first thing ever done by the Government of Canada to put in force the Act they themselves had passed was on the 28th January, 1885. Six long years elapsed before they attempted to do that justice to the half-breeds which they had taken power from Parliament to do at the time. During all that time the Government was perfectly immovable. . . . Sir, if the Government had done their duty by the half-breeds, how is it that the half-breeds so often petitioned the Government to grant them their rights? How is it that they so often deluged the Department with petitions and deputations? . . . How is it that these men, in order to obtain the rights which were denied them, have gone through such an ordeal as they have, if the Government did justice by them? Is this not the greatest condemnation that could be pronounced against them? . . . The Government had been refusing for years, and at last these men took their lives and liberties in their hands, and at last the Government came down and gave them what they were entitled to. I appeal now to any friend of liberty in this House; I appeal not only to the Liberals who sit beside me, but to any man who has a British heart in his breast, and I ask, when subjects of Her Majesty have been petitioning for years for their rights, and those rights have not only been ignored, but have been denied, and when these men take their lives in their hands and rebel, will anyone in this House say that these men, when they got their rights, should not have saved their heads as well, and that the criminals, if criminals there were in this rebellion, are not those who fought, and bled and died, but the men who sit on those Treasury benches? Sir, rebellion is always an evil, it is always an offence against the positive law of a nation; it is not always a moral crime. The Minister of Militia [Adolphe Caron] in the week that preceded the execution of Riel, stated his sentiments of rebellion in these words: "I hate all rebels; I have no sympathy, good, bad or indifferent with rebellion." Sir, what is hateful—I use the word which the hon. gentleman made use of—what is hateful is not rebellion, but is the despotism which induces that rebellion; what is hateful are not rebels, but the men who, having the enjoyment of power, do not discharge the duties of power; they are the men who, having the power to redress wrongs, refuse to listen to the petitions that are sent to them; they are the men who, when they are asked for a loaf, give a stone. . . .Where would be the half-breeds to-day if it had not been for this rebellion? Would they have obtained the rights which they now enjoy? I say, Sir, that the Canadian Government stands convicted of having yielded their rights only to rebellion, and not to the just representation of the half-breeds and

of having actually forced them into insurrection. . . . Though, Mr. Speaker, these men were in the wrong; though the rebellion had to be put down; though it was the duty of the Canadian Government to assert its authority and vindicate the law, still, I ask any friend of liberty, if there is not a feeling rising in his heart, stronger than all reasoning to the contrary, that these men were excusable? . . . I am a British subject, and I value the proud title as much as anyone in this House. But if it is expected of me that I shall allow fellow countrymen unfriended, undefended, unprotected and unrepresented in this House, to be trampled under foot by this Government, I say that is not what I understand by loyalty, and I would call that slavery. I am a British subject, but my loyalty is not of the lips. If hon. gentlemen opposite will read history, they will find that my ancestors, in all their struggles against the British Crown in the past, never sought anything else than to be treated as British subjects, and as soon as they were treated as British subjects, though they had not forgotten the land of their ancestors, they became amongst the most loyal subjects that England ever had. . . . But loyalty must be reciprocal. It is not enough for the subject to be loyal to the Crown; the Crown must also be loyal to the subject. So far as England is concerned she has done her duty nobly, generously; but this Government has not done its duty towards the half-breeds. The Government are shocked, and their friends profess to be shocked, because those men claim their rights and demanded them with bullets. Have the Government been loyal to those half-breeds? If they had been loyal to the half-breeds no such trouble would have occurred. But the Government have not been loyal to the laws. If the Government do not respect the law themselves, and if afterwards men, to vindicate their rights, take weapons in their hands and brave the laws, I say the Government are bound to search their consciences and see if they have given occasion for rebellion, and if they have, to give the benefit to the guilty ones. This is what we, in Lower Canada, have been claiming, and this is one of the reasons why we have felt so warmly upon this question. But such is not, however, the doctrine of the Government. . . . Sir, I am not of those who look upon Louis Riel as a hero. Nature had endowed him with many brilliant qualities, but nature denied him that supreme quality without which all other qualities, however brilliant, are of no avail. Nature denied him a well-balanced mind. At his worst he was a subject fit for an asylum; at his best he was a religious and political monomaniac. But he was not a bad man—do not believe at least that he was the bad man that he has been represented to be in a certain press. It is true that at the trial a most damaging fact was brought against him; it is true that he had offered to accept a bribe from the Government. But justice to his memory requires that all the circumstances connected with that fact should be laid before the House. If he accepted this money, it is evident that in his own confused mind it was not with a view of betraying the cause of his fellow countrymen— . . . I grant that if that reasoning had been made by a man in his senses, such as an hon. gentleman on the other side, it would be enough to stifle any sympathy we could have for him; but we must make due allowances for the fact that it is proved that if he was not actually insane, no man can deny that upon this subject of politics his mind was not right or sound; and of course in the case of a mind unsound or insane we

cannot apply the same tests that we should apply to a reasonable mind—it would be unfair to him. But that he was insane seems to me beyond the possibility of controversy. . . . But we never knew, until the Minister of Public Works [H. L. Langevin] spoke the other day, what was the true reason of the execution of Riel. We have it now; he has spoken and we know what was the true inwardness of it. The Government had written a pamphlet in order to justify themselves. The utility of that pamphlet is gone; it never had any; not one of the reasons it gave for the execution of Riel was the true reason. It never had any usefulness at all, except, perhaps, as affording to the Government job printing to settle the wavering consciences of some of their followers. But now we know the true reason why Riel was executed, and here it is in the language of the Minister of Public Works:

"We had this before us, we had the fact that Louis Riel had, fifteen years before this, committed an act which was considered at the time one that should have been punished in the most severe way. The prisoner, Louis Riel, at that time was not condemned to a severe punishment; he was allowed to remain out of the country for five years, and he was not brought before a tribunal to be tried, and punished or absolved, for the death of Thomas Scott."

Here is the reason—the death of Thomas Scott. . . . The death of Scott is the cause of the death of Riel to-day. Why, if the hon. gentleman thinks that the death of Scott was a crime, did he not punish Riel at the time? Scott was executed in the early days of 1870, the Government remained in power until the fall of 1873, yet they never did anything to bring that man to justice, who had committed such a crime as they say now he committed. 1870-71-72-73, almost four full years, passed away, and yet the Government, knowing such a crime as it has been represented here had been committed, never took any step to have the crime punished. What was their reason? The reason was that the Government had promised to condone the offence; the reason was that the Government were not willing to let that man come to trial, but, on the contrary, actually supplied him with money to induce him to leave the country, and, Sir, I ask any man on the other side of the House, if this offence was punishable, why was it not punished then? and if it was not punishable then, why should it be punished now? . . . Indeed the Government have convinced all the people here mentioned, the half-breeds, the Indians, the white settlers, that their arm is long and strong, and that they are powerful to punish. Would to heaven that they had taken as much pains to convince them all, the half-breeds, Indians and white settlers, of their desire and their willingness to do them justice, to treat them fairly. Had they taken as much pains to do right, as they have taken to punish wrong, they never would have had any occasion to convince those people that the law cannot be violated with impunity, because the law would never have been violated at all. But to-day, not to speak of those who have lost their lives, our prisons are full of men who, despairing ever to get justice by peace, sought to obtain it by war, who, despairing of ever being treated like freemen, took their lives in their hands, rather than be treated as slaves. They have suffered a great deal, they are suffering yet, their sacrifices will not be without reward. Their leader is in the grave; they are in durance, but from their prisons they can see that that justice, that liberty which they sought in vain, and for which they fought not in vain, has at last dawned upon their country. . . . Yes, their country has conquered with their martyrdom. They are in durance to-day; but the rights for which they were fighting have been acknowledged. We have not the report of the commission yet, but we know that more than two thousand claims so long denied have been at last granted. And more—still more. We have it in the Speech from the Throne that at last representation is to be granted to those Territories. This side of the House long fought, but fought in vain, to obtain that measure of justice. It could not come then, but it came after the war; it came as the last conquest of that insurrection. And again I say that their country has conquered with their martyrdom, and if we look at that one fact alone there was cause sufficient, independent of all others, to extend mercy to the one who is dead and to those who live.

## Conclusions

Charles A. Boulton, *Reminiscences of the North West Rebellions*, (Toronto, Grip Printing & Publishing Co., 1886), pp. 405-408.

## Ambitious and Criminal

His career and fate teach lessons which it is worth while for a moment to dwell on. The constitution under which British subjects are governed is of the most liberal character, and affords a legitimate vent for the expression of opinions and the redress of grievances that no other constitution so liberally provides. In 1869, the French half-breeds can fairly claim they had a legitimate right to know what terms were going to be accorded to them in the transfer of the country to Canada, and up to the point of forbidding the entrance of the Hon. Mr. Macdougall [*sic*] into the country, until some guarantee had been provided for the protection of their interests, the agitation that was commenced may be called legitimate. But the moment they took up arms, threatened the peace of the country, and prevented by bodily fear a free expression of the wants of the people in their negotiations with the Canadian Governor or Commissioners, it became rebellion, and any loss of life or property in consequence of this, the rebellious become responsible for.

Riel, however, realizing that the people had a grievance, took advantage of the circumstances to arouse their fears and hostilities, to obtain their support and enable him to usurp authority, not scrupling to take life, that he might occupy the position of autocrat of the country. After the arrival of the Canadian Commissioners, with power to treat with the people, Riel was criminal in every act that he committed. He was going beyond the constitutional privileges which are the great safeguard and protection of the people. In retaining prisoners and keeping them confined in unwholesome prisons, he was cruel; vindictive, and tyrannical. In taking the life of Scott, for no other reason than to make his power felt as dictator and autocrat of the country, he was a murderer. That crime was done at his bidding and for the purpose of advancing his personal ends. The circumstances of the country at the time were such that the Government could not bring him to justice for his crime. The amnesty having once been promised by Archbishop Taché put a different phase upon the circumstances, and Riel escaped the consequences of his act with the moderate punishment of banishment for five years to the United States—a country where he had for some time previously resided and where he was quite satisfied to make his home.

The years go by, and the half-breeds recollect the excitement and the profit they derived from the rebellion of 1869-70, and remember that the benefits of scrip which had been accorded to them at that time were withheld, or rather that the principle of issuing scrip had not yet been extended to the North-West Territory. More than that, the half-breeds who had left the Province of Manitoba, and who had there secured the patents for their lands, and obtained the scrip for themselves and families, now thought that they could claim the same privileges over again as residents of the North-West Territory. In order to obtain the pecuniary advantage of the scrip which the Government issued, they sent for Riel as having the ability to make this demand in such a forcible way that they might have some hope of obtaining it. The secret of the rebellion lies in the fact that the majority of the half-breeds were petitioning for something they were not entitled to, and were not likely to get by constitutional means, but which might be obtained by extreme measures of violence if successful. Riel also formulated a scheme which raised the hopes and ambitions of the half-breeds and Indians. The half-breed reserve in the Province of Manitoba was allotted on the proportion of one-seventh of the lands contained in the Province at that time created, which, upon computation, was found to be 1,400,000 acres, or 240 acres of land to each resident half-breed then born. Riel at once made the bold claim that the principle of one-seventh of the land which had been accorded in the Province of Manitoba should be carried out in the North-West Territory, and held out hopes to the Indians that one-seventh of the land should be theirs also. It was those ambitious ideas that enabled him to exercise a control over the half-breeds and Indians, in leading them to break out into open and murderous rebellion, while Riel hoped to make a big stake for himself in consequence, as he supposed, of the weakness of the Government.

Guy Frégault, "Louis Riel, Patriote Persécuté", *L'Action Nationale,* February 1945, pp. 15-22. Reprinted by permission of the Author.

# A Résumé

Louis Riel was born at St. Boniface, a hundred years ago, October 28, 1844. This centenary is not that of a chief of a savage tribe; it is the celebration of a great French Canadian. Since the nation defines itself functionally as a "spiritual vibration" which transcends the racial element; since it rests on still greater realities than those of flesh and blood, we can affirm that every Canadian—by birth or by adoption—whatever his race, provided his culture is French, is a true son of French Canada and belongs incontestably to our nation. Such was the case of Louis Riel.

He was thirteen years old, in 1858, when he left his little home to attend classes at the College of Montreal. Called home after several years by the death of his father, the young man resumed contact with the country of his birth just before the Canadian government was preparing to acquire the North-West. Returning from London in April 1869, Sir Georges-Etienne Cartier, Baronet, declared in fact in Montreal: "In a few months,

Canada will extend from the Atlantic to the Pacific!"

It was a grandiose project, but one which was going to create injustices and cause blood to run. The Dominion had not yet legally annexed Rupert's Land and the North-West Territories when already English-speaking surveyors invaded it and conducted themselves as in an occupied country, throwing the Métis of Red River into confusion, rallying the blustering, the exploiting "Canadian Party," making plots to reserve the best lands for themselves and their friends. The Métis were determined, intense and impulsive people, submissive to authority but strong in defence of their rights. Unjustly the Ontario press, animated by racism, which exemplified its lack of all spiritual feeling, compared these men to herds of buffalo: on the contrary, they formed a civilized society, endowed with stable religious, political and judicial institutions. And especially they did not understand that they were being dealt with as one does worthless cattle. They stood up to the surveyors and even turned back the Lieutenant-Governor named in September 1869 by the federal government, that is to say ten months before the date Ottawa would have jurisdiction in the Territories.

Riel, then 25 years old, was the mainspring of the resistance. He organized with his friends a National Committee of Defence, seized Fort Garry (later Winnipeg) and assumed the leadership of a legally constituted Provisional Government to which 12,000 Métis confided their destinies. The government at Ottawa soon undertook negotiations with that at Fort Garry, which found itself, thus, recognized. In mid-February 1870 a group of 600 English Canadians attempted to seize the little capital and left 48 prisoners in the hands of the Métis. The Orangeman Thomas Scott who had boasted of going to assassinate Riel, was among the prisoners; he appeared before a court martial, was condemned and shot. This incident aroused violent indignation in Ontario; they cried murder; they demanded Riel's head. The federal government sent 1,150 soldiers to the North-West and promised formally to Mgr. Taché that Riel and his followers would enjoy an amnesty. The Provisional Government yielded, ceased all resistance; but in the face of the brutalities inflicted by Colonel Wolseley's troops on his countrymen, the Métis leader understood what value he could attach to the promises of the politicians and he sought refuge in the United States. . . .

During the whole Red River affair, despite the tight discipline of the parties, the people of Quebec who had nothing to gain by injustice or persecution, showed an instinctive sympathy for the hero of the North-West. It is at this time that the first French-Canadian nationalist movement under Confederation took shape with a thirty-year old chief, Honoré Mercier; at this time also developed the New Brunswick schools affair; the Acadians were plundered and insulted, the federal government, protector of minorities, drew back in the face of fanaticism. Cartier heaped indignities on his followers and the patriots were divided by shame, anger and deception. In the elections that followed [1872], the constituency of Montreal East, inspired by Mercier, imparted a resounding slap on Sir Georges-Etienne's shrivelled cheek through personal defeat. Then there was the surprise of seeing the outlawed Riel, who had been elected in Provencher, give up his seat to the honourable baronet. Mgr. Taché had conceived this audacious manoeuvre to place Cartier under a moral obligation to

see the amnesty finally accorded to the Métis chief. But the Conservative leader, sick, went to Europe and died in London May 23, 1873.

He was still alive at the time the Pacific scandal burst like a bomb on the party house of cards. The opposition threw itself passionately into the attack on the government; the administration was overthrown and replaced by the Liberal Ministry of Alexander Mackenzie. A short time previously the Riel affair had become bound up with the Lépine affair. Ambroise Lépine had been one of Riel's chief lieutenants in 1870. Arrested December 27, 1873, he saw rising before him the Orangemen who demanded his head. When the Conservatives were in office, the Liberals had been ardent in demanding the amnesty; what would they do now that they had power? At first they made promises, then they distributed good advice when it was a question of wisdom and prudence, finally they effected a strategic retreat. On their side, the Conservatives, who had beaten a retreat as long as their great men held power, sought to exhibit sentiments of outraged justice and patriotism. The actors had simply changed roles. The comedy continued.

Chapleau, who was no longer a Minister, was begged to go to Manitoba to defend Lépine's cause. He left without asking a fee, without even asking to be paid the expense of the trip. In Winnipeg he placed at the service of the Métis his talents as a writer on criminal law, his loud and metallic voice, his captivating gestures and his brilliant rhetoric; he was finer than ever. Lépine, nevertheless, was condemned to death. When the marvellous orator returned to Montreal in mid-November 1874, he received gifts and ovations; they pampered him, they fêted him, they waved the flag for him. But they did not forget that the Métis had been sacrificed and they accused the Liberal ministers of having betrayed them. The accusations continued when the Governor-General commuted the death sentence to two years' detention. It is not generosity, it is shame, cried the Conservatives, who readily forgot the evasions of Macdonald and Cartier. Their protests resumed with renewed indignation when they learned that the Rouge government at Ottawa had granted a partial amnesty to the Métis, excluding Riel and Lépine, and that the Liberal members from Quebec supported the ministry: "This vote," wrote a Conservative journalist, "will remain as an eternal stain on the history of the third federal Parliament, and on the name of the members of our province who have sanctioned this act of iniquity."

While this vigorous eloquence was being savoured, Riel, expulsed from the Commons, had to enter a mental hospital, then fled to the United States, far from the Orangemen. It was to Montana, where he was a teacher, that a delegation of Métis, in June 1884, sought him out to ask him to head a protest movement. The mounting flood of immigration had already submerged the essential rights of the first inhabitants of Manitoba. Vexations, ill-treatment, and humiliations accumulated. Since 1878, the Métis had signed petitions outlining their grievances. Ottawa contented itself with sending to the petitioners assurance of distinguished sentiments, at the same time sending back their papers. And as the situation worsened, Riel took it in hand, at first with great moderation. Then, faced with the rebuffs his men experienced, he was overcome by delirium and seized with anger, a hallucinatory anger which welled up in him like water. He formed a Provisional

Government in March 1885. In Ottawa the Conservatives had regained power with the eternal Sir John Macdonald.

A first engagement between the Métis and regulars took place near Duck Lake; the soldiers of Her Majesty were forced to take to their heels. The government raised a little more than 4,000 men to go to fight the North-West insurgents. The cause was holy and the enthusiasm frenzied. They fought at Fish Creek April 24 and at Cut Knife May 2. On the 13th, after a four days' siege, the troops entered Batoche, where Riel had established his headquarters. Accompanied by some of his followers, the Métis leader plunged into the forest. General Middleton promised them they would not be molested if they surrendered. Riel came out. Middleton announced that he had captured him, which was quite otherwise. The hero of the North-West was a soldier and it was in this capacity that he gave himself up to another soldier. Nevertheless he was treated as a criminal. In Regina he appeared before Judge Richardson and a half-jury of Englishmen, was condemned to death August 1st and hanged November 16, 1885.

This series of striking events had a profound repercussion in Quebec. In the beginning, Conservatives as well as Liberals recognized the Métis grievances, but the former were no longer in opposition, and inspired by fine sentiments, they were not slow to change sides. In Quebec, Mercier, always more nationalist than Liberal, undertook at once to arouse public opinion—while the Conservatives stole away. Little by little, the situation became clear. The French-Canadian nation unanimously sympathized with the persecuted; Mercier and the nationalists expressed the profound instincts of their people; the Liberals, if lukewarm ten years earlier, became Rielists; and the Conservatives, if Rielists ten years earlier, became lukewarm.

It was towards Chapleau, who had done so much to save Lépine from the gallows, it was towards the fine, noble Chapleau that they directed their hopes. The French Canadians begged him to save Riel. They expected at least of him that he would resign his position as a Minister, which would create a crisis out of which would come, they believed, the salvation of the Métis. In a fine gesture of self-sacrifice, Mercier wrote this moving note: "I have everything to gain as chief of the party if you stay in. You have everything to gain if you resign. Resign, Chapleau and place yourself at the head of the province. I will be at your side to assist you with my feeble efforts, and bless your name with our brother Riel saved from the scaffold."

Chapleau felt his popularity waning. But he was afraid. He did not move. It was then that Mercier stood forth. He was magnificent. All the grief, all the shame, all the humiliation of his people passed through his lips, when he cried: "Riel, our brother, is dead, . . . a victim of fanaticism and of betrayal." It was a great day. Fifty thousand French Canadians, gathered together on the Champ de Mars, cried out for vengeance. Laurier, then as nationalist as anyone, declared to a tempest of applause: "If I had been on the banks of the Saskatchewan, I too would have shouldered my musket." Quebec was on fire. A slight fire, said Sir John Macdonald with a small smile at the corner of his mouth. But the old fox was wrong.

The fire ran from the valley of the Ottawa to the Gaspé peninsula. Nationalist sentiment broke the most solid organizations into pieces, destroyed the most deep-rooted habits; nationalist sentiment asserted itself with a violence which carried a whole people together in a torrent. Of course, some served it with all their strength, while others, alas! exploited it. Through the shortcoming of the latter, instead of having arrived at a turning point in our national history, we were at a turning point in our political history. Two stars arose on our horizon; the one, more pure, of Mercier, and one, more brilliant, of Laurier. In 1886, Mercier carried off the first victory, the ephemeral victory of French Canadian nationalism. Ten years later, Laurier registered an important Liberal success.

From all these events three conclusions may be drawn. The first is that the French Canadian nation possesses a formidable reservoir of energy and a marvellous faculty of regeneration. The second is that the French Canadian nation has a pressing duty to be always more lucid than generous. These events, finally, teach us that national unity is possible for us and that it remains, today still more than yesterday, a condition of strength and grandeur.

# Suggested Reading

Anderson, Frank W., *The Riel Rebellion, 1885,* Calgary Frontiers Unlimited, 1962.

Begg, Alexander, *The Creation of Manitoba; or, a History of the Red River Troubles,* Toronto, A. H. Hovey, 1871.

Boulton, Charles A., *Reminiscences of the North West Rebellions,* Toronto, Grip Printing & Publishing Co., 1886.

Canada: Journals of the House of Commons 1874, Vol. 8, Appendix 6, *Report of the Select Committee on the Causes of the Difficulties in the North-West Territory in 1869-70.*

Canada: Sessional Papers 1870, Vol. 5, No. 12, *Correspondence and Papers Connected with Recent Occurrences in the North-West Territories.*

Canada: Sessional Papers 1886, Vol. 19, No. 43c *(The Trial of Louis Riel).*

Davidson, W. M., *The Life and Times of Louis Riel,* Calgary, Albertan Printers, 1952.

Dugas, Georges, *Histoire Véridique des Faits Qui Ont Préparé le Mouvement des Métis à la Rivière-Rouge en 1869,* Montreal, Librairie Beauchemin, 1905.

Frémont, Donatien, *Les Secrétaires de Riel, Louis Schmidt, Henry Jackson, Philippe Garnot,* Montreal, Les Editions Chantecler, 1953.

Howard, Joseph Kinsey, *Strange Empire, a Narrative of the Northwest,* New York, William Morrow & Co., 1952.

Lamb, R. E., *Thunder in the North, Conflict over the Riel Risings 1870 . . . 1885,* New York, Pageant Press. 1957.

Morice, A. G., *A Critical History of the Red River Insurrection after Official Documents and Non-Catholic Sources,* Winnipeg, Canadian Publishers, 1935.

Morton, W. L. (ed.), *Alexander Begg's Red River Journal and Other Papers Relative to the Red River Resistance of 1869-1870,* Toronto, The Champlain Society, 1960.

Morton, W. L. (ed.), *Manitoba: The Birth of a Province,* Altona, Manitoba Record Society, 1965.

Mulvaney, C. P., *The History of the Northwest Rebellion of 1885,* Toronto, A. H. Hovey, 1885.

Osler, E. B., *The Man Who Had To Hang, Louis Riel,* Toronto, Longmans Green, 1961.

Rumilly, Robert, *Histoire de la Province de Québec* (Vol. 5, Riel), Montreal, Editions Bernard Valiquette, 1942.

Stanley, George F. G., *Louis Riel,* Toronto, The Ryerson Press, 1963.

Stanley, George F. G., *Louis Riel: Patriot or Rebel?,* Ottawa, Canadian Historical Association, Historical Booklet No. 2, 1954.

Stanley, George F. G., *The Birth of Western Canada, a History of the Riel Rebellions,* London, Longmans Green, 1936.

Trémaudan, Auguste Henri de, *Histoire de la Nation Métisse dans l'Ouest Canadien,* Montreal, Editions Albert Lévesque, 1935.